PEACE, LOVE & MURDER

PEACE, LOVE & MURDER

THE CHARLES MANSON STORY

ALAN R. WARREN

COPYRIGHT

Peace, Love & Murder: The Charles Manson Story

Written by Alan R. Warren
Published by House of Mystery

Copyright @ 2025 by Alan R. Warren

Cover design, formatting, layout, and editing by Evening Sky Publishing Services

Published in the United States of America
ISBN (Paperback): 978-1-998680-12-2
ISBN (eBook): 978–1-998680-13-9

CONTENTS

INTRODUCTION

When I think of the Charles Manson crimes, I often think that this was
something that could have only happened in this one particular place in
time. Manson could not have been who he was or done what he did at
any other place or time. He needed aid from several events to support
his behaviours. And because those events happened, he was able to start
his family of supporters who committed his crimes for him.

During the 1960s, many American teenagers had become
disillusioned with the police and felt different from their parents. They
thought that they had become alienated. The Vietnam War raged on,
causing several protests amongst the young people in colleges and
universities around the country. African Americans were now becoming
militant in their pursuit of equal rights, starting groups like the Black
Panthers. Gloria Steinem led the fight for feminism, winning women
the freedoms of simple things we take for granted today. Some of these
included the right to have their own bank accounts, the choice of
working outside the home, rather than being confined to homemaking
and motherhood, reproductive rights, including the right to make
decisions about their own bodies.

In contrast, the hippie movement in San Francisco, centered on
open and free love, had become a place for those seeking a new belief

system, completely different from what the youth knew to that point. It was a ray of sunshine cutting through a country that seemed full of anger and hate.

Add the cultural cocktail of mind-altering drugs, such as marijuana and LSD, which had become widely available on the streets, and it added the comforting feeling of a warm jacket during winter. While wearing it, everything felt great. Nothing was wrong. The world was now exactly where it needed to be for Manson to be successful.

Opportunity. Chance. Chaos.

PART I

CHARLES MANSON - THE STORY

1

THE EARLY YEARS

Charles Manson, as we know him, was born Charles Miles Maddox Manson in Cincinnati, Ohio, to a single teenage mother, Ada Kathleen Maddox, on November 12, 1934. His mother listed his last name as Manson, even though his biological father's name was Colonel Walker Henderson Scott Sr. from Catlettsburg, Kentucky. We know this because Ada had filed a paternity lawsuit against Scott in 1937, which she won.

Scott Sr. told Ada that he was a colonel in the army, but it was later revealed that he was a mill worker who frequently changed jobs. "Colonel" was a nickname, not his official rank in any military unit. Scott was a well-known con artist and liar throughout Kentucky. When Ada informed Scott that she was pregnant, he told her that he was being transferred to a new location by the army, and he disappeared. She never saw him again.

Not long after that, Ada decided to marry William Manson. Three months before Charles was born in the Summer of 1934, she realized that she couldn't rely on his biological father. William Manson worked at their local dry-cleaning store and was reliable. However, the couple divorced after only three short years. Despite being married with a child, Ada still enjoyed partying and drinking. And as soon as William left for work, Ada would leave to go out drinking, often with her brother Luther Maddox.

William filed for divorce, claiming that Ada neglected her duty as a wife and mother by going out daily and getting drunk, never being home to clean or cook dinner for the family, and also leaving Charles with strange people to babysit him.

After the divorce was final, Charles lived with his mother; however, he kept Manson as his last name.

Within two years, Ada and her brother Luther were both arrested for robbery and theft using physical violence during the crime. They were both convicted. Ada received a five-year prison sentence, and Luther received a ten-year prison sentence. Charles was sent to live in McMechan, West Virginia, with his uncle and aunt.

Ada was released on parole in 1942 and went to McMechen to be with her family. About a month later, Ada took Charles and moved to Charleston. While they were living there, she went back to her old lifestyle and drank daily, leaving Charles alone to fend for himself. He started skipping school regularly.

Ada was arrested again and charged with grand larceny. She was never convicted of the charge, but after her release, she took Charlie, and they moved to Indianapolis. It was there that Ada met a man named Woodson Cavender Jr. at an Alcoholics Anonymous meeting. They were married in August 1943.

Around this time, Charles began to misbehave at school more than ever before. He was no longer just skipping out of class. He was getting into fights and even attempted to set the school on fire. Charles also began stealing from others at school and from a few stores. But he was always caught.

After four years of this kind of behavior, Charles was sent to the Gibault School for Boys in Terre Haute, Indiana. It was a reform school meant for reform delinquent boys who were repeat offenders. The school was run by Catholic priests who would beat the boys who broke any of the rules with large wooden paddles or leather straps.

Charles hated the reform school so much that he decided to run away. He spent several days sleeping in the woods before returning home to his mother. Ada allowed him to stay home throughout the

Christmas holidays, but would return him to the school in early January 1948.

Charles stayed at the reform school for another ten months before he ran away again in October 1948. This time, he traveled to Indianapolis, where he committed his first known felony by stealing food from a local grocery store. When he got away with that, he continued to rob other stores. In one of them, he found a hidden box containing $100. The cash allowed him to rent a room instead of sleeping in the forest.

Charles now has a residence, and with a few dollars, he was able to get himself a job working for Western Union, delivering messages for them. When the hundred dollars he found ran out and he wasn't earning enough money from his work, he began to steal again. And in early 1949, Manson was caught stealing. He was arrested and charged. The judge sentenced him to serve time in Boys Town in Omaha, Nebraska.

Manson was only there four days when he and another juvenile, Blackie Nielson, got a gun and stole a car. The two of them decided to travel to Peoria, Illinois, where Nielson's uncle lived. On their travels, they stopped and robbed two different stores. In both cases, they used their gun to get money.

According to Manson, Nielson's uncle made his living as a thief, and when the two boys arrived at his place, he agreed to show them how to steal without getting caught. That never worked out too well for either of them. Within two weeks, Manson was arrested for robbery. Police were able to link him to the two other robberies he committed with his friend Nielson. In the end, he was convicted of all three crimes and sent to another reform school. This one was a strict, lock-down facility located in Plainfield, Indiana.

While Manson was in that reform school, another boy raped him. During the rape, the boy was being cheered on by other reformers as well as some of the orderlies who worked there. Manson said that it was because of these attacks that he created what he would call the "Insane Game" as a way of defending himself. When it looked like they were going to attack him, he would begin to scream in high-pitched screech-like sounds, while making strange grimacing looks on his face. He would wave his arms around as if he were a monkey, in hopes that it would make his attackers think that he had gone insane.

It didn't always work. After being attacked several times by other boys and staff at the school, Manson began to run away when any possible opportunity came up. The school claimed that he ran away over eighteen times while he was there. In the first two years, every time he escaped, he was caught and brought back. But in February 1951, Manson and two other boys in the school escaped successfully. The three wanted to go to California, so they stole a series of cars and robbed several gas stations for both gasoline and money, and also grocery stores for food. The police caught them in Utah, where they were all charged with federal offenses as they had driven stolen cars across state lines.

Manson was convicted and this time sent to the National Training School for Boys located in Washington, D.C. He was seventeen years old at the time. While there, he was given an aptitude test and a psychological evaluation. Even though he was unable to read or write, he still scored 109 on his IQ test, which was above average, especially for someone his age.

Manson was determined to have an aggressive, antisocial personality. The training school for boys decided that they were not equipped to handle Manson, so he was transferred to a minimum-security jail located in Virginia in October 1951.

In February the following year, Manson had a parole hearing in which his aunt appeared before the board and agreed to let him stay with her, and she would help him find work. But before he was released, the guards caught Manson raping another boy at knifepoint at the prison.

Manson was then transferred to the Federal Reformatory located in Petersburg, Virginia, because of the sexual assault that he committed. It was a medium security prison, and while there, he was caught committing three more sexual assaults and five other disciplinary offenses. So he was transferred again. This time to a maximum-security prison for boys in Ohio. His scheduled release date was set for his twenty-first birthday, November 12, 1955, but he was well-behaved at this reformatory and was released early in May 1954 for good behavior. He went back to live with his aunt in West Virginia.

In January 1955, Manson married Rosalie "Rosie" Jean Willis, a sixteen-year-old waitress who worked at the hospital restaurant. That Summer, Rosalie was pregnant, and in the Fall, the couple decided to move to Los Angeles. In Los Angeles, they were stopped by the police, who discovered that the couple was driving in a stolen vehicle. Manson had stolen the car in Ohio, so again he was charged with transporting a stolen vehicle across state lines.

The court decided to give him another psychological evaluation because he was newly married and about to become a father. He did well enough that they released him on a five-year probation. The following Spring of 1956, he failed to appear for another charge of auto theft from Florida. That led to his arrest when he was pulled over in Indianapolis. His probation was revoked, and he was sentenced to serve three years in prison at Terminal Island in Los Angeles.

The following month, on April 10, 1956, Rosalie gave birth to their son, Charles Manson Jr., and they moved in with Charles' mother, Ada. Ada and Rosalie would often visit Charles in prison for about a year. Eventually, only his mother came to see him. Ada explained to Charles that Rosalie had met another man and moved in with him. Manson got angry after hearing the news about his wife and attempted to break out of prison, but was caught. The attempted breakout happened less than two weeks before his parole hearing, causing him to be denied, and leaving him to stay in jail until September 1958. By then, Rosalie had divorced Manson and remarried her new boyfriend.

Manson was released but on parole for five more years. Two months later, in November, he was already pimping out a sixteen-year-old girl while dating another who was wealthy and from whom he would get money.

In September 1959, Manson was arrested again, this time for trying to cash a stolen U.S. Treasury check. At the sentencing, he had a young woman, Leona Rae Stevens, appear before the judge, claiming that she was in love with Manson and would marry him if he weren't put in prison. The judge gave him a ten-year suspended sentence and placed him on probation.

The two did get married, but it was thought that Manson only married Stevens so that she could not testify against him for the crimes he had committed while with her, or the ones he had her commit for him. Stevens had a long record of prostitution.

Manson and his wife, along with another prostitute friend of theirs, went to New Mexico. Once they were settled, Manson began pimping the two women out on the streets. They were both arrested, and later, police charged Manson with the Mann Act, which was a trafficking law. They released Manson, and because he was scared of being convicted, he disappeared and stopped showing up to see his parole officer.

It wasn't long before a bench warrant was issued for Manson for violating his parole. In April 1960, there was also an indictment for Manson issued for violating the Mann Act. While Manson was in Laredo, Texas, in April 1960, he was arrested and extradited to Los Angeles. He was sentenced to serve ten years in prison.

In July 1961, Manson was transferred to McNeil Island, Washington, to serve his time in the United States Penitentiary. It was there that Manson met Alvin "Creepy" Karpis, who was the leader of the Barker-Karpis gang. The two men became friends, and it was Karpis who taught him how to play guitar. He was also able to get the contact information for Universal Studios Producer Phil Kaufman.

Manson's mother decided to move to Washington State so that she could be close to him and would be able to visit him in prison regularly. She worked in a nearby town as a waitress. Two years later, in 1963, Manson's second wife, Leona Stevens, divorced him. During the divorce proceedings, she claimed to have had his son, Charles Manson.

In June 1966, Manson was sent back to Terminal Island Prison in Los Angeles to prepare him for release on March 21, 1967.

There was a rumor that Charles Manson had auditioned for a role as one of the Monkees for the 1965 television show. But this has been refuted, mainly because he was still in prison during the auditions.

2

SAN FRANCISCO YEAR

After he was released from prison, Manson went to Berkley, California. Within a month of calling his probation officer, he was sent to San Francisco. Roger Smith, a doctoral researcher in criminology at the Haight-Ashbury Free Medical Clinic, was now supervising him.

At the same time and same medical clinic, the CIA was paying for them to study the effects of LSD on patients. David Smith was the head of the clinic. It was later claimed that Manson and many of his new family members were all being tested in the LSD project, but there is no conclusive evidence of such.

Also, during this time, Manson began to read the book *Stranger in a Strange Land* by Robert Heinlein and had been going to a Scientology group after meeting an inmate, Lanier Rayner, who began to train Manson in Scientology. In 1966, there was a prison report stating that Manson was no longer a Scientologist. After his release in 1967, he traveled to Los Angeles, and it was reported that he attended several parties with movie stars where there were Scientologists. Manson completed 150 hours of auditing, and his friend Bruce Davis also worked at the Church of Scientology in London from November 1968 to April 1969.

Manson met 23-year-old Mary Brunner, who was working in the library at the University of California, Berkley. Manson, who had been living on the street and panhandling, then moved in with Brunner. He often brought different girls back to Brunner's apartment while she was at work, and some of them he would have sex with. Even though that upset Brunner, she stayed with him.

One of the girls that Manson brought home was Lynette Fromme, whom he would later nickname "Squeaky." She had been a teenage runaway. Manson convinced Brunner to let Fromme move in with them.

Eventually, there were seventeen girls or young women living at Brunner's apartment with them, most of whom were young runaways, loners, and had insecurities. He could easily take advantage of them.

1967 became known as the "Summer of Love," when the hippie movement reached its peak in San Francisco. It attracted teens from all over the country to experience it. The Haight-Ashbury district, where those two streets crossed, became the center of many activities. It was a non-stop party, with concerts and festivals taking place almost daily. It seemed that every second hippie had free pills or marijuana to share with others. Several hippies lived together, and free love was the prevailing theme of their lifestyle. Along with all of that, there was every kind of religion available to you on the streets—Buddhists, Satanists, and many other gurus preaching their version of the gospel to everyone who walked by them.

Manson was one of those gurus in Haight-Ashbury. It wasn't long before he had several groupies following him—most were female. He told his followers that they were the reincarnation of the original Christians who lived on Earth. He often characterized what was then called "The Establishment" as Roman. To him, anyone who was in some position of authority, be it cops, politicians, or even doctors, was The Establishment.

Manson started using the name Charles Manson and found an old school bus that he had modified by removing many of the seats and adding colored rugs and pillows. He often took trips with his followers in the bus to Topanga Canyon, Malibu, and Venice.

Brunner became pregnant with Manson's son in 1967, giving birth to him on April 15, 1968. The couple named the boy Valentine Michael. After the birth, Mary Brunner was then dubbed "Mother Mary" by Manson.

During Manson's brief tenure in the Haight-Ashbury district of San Francisco, he managed to acquire around twenty devoted followers. The prominent members who moved with him to Los Angeles were Charles "Tex" Watson, Bobby Beausoleil, Susan Atkins, Patricia Krenwinkel, and Leslie Van Houten.

On July 31, 1967, Manson was arrested when he tried to stop police from arresting one of his followers, Ruth Ann Moorehouse, for prostitution. Manson received a misdemeanor charge, and the judge added two more years of probation to his existing probation.

In July 1968, when Manson and his family were moving to Los Angeles, they ran their bus into a ditch. When police came, they found drugs on the bus and several, including Manson, were arrested. They were all released within three days.

BEACH BOYS AND DENNIS WILSON

Dennis Wilson had moved into the old Will Rogers hunting lodge on Sunset Boulevard after separating from his wife. It had the log cabin-type exterior, while inside was a beautifully designed estate. Since renting the place, he had been hosting parties nonstop. His guests often stayed for days, utilizing all the luxury amenities, including a large swimming pool and several guest bedrooms.

Wilson was driving home one day when he saw two beautiful girls, Ella Jo Bailey "Yeller" and Patricia Krenwinkel, hitchhiking. As Wilson often did, he picked up the girls and brought them back to his house. In addition to offering to give the girls a ride, he also asked them if they wanted to come over to his place for some milk and cookies. The girls both agreed and laughed, thinking he was joking.

After the three of them shared some raw milk and cookies, Wilson had to go to his recording studio, which was located in a separate house at the back of his property. He said goodbye to the girls and sent them on their way, telling them that he hoped to see them again. He added that next time, maybe he could meet the guy named Charlie they had told him about.

When Yeller and Patricia made it back home to Charlie, they told him about meeting a cool guy who had picked them up and taken them both to his house, where they had a great time. Once Charlie heard the name Dennis Wilson, his eyes lit up. "You mean of the Beach Boys?" He asked. Neither of the girls knew who the Beach Boys were, and both just smiled and shrugged. "I guess so," Krenwinkel answered.

After Wilson finished his recording session sometime after midnight, he returned home. When he pulled into the driveway, he noticed that several lights were on in the house, confusing him. As he was getting out of his car, the back door swung open, and out came a petite man waving his arms and talking to Wilson. It was Charles Manson. Initially, the meeting frightened Wilson, who stood beside his car, his back to the open door. He asked Manson if he was going to hurt him. Manson laughed and answered, "Do I look like I'm going to hurt you?" Oddly, Manson fell to the ground and, while on all fours like a dog, bowed his head and kissed Wilson's feet.

Wilson went into the house with Manson, who now had placed his arm around Wilson's back, as he wasn't tall enough to put it around his shoulder comfortably. Manson continued talking to Wilson, who was still nervous and wondered who else was in his house and what was going on.

Once inside, Wilson saw the two girls that he had picked up earlier that day and looked at them. Both came running over to him and lovingly put their arms around him, hugging him. Yeller told Wilson that they liked being with him so much that they thought he wouldn't mind them bringing some of their other friends over. Of course, Wilson, being a passive-natured soul, just responded with a nod and a smile. Krenwinkel then grabbed Charlie's arm and, with excitement, screeched, "Oh, and you have met Charlie. Wonderful!"

In the background, Wilson heard a Beatles album playing on his stereo. As he looked around and took in the scene, he saw several girls. Most of them were topless. He began to relax and smiled. That night, Wilson met one of the girls, Nancy Pittman, whom he liked mainly because she would do anything sexually that he wanted to do.

Wilson and Manson started to have some intense conversations over the following week, and they grew close. As usual, Manson knew how to spot any weakness or need Dennis had—there was a bad history with his father, Murray Wilson, who had often beaten him and his brothers.

Murry had a machinist business and was a musician himself, but he didn't have any success with music and even made fun of his sons' band and their songs.

As the Beach Boys gained popularity and people started buying their records, Murry took over running the band, which the band members hated. Every day, their father would lose his temper and yell at them until he hit one or all of the boys. Manson picked up on Wilson's troubled childhood and hatred for his father, explaining that this was a regular part of life, where parents often ruin their kids.

Wilson came to believe that Manson was wise and spiritual. He started introducing him to all his friends, family, and colleagues in the music business. At the time, Wilson had been writing songs with a talent scout, Gregg Jakobson, as the Beach Boys had been struggling to have a hit.

What started in 1961 with the hit song "Surfin'" until their last hit in the fall of 1966, "Good Vibrations," the band was the biggest-selling American rock band going. Throughout their success, Brian Wilson was the major songwriter, and his brother Carl was the lead guitarist. Meanwhile, their lead singer was Mike Love. Those three members of the band often excluded Dennis from the creative process and never considered him a great drummer. Dennis hated being left out. That and his good looks made his life a party with lots of sex, drugs, and alcohol.

By the time of their 1968 album, "Friends," which failed to chart, reaching only number 126 on the album chart and producing no hits, Dennis began to think that he could write songs that would save the band and take them back to the top of the charts again.

Dennis was good enough on a guitar or piano to write the music or even the melody of a song, but couldn't seem to get a handle on writing the words. So, he began searching for a writing partner, and after a few unsuccessful attempts, he found Jakobson in 1963. The two hit it off and often hung out with producer Terry Melcher.

Now that he had met Manson, he decided to introduce the two and see what happened. When Jakobson came over to Wilson's house, he initially didn't care for Manson very much and figured him to be another stray that Wilson had picked up. He did that a lot. However, as Manson often did, he picked up on Jakobson's goals and explained to him how to achieve them. Manson also gave him Ruth Ann, another of his girls, who Jakobson liked, even though he was already married to the famous comedian Lou Costello's daughter.

Eventually, Charlie got what he wanted. He got to know and meet all of Wilson and Jakobson's contacts in the music business. Manson then got to play some of his songs with the two of them, while his girls served as backup singers. While Jakobson thought that there might be something there, he considered Charlie far better to watch than to listen to.

Wilson took the opposite belief that Manson was a true genius and wanted his band's record label to record him. He immediately took Manson over to the studio to have him audition for the label's management. Nobody was impressed.

The brothers had a rule amongst themselves that each of them had the right to record whoever they chose. At this time, though, the band had been struggling to have a hit, and the money wasn't rolling in as it once was. So they told Dennis that they couldn't record Charlie. It didn't help either that when Charlie came in to do a demo, he was filthy and smelled bad. Everyone around the studio called him "Pig Pen" after the filthy character on the popular comic strip of the time, *Charlie Brown*. Manson also tried ordering everyone around and just sat, playing sporadically for hours, but came out with nothing worth recording.

Dennis continued to move forward with the idea of working with Manson. He did interviews with newspapers, magazines, and even radio, and in them, he would mention his discovery of Charles Manson. Dennis had even come up with a new name for Manson: "Wizard." Dennis was feeling desperate as Manson kept the pressure on by asking him to sit with him to work on some songs together. Manson also had the girls close by to help sing and flirt with Dennis.

A distance developed between Dennis and the other Beach Boys, so much so that whenever they came over to visit him, Dennis became quiet and reserved and did not act as freely and openly as when they weren't there.

Jacobson said that every time he went to Dennis' house, several girls were lying around the pool, and they ate and drank all of his food.

Manson told the girls to sleep with whoever Dennis had over so that nobody complained.

Getting tired of Manson and his Family, the other Beach Boys hired a private detective to see what they could find out about Manson. They thought that they hit pay dirt when they learned that Manson was an ex-con who had served time in prison and was still on parole. But when they told Dennis about their discovery, he reacted in the opposite way they had expected. Instead of being worried or upset, Dennis was intrigued and wanted to know more. His reaction only caused an alienation between Dennis and his brothers, who no longer came over to his house as long as Manson was there.

After a few months of Dennis having to handle Manson and his followers at his house and studio on his own, without the help of his brothers, he began to feel pestered by Manson. Everywhere Dennis went, Manson was right there with him. To make things worse, some of the Manson Family members crashed Dennis' Ferrari, and of course, didn't have any money to pay for the repairs.

He knew it was time to get Manson and his followers out of his house. But how was he going to do that? He didn't know how without making an enemy of them. Eventually, he decided the easiest way was to move out of the house. Since he was only renting it, he gave notice to the owner. He moved to the beach as soon as he returned from Europe, where he was on a shorter three-month tour with the Beach Boys.

Dennis told Manson immediately so he would have time to find a new place to live. After the Beach Boys left the country, Manson and his followers began to party heavily at Dennis' rented place, and started to get complaints. The landlord ultimately evicted them from the house before the lease was due and before Dennis got back to the States.

Dennis was so relieved to return from his tour with the Beach Boys and to have Manson and the Family gone. He could now select when and where he would see Manson and not be in the situation where he was unable to get away from him.

He began going out to the Spahn Ranch occasionally to visit Manson and some of his favorite girls. It was far easier this way, as he could leave whenever he wanted to and go home to some peace without the group being there.

Dennis also gave Manson money each time he visited the ranch. He still cared for quite a few of them, plus it gave him a chance to have sex with some of the girls there. Manson wanted to maintain their friendship, and he was still seeking a recording deal and possibly collaborating with Wilson on some songs. Although none of them were living with him anymore, Manson remained on good terms with Wilson.

Dennis kept telling Manson on each visit that the Beach Boys were going to record one of his songs, "Cease to Exist." Even though Manson thought that he was talented enough to get a record deal so that he could record his album with his songs only, he would take whatever he could get. And he figured that after the Beach Boys recorded the song and it became a hit, heard on the radio, he would surely receive offers to record an album.

The next visit that Manson was excited about was with producer Terry Melcher. Now, Melcher didn't seem to be as committed to Manson getting a recording contract. But at least he was visiting the ranch. So the least Manson could do was get some of the girls to have sex with him. Melcher usually chose to be with Ruth Ann, who was his favorite girl in the group.

Another person in the music business who frequently visited the ranch was Gregg Jakobson. He never came by himself but was always tagging along with either Terry Melcher or Dennis Wilson. Jakobson wasn't impressed by Charlie's music, but he thought that he had a significant presence and would be good in a film of some sort. The two men would often get caught up in deep conversations, where Jakobson was trying to learn about Manson's history. Instead, he would hear one of the many wild stories that Manson liked to tell.

Another regular group of visitors to the ranch to visit Manson and his Family was a couple of motorcycle gangs. The bikers caused some conflict for Charlie, as the bikers all loved to drink beer and whiskey, which he disapproved of. When they went out on their scrounging or shoplifting raids, they would also have to include getting beer for the bikers, which would mean using some of the money they got from panhandling. However, Manson tolerated the bikers' behavior, as they often repaired the bikes and dune buggies that the family used at the ranch.

4

SPAHN RANCH

George Spahn owned one of the most famous television and movie sets of the 1960s, which was used for many Western series and movies. It was hundreds of acres of beautifully rugged foothills, containing several rivers and caves, and teeming with a variety of animals, including deer, bears, rabbits, and snakes. It would be easily recognizable to anyone who had ever watched one of those older black-and-white Western shows.

Throughout the land, several sets consisted mainly of town settings with storefronts and businesses reminiscent of those found in old Western towns. There were also numerous complete buildings on site, which were used for interior shots, such as bars, saloons, and residential family homes.

However, by the mid-sixties, television production companies had mainly moved away from westerns. As a result, they were no longer using the Spahn Ranch. So George Spahn turned it into a place for tourists to visit the old sets of some of their favorite shows. He also offered tours of the location, which included guided horseback riding around the trails of the property. For only a buck fifty, you could saddle up a horse and be taken around the land, and into some of the places where great western battles had been filmed.

Now in his eighties, George Spahn started to slow down. Arthritis had set in, and his vision was fading rapidly. He had hired several staff members to handle the visitors who came to the ranch from the city, allowing him to take it easy and manage the finances.

One of the many times when the Manson bus broke down, it happened on the Spahn Ranch. They were unable to fix it. Sandy Good told Manson that she had a friend who could fix it, but he lived on a ranch about thirty-five miles out of town.

When Manson arrived at that ranch, he was impressed. He thought it would be a great place to live, as it was private and far enough away from the city that they wouldn't be bothered by people. Another great advantage of the ranch was that it rested on the line between Los Angeles and Ventura city districts, and neither city wanted to take care of it. This mindset was also held by both police forces, knowing it was just a group of hippies hanging out there. They figured it would be a waste of time following them around, as all they would get were arrests for drug possession and other minor things.

Once Manson met George Spahn, he knew he would have no problem convincing him to let Charlie and his girls stay at the ranch for free. Manson offered George a deal where they would keep the ranch clean, take care of the horses, and assist with visitors by leading them on tours. In return, George wouldn't have to pay them a penny. To top it off, Manson offered to have the girls help take care of George, do his housework for him, and even keep him company.

George was already running a fairly relaxed ranch and had others who were living there for free. They all worked around the ranch in exchange for their keep. To help seal the deal, Manson sent Lynette into George's house to make him his meals and to clean it up, but while she was there, she was given the job to have sex with George.

George liked Lynette and enjoyed being with her. She didn't mind George either. Within a few days, whenever the couple was out in public on the ranch, George would try to pinch Lynette on her backside, and she would let out a loud squeal. Soon, Lynette was given the nickname "Squeaky."

George thought Manson was bringing just a few other girls with him. But when he showed up to move in, he brought seventeen girls with him. In only a few more months, eighteen people turned into thirty-five or six. When George approached Manson about how many people he had living there, Manson told him that they were just there for a day or two. He said they were only friends who were visiting him and hadn't come there to live. Of course, none of that was true. They had all come to live there.

It wasn't long before Manson began making the others who were already living and working at the ranch feel uncomfortable, to the point where they decided to leave. All along, this was Manson's plan. He wanted to have the best buildings for himself and his Family to live in.

Since there were now too many people living on the ranch and not enough cabins to house them all, Manson had Tex Watson start constructing new buildings. They were built off the storefronts of the movie set that were already there. Manson and Watson had a strained relationship at the time. Manson wouldn't give Watson full membership because, according to Manson, he hadn't surrendered his ego. He wanted Watson to work hard and never complain to prove his commitment to the Family.

The ranch had very primitive living standards. There was no running water, no toilets, and no facilities for cleaning up. Most of the shacks had no beds or furniture, at least none that could be used for sleeping. But it was all okay for everyone who was there. The Family also had to scrounge through garbage to find food. Often, different members would go into town to find garbage from restaurants or people's homes, then bring it back to the ranch.

The female members of the Family were expected to panhandle on the city streets. When they received some money from a passerby, they had to give it to a male Family member who was also present. Manson had a strict rule that no female was ever allowed to hold onto any money, regardless of the amount. Most likely, this rule was another method of Manson keeping control over the female members of the Family. Without money, it was harder for them if they decided to leave.

In addition to looking for food, Manson always had his Family members looking for potential new members to bring back to the ranch. They would find younger people, often alone and living on the streets. Once they were back at the ranch, Manson drilled them to find out if they had any money or items that they could use or even sell. If they had something he felt would be helpful to them, Manson invited them to join the Family. Once this was decided, he would place the new member under probation and assign one of his principal members to train and supervise them. If the only thing they had to offer was money, once that ran out, they would never be accepted into the Family as a member. Instead, they would be told to leave the ranch.

Besides the Family's fundamental needs being met at the ranch, it was pretty isolated from the public. Not so much that Manson considered it a hideout, but he had the Family's complete attention. They would only hear the stories he told, so they had no outside influence on them. He couldn't do this when they were living in other people's homes, like Wilson's. There were far too many distractions.

George had a few regular ranch hands working there for a little while. Juan Flynn was the supervisor in charge of the ranch's workers. Shorty Shea, who had worked as an extra for several television shows filmed at the ranch, also stayed on and worked there, giving tours to many of the visitors.

The two hands that were most popular with Manson were Johnny Schwartz and Steve Grogan. Grogan was only a teenager and appeared to be of lower intelligence. Most of the Family considered him to be mentally disabled, and they all called him "Scramblehead." It was only a few months before he became a full member of the Manson Family.

Schwartz became a favorite of the Family because he owned a 1959 Ford that he let any of them drive into the city for their garbage runs to get food. He gave them the keys to the car and never imposed any restrictions on when they could use it, so they came and went with it whenever they felt like it.

Flynn, though, ran a tight ship. He expected everyone living at the ranch to work hard to pay their way. Manson liked that as he knew it would keep the Family occupied when he wasn't using them for his errands or preaching something to them. It also kept them from thinking too much about what Manson was telling them.

Manson and Flynn didn't like each other personally, and both were trying to show the ranch employees that they were in charge of what went on there. Manson attempted to create conflict and posed a challenge that would force his followers to choose him over others. An example of this was once when Flynn assigned everyone a job to do around the ranch early one morning. Manson told them all not to work, but instead to follow him to the saloon at the ranch so that he could give them a sermon.

Once Flynn realized that nobody was at work, he searched for them and found everyone at the saloon. He had a bad temper and constantly yelled at people, so when he arrived and found Manson preaching to them, he ran up and began screaming at him face-to-face. Manson knew he was no match for Flynn, as he was at least a foot shorter than him, so instead, he pulled out a book of matches. He lit one and placed the flame under his wrist, and it began to burn his arm. Then, with a calm, straight face, he looked up at Flynn and said, "You know, brother, there's no such thing as pain." The act made Flynn feel uncomfortable, so he left the saloon. These kinds of scenes would reinforce Manson's control over his followers.

During the first Summer that Manson and his Family lived at Spahn Ranch, he gained several new members: Cathy Gillies, or Capistrano, Tom Walleman, named "T.J.," John Phillip Haught, called "Zero," and Simi Valley Sherri.

Gypsy, and Leslie Van Houten, who were living with Manson's friend Boby Beausoleil, had suddenly shown up at Spahn Ranch and told Manson that they had decided to leave him. Manson was angry and told them to go back to Beausoleil immediately. It wasn't that he cared about them. It was more than he wanted to remain friends with Beausoleil, who did a lot of work for him.

Gypsy began to cry and begged Manson to let her stay, that she couldn't go back to Beausoleil, and that if he made her leave, she would just run away. Manson liked Gypsy's ability to recruit and bring him new devotees, so after a while, he decided that it would be okay if she stayed.

Manson had never met Leslie Van Houten before, and even though she was beautiful, he didn't like that she seemed very smart. He didn't like girls who were too bright, as they often challenged his beliefs and his preaching to others. Gypsy began to sell Leslie to him by telling him that Leslie was a great writer and knew how to take shorthand.

Manson began to think of a way to use Leslie. While she was home around the ranch, she could follow him everywhere he went and take notes. So, whether he was writing song lyrics or discussing issues or plans, she could help him keep track of such things. And being so pretty, he could pair her up with Ruth Ann, and the pair could use their looks to lure men into the group.

The most significant change that resulted from the two women joining the Family was when Gypsy became the leader of all the girls who lived on the ranch. She became very strict with the girls and made sure that they followed Manson's orders completely.

5

ALAN ROSE

When Manson was in San Francisco, in the Haight-Ashbury district, he frequently visited the free medical clinic located there. One of its workers, Alan Rose, was fascinated by Manson and had several conversations with him. Rose often thought about joining Manson's group but never did.

He stayed in touch with the Manson Family, though, and decided to visit them for a while to see if it was right for him to join. Rose only spent two weeks there before returning home to San Francisco and resuming work at the clinic.

Later, Rose and the free clinic founder, David E. Smith, wrote an article in the Fall of 1970 for the *Journal of Psychedelic Drugs*, which centered around Manson, his teachings, and his heavy influence over his followers. The timing of the article led to the belief that it was the primary reason for Rose's visit to the Spahn Ranch. They wanted to get insider details about what went on among Manson and his followers.

The article explained the various ways Mason controlled his followers. He often used sexual behavior on the women in the group to break them down emotionally. If they were fragile enough for him to control, he would let them join the group and live there. Manson liked to take everything his followers owned and any money they had, thereby making them dependent on the group to survive. He had his group talks daily, but always drugged his followers beforehand. He also took away their personal items, such as glasses, because he thought that they should only see the world as they could and that lenses shouldn't enhance their vision.

Manson wouldn't allow any books except for the bible on the commune. He believed that authors and writers were only trying to deceive people by creating stories that would trick people into doing things they wouldn't normally do. Manson held book-burning sessions in front of everyone, telling them that if they needed to know anything, they could find out from him.

Another form of control that Manson used was to keep everybody working as much as possible. This type of work involved a significant amount of labor, including building, cleaning, and caring for the horses at the ranch.

Life on the ranch was a very unique experience in itself. There were no bathrooms with showers or bathtubs, and the facility lacked running water. Most of the cabins in which they all lived didn't have much in them. Each room had a homemade bed built from pieces of old wood found around the land, covered with blankets. There were no clocks, watches, or calendars around, as Manson had forbidden anyone to have them. He wanted them to be focused on the present, the right now, and not some time in the future.

The family had a schedule of rising early every morning. Then the men would take the horses out into the fields so that they could eat, and the women would gather up the last night's dinner and create some breakfast out of it for them all to eat. After eating, they would prepare the horses for visitors to take riding tours around the ranch.

There was no time to relax. The moment Juan Flynn caught someone just sitting, he would order them to work. There was always something that needed fixing or hay to fetch. Landscaping and cleaning of the old movie set were done before any visitors arrived. Nobody would ever dare to challenge any of the work orders. They all worked until it was dinner time, and dinner consisted of whatever scraps could be found by some of the women who had been sent out earlier that day to gather food from the garbage of people's homes or businesses in the city. During dinner, the men always ate first, then the women who found and cooked the dinner ate whatever the men left behind, and then everyone else ate what was left.

In the Manson Family, the men always led and took control. Manson believed that women were never to be trusted because they knew how to trick men with their sex and love. He thought that this was the biggest problem in the world at that time.

After they ate, Manson usually started one of his meetings by giving everyone some LSD, which he believed to be holy. He thought it allowed the person to be in touch with their soul and to learn something about themselves. He gave the LSD to everyone personally. Once the Family got high, Manson started one of his teachings or sermons. He never took much or any of the LSD himself, as he wanted to keep control of his behavior. Manson never allowed the group to drink alcohol, though, as he thought that it destroyed their minds and made them less productive around the ranch.

Sometimes, he would act out some event from the bible, including the crucifixion of Christ, which he considered himself to be. At other times, Manson would play his guitar and sing, which inspired the women of the Family to dance. When Manson wasn't preaching or singing with his guitar, the Family would listen to music on albums from mainly the Beatles, Steppenwolf, The Doors, Jefferson Airplane, and sometimes the Moody Blues.

Most of the other women were jealous of Squeaky because she lived in the main house with the owner of the Spahn Ranch, George. In the main house, she got to listen to his radio, which played something different. Some of the girls were getting tired of hearing "Magical Mystery Tour" by the Beatles repeatedly every night. Yet nobody ever complained about it. They may have said a little about it to each other, but they couldn't let Gypsy or Tex Watson hear them. They knew it would get back to Manson if they heard them complain.

After the music, or sometimes during, members paired up with each other to have sex. The basic rule of the Family was that everyone was willing to have sex with anyone else in the Family, and no two people could pair up as a couple permanently. Usually, the only time Manson would make a couple that could stay together was for a different reason.

For instance, if he didn't trust one of them and wanted the other to keep an eye on that person. Sometimes, it was that both members had reservations about it, but he would tell each of them to watch out for the other on his behalf.

Manson had recruited fourteen-year-old Dianne Lake, whom he called "Snake," from her parents, and he had taken ownership of her. He continued to sleep with all the other women in the Family, which would often cause an issue between Dianne and whichever woman he was sleeping with the night before. Manson believed that it was his duty to have sex with each of his members and that for them, it was not only an honor but something that would empower them.

At times, Manson selected who was going to be with whom sexually, and what they should do when they were together. He believed that these sexual acts that he asked them to do were sacred and would help them grow as human beings.

6

CHILDREN OF THE FAMILY

Manson was very strict about when a child was born in the Family. He believed that a newborn needed to be removed from their biological parents. It was not that they couldn't see or talk to their kids, however. It was that Manson believed that if they raised their flesh and blood, it would only ruin them. Therefore, he made it so that the entire group raised all children born to Family members, and they were considered independent Family members in their own right.

When Mary Brunner had "Pooh Bear," Manson's son, he was considered to belong to the whole Family, and every member took part in raising him. When Susan Atkins had her son, Ze Zo Ze Cee Zadfrack, later that year, he too was kept with Pooh Bear in a different part of the commune. Manson wanted all the women to get pregnant as many times as they could and have as many children as possible. He thought that it was their job and a perfectly natural position for a woman to be in. However, Manson himself didn't want to produce any children with his Family of women.

7

CEASE TO EXIST

In the Fall of 1968, the civil unrest continued with protesters of the Vietnam War who were at the Democratic Presidential Convention in Chicago. All the television networks caught the police attacking the protesters, hitting them with their batons while choking them with tear gas bombs.

After a few years of assassinations, race riots, war protests, hippies, rock and roll, and drugs, the Republican party was elected with promises to clean things up. Richard Nixon got in with a narrow win over Hubert Humphrey. Within America, generational differences often divide people out of fear.

As the country appeared to be in turmoil, the Beach Boys were in the studio recording new music. Dennis Wilson decided that he needed to make some changes to Manson's song, "Cease to Exist," which he was going to record. Not only did he end up changing the music, but he also changed some of the words, including the title. In essence, Wilson altered the spiritual meaning behind the song, transforming it into something more sexually charged. After all those changes, he decided to call the song "Never Learn Not to Love."

After the album was completed, Dennis Wilson also failed to list Manson as a writer of the song. He had decided that, after all the money

Manson had cost him by letting the Family stay at his house and supporting them with everything, he figured he had it coming to him. As well, he just thought Manson owed him for the cost of replacing the Ferrari that one of his Family members, Clem Grogan, totaled. He was one of the workers at the Spahn Ranch and one of Manson's Family who jumped into Wilson's Ferrari and drove off into town, where he later got into an accident and demolished the car. The way that Wilson saw it, he had some money coming back to him from Manson, and this was just a start to pay him back.

During the time of the new Beach Boys album release, Manson was focused on other things, such as finding a new place for him and his Family to live. He was growing tired of the constant influx of drifters arriving at the ranch and wanting to stay. At the same time, Family members were wandering off with bikers or whoever came out to visit at the ranch, which made Manson feel like he was losing control over them. He already had enough of a flock that he didn't need to find any new members, but instead he had to focus on getting a tighter control over the members he already had.

Manson's main goal was to get a recording contract and become a rock star. He needed his Family to be behind him, following everything he said and doing the things he needed done, to secure that record contract.

All of these reasons are what led Manson to find another location for them to move to. One that was even further away from Los Angeles.

One of Charlie's girls, Cathy Gilles, often talked about a property out in Death Valley that she would call "Grandma's Place." When he asked her about some of the property's details, one of the first things that attracted him to it was that it was complicated to access, even by car.

When Manson finally ventured out to find the property, he was thrilled. It took hours to get to it from Los Angeles. After taking the highway to the turnoff, you had to follow this rough, gravel trail through mountains and harsh ranges with a population of only two people per square mile in the area. There were far more animals than humans, and the people present were usually prospectors searching for something or transients. Even more attractive to Manson was that there were only a few police officers to cover the entire county, and park rangers oversaw Death Valley National Park.

When they arrived at Cathy Gilles' family's ranch, they were impressed. It had been beautifully renovated, and they had several gardens where they grew their food. Across from their property was the Barker Ranch. Manson was immediately in love with it and could foresee what it could become.

It consisted of two buildings. The larger house included running water, which supplied a bathroom with a full shower and sink, as well as a workshop or tool shed. The property also had a pool and a generator, which could supply the buildings with power, as they were over fifty miles away from the closest electricity hookup location.

Manson found out where the owner, Arlene Barker, lived and went to her house to ask permission for him to move into her ranch. He told her that he was a musician recording a new album for the Beach Boys, and he needed the solitude and quiet that her ranch could offer. While he was telling her his story, he gave her one of the Beach Boys' gold records that he had stolen from Wilson's house when they were living there. The gift helped to prove his story to Barker, and she agreed to let him move in. After that, Manson relocated several of his Family members to Barker Ranch, but left a few behind at Spahn Ranch.

The members who ended up living at Barker Ranch were very unhappy with the move. They didn't like that it was so much hotter out in Death Valley. They didn't have any radio reception, no telephones, and no trees to hide from the sun. It was even harder for them to do simple things like cooking a meal, as they would have to chop wood and build a fire to cook something, and the outside temperature was excessively high.

Manson had to convince the family that Barker Ranch was the place they all needed to be during the Black revolution against the whites. He set a new goal for them to find the hidden hole, which would lead them down into the Earth, where they would discover a beautiful, wondrous world to live in.

Like he did before at Spahn Ranch, after they all ate dinner, he started everyone on an LSD trip. He began by telling them all stories about the wonderful world they would find in the hidden hole when they found it.

The primary issue they now had was finding food for the family to eat. When they were at Spahn Ranch, Manson could send a few members into the city, where they could panhandle or scrounge for food by going through people's or businesses' garbage cans. He couldn't do that now. Not in this remote place. Not to mention that whenever he sent the girls out into the desert to find some food or plants to eat, they not only couldn't find anything, but they had to fight off snakes and other creatures they had never dealt with at Spahn Ranch.

In Late November, just before Thanksgiving Day, Dennis Wilson and Jakobson decided to travel out to Barker Ranch and inform Manson that his song had been recorded and would be included on the new Beach Boys album. Once they arrived and told him the news, Manson wanted to go back to Los Angeles to attend the release of the song and album.

Manson told his family that they were going back to live on Spahn Ranch because the winters were too rough in Death Valley, and they would return there again in the following Spring. He didn't want any of them to know that the move was really because of his song being released on the new Beach Boys album. It wasn't a problem getting them to return to Spahn Ranch. In fact, they were thrilled. They liked it better at Spahn Ranch anyway.

Manson had to find a place to rent for a lot of his Family members because when Squeaky asked George Spahn if the Family could all return to the ranch, he told her no. He didn't want all of those long-haired hippies around the ranch anymore, as it made the place look run-down, and customers didn't like it.

Manson found a house in Canoga Park just above Topanga, where the Family continued their normal lifestyle of raiding garbage cans for food, panhandling, and doing their LSD preaching parties every night. The talks by Charlie were becoming more intense then, and he started asking them to do weird things, such as baa like a sheep. Around this time, the Beatles launched their new double album, named the *White Album*.

8

THE BEATLES

The *White Album* was released on November 22, 1968. It was like nothing The Beatles had done before. The album was far more a postmodern work than their usual folk and pop-rock style, for which they were well known. The thirty songs comprised an eclectic set of rock songs, heavily influenced by the band members who were constantly at odds during the five-month recording sessions.

The issues between the four band members were primarily due to John Lennon's new wife, Yoko Ono. By having her attend the recording sessions, he was violating the band's rule of never allowing any band member's spouse to be in the studio while they were recording. Later, Lennon would say that you could hear the breakup of the Beatles on the *White Album*. Additionally, during the recording sessions, their longtime engineer grew tired of the constant fighting within the group and quit, leaving halfway through the recording.

During the recording of "Back in the USSR," Ringo Starr got frustrated and upset with Paul McCartney's constant complaints about his drumming. Starr quit the band and walked out. A couple of weeks later, after the other band members asked him to return, he rejoined and resumed work in the studio to complete the album.

Nineteen of the thirty songs were significantly influenced by the

Beatles' visit to the Maharishi in India, where they took a Transcendental Meditation course in February 1968. Those nineteen songs were written during this time.

All four of the Beatles left before the Transcendental Meditation course was finished for different reasons. Ringo Starr couldn't stand the food that was served there and left after only two weeks. Paul McCartney left next within the first four weeks of March. John Lennon and George Harrison stayed longer, as they were both drawn to the religion of India, as well as meditation. But Lennon heard that the Maharaja had made sexual advances towards some of the women who came to India with the Beatles and worked for them, and so he left. Harrison ended up staying the longest, where the mediation course had the most effect.

While they were in India, the only instrument they had access to was the acoustic guitar. So it became the primary way that they wrote and performed their new songs. Five of the songs on the album remained acoustic even when they returned to their studio in England.

Manson and the White Album

Manson had to go out and buy the album on the day that it was released. He took it back to his newly rented house and gathered the Family to listen to it. He sank deeply into every song on the record and demanded that it be played repeatedly. Nothing else was to be played anymore, just the *White Album*.

Manson told his Family that it was most vital for them to listen to and understand certain songs on the album. "Piggies," "Blackbird, "Revolution #1, "Revolution #9," and "Helter Skelter." Manson believed these songs to be, as he called it, "a musical road map to the immediate future."

So, what did each of these songs mean?

"Piggies" – The song talks about the wealthy and powerful people and their entitlement and says that they needed a "good whacking."

"Blackbird" - The song described the days when the downtrodden Blacks in America were going to rise and take over.

"Revolution #1" – This was a call to arms for Blacks.

"Revolution #9" – This recording featured several sound effects, including a machine gun clattering, people screaming, and eerie electronic sounds, which were intended to represent the impending destruction and violence.

"Helter Skelter" – This represented the official name of the war that was coming.

Manson believed that the Beatles' *White Album* was a collective call to arms for everyone in the world, aimed explicitly at Manson and his followers. He told his Family that the day would come when they would all return to Barker Ranch, sometime in 1969, and the Beatles would meet them there. He said that this came from a verse, "Crossing the Atlantic," found in the song named "Honey Pie."

The message he believed to be true prompted Manson to send several invitations via telegrams and mail, inviting the Beatles to join him and his Family at the ranch, or for them to visit their management office in London. Manson never received any response from the Beatles, but that didn't deter him at all. He thought that the Beatles were just one part of the war that was coming.

Manson believed that the Beatles were mentioned in the final book of the New Testament version of the Bible. In the "Revelation to John," John had been exiled to an island for preaching the gospel of Jesus. His reward from Jesus was to understand the signs that would indicate when Jesus would return to Earth.

Charlie believed that Revelation predicted that locusts would come to the Earth. To him, because locusts were beetles, the prophecy was about The Beatles. It also said that the locusts would have "scales like iron breastplates." He believed that these were the Beatles' guitars.

Revelations also spoke of a fifth angel coming to Earth who was given the key to the shaft of the bottomless pit, and Manson believed that he was that angel and that the pit was in Death Valley.

Manson said that this was the time when the oppressed of the world, led by Blacks, were to rise and take power over the Whites. And that the uprising was known as the "Helter Skelter." He told his followers that the Blacks were going to kill most of the Whites, and the remaining would be held and used as their slaves.

According to Manson, the Bible told him to lead his Family into the bottomless pit, where they would be safe until the battle between the Blacks and Whites was over. During this time of seclusion, Manson's Family would grow to the size of the twelve tribes of Israel, with approximately 144,000 members.

He also preached that the Blacks who were now in charge of the world would figure out that they didn't know how to run the world properly. This realization would be the time when Manson and his followers came out of the pit and returned to the world. The Blacks would then ask Manson to take charge of the world and show them the way.

To help maintain control over his followers, Manson told his story of the coming race war. He added that anyone who was white who left the Family would end up enslaved by the new Black leaders.

Tex Watson's Departure

Even with all this new information, Tex Watson left the group. Watson was a devout follower of Manson but found that he couldn't stand to live with the Family. It made him feel claustrophobic, and it lacked privacy. So he snuck away from the ranch late one night. He moved to Los Angeles and found a place to live with a new girlfriend, and supported himself by selling drugs.

Manson was too preoccupied to notice Tex's disappearance between the upcoming race war and the new Beach Boys' album, containing his song, "Cease to Exist," which was about to be released on January 27, 1969. Only at that time, he still had no idea that Wilson had not only rearranged the song both musically and lyrically, but he also wasn't given any credit on the album for the song as a writer.

9

"CEASE TO EXIST" CEASED TO EXIST

In early January, the Beach Boys released their first singles from the album. The second single they released was "Bluebirds over the Mountain," which had Manson's reworked song "Cease to Exist" on the B-side. The new title was "Never Learn Not to Love."

The day that Manson heard the new single, he was enraged. He couldn't understand how or why Dennis Wilson betrayed him. He knew that Wilson could no longer be trusted. Not only had he taken Manson's song, but he had also changed the words and music, then put it on the album without giving Manson any credit for writing the song. To add salt to the wound, the single only managed to go to number sixty-six on the charts, so it was considered a flop as well.

All Charlie had left was the hope that producer Terry Melcher would get him a record deal. He knew that he couldn't attack Dennis Wilson verbally or physically because he was still best friends with Melcher. Manson would have to pretend to like Wilson still until he got a deal arranged with Melcher.

Melcher was preoccupied with dealing with his mother, Doris Day's, financial problems. After her husband, Marty Melcher, died in early 1968, it was discovered that Marty and his business partner at the time had spent all of her money. This left Day deep in debt and owing some back taxes to the government. It took almost five years for them to win a lawsuit against Marty's business partner, and even longer to collect any damages.

Melcher and his then live-in girlfriend, actress Candice Bergen, moved out of their rental property on Cielo Drive to save money. They moved into one of his mother's beachfront properties instead. He tried to keep his move quiet because if it got out to the public, it would only create more talk about his mother, so he only told his closest friends about his move.

Melcher was also taking some time off from working in the studios with bands or attending Hollywood parties to address his mother's financial problems. His stepping back made it virtually impossible for Manson to talk with him. Melcher was no longer seeing him. Manson asked both Wilson and Jakobson to tell Melcher that he was looking for him, and even though they both said that they would, Manson still wasn't hearing from Melcher.

10

ROMAN POLANSKI & SHARON TATE

Filmmaker Roman Polanski and his wife, actress and model Sharon Tate, began renting the home on Cielo Drive in February 1969. The couple settled into their new home quickly, having some of the most lavish parties in Hollywood. Polanski's recent success had thrown him into the spotlight, and Tate's beauty and kindness only added to the attention. In addition to everything else, Polanski gained a reputation for being quite the partygoer and the subject of much gossip around town.

A noticeable difference at the Cielo Drive residence after the couple moved in was the ease of access to the property. When Melcher lived there, the electronic gate was always closed, and no one was allowed in unless he knew who they were and why they were there. In comparison, Polanski and Tate were more open to guests.

The couple had some regular visitors who stayed over for several nights at a time. Jay Sebring, known as the "hairdresser to the stars," had dated Tate before she met and later married Polanski, and had become close to the couple, often visiting them. Voytek Frykowski, who had grown up with Polanski in Poland, was always there, especially if Polanski was away filming in a different country. Frykowski's girlfriend, Abigail Folger, also known as "Gibby" to her friends, would often be with him. They all became quite close. Folger even invested in Sebring's hair salons that he had been opening. She was already wealthy, having been born into the Folger's Coffee family. But Folger never let her own wealth get in the way of her commitment to helping people experiencing poverty. She was a volunteer social worker for the Los Angeles County Department of Welfare.

Another frequent visitor to the Polanski house was Tate's photographer, Shahrokh Hatami. On Sunday, March 23rd, Hatami was at Cielo Drive to do a photo shoot with Tate. He was waiting for Sharon to come out to the pool area so that he could take some pictures of her. Suddenly, a stranger appeared, surprising him. "Hey, man, what do you want?" Hatami shouts out to the man who had a more petite frame, long hair, and a beard. "I'm looking for someone." The man replied in a quieter, lighter tone. "He's not here!" Hatami says, still in a firm tone. "Maybe you'll find it in the guesthouse." Hatami then pointed down the alley towards the guesthouse. He was thinking that perhaps the owner of the residence, Rudi Altobelli, who was living at the guesthouse, was expecting a visitor.

At that moment, Sharon Tate walked out onto the porch and asked Hatami what was going on. She looked up at the man, and the two of them stared each other in the eyes before the man walked towards the guesthouse. "It was nobody, Sharon, just someone probably looking for Rudi." Tate smiled, and the two of them began planning their photo shoots.

Altobelli was in the shower when his dog started barking aggressively. He got out and put on a robe to look out the window to see what was going on. He noticed a figure standing outside his door, so he walked over and opened the door. The long-haired, short-bearded man smiles slightly and introduces himself, "Hello, I'm Charlie, and I am…" Abruptly, Rudi says quickly, "I know who you are, Charlie. What do you want here?" Still speaking softly, Charlie continues, "I am looking to speak with Terry Melcher." Annoyed, Rudi says, "He's moved, he doesn't live here anymore." Then he began to close his front door when Charlie asked, "Do you know where he's moved, man?" Rudi had met Charlie a few times before and didn't like him at all. Charlie knew that Rudi was an agent and had given him some of his music on tapes before, which Rudi hated. "No!" he answers firmly. All of a sudden, Charlie changed his tune. "What do you do for a living?" Rudi now said, "I would love to talk some more to you, Charlie, only I have to get packed quickly as I am leaving the country tomorrow." Rudi and Tate were leaving for Italy as she was starring in a film being made there. "How did you get here? Why did you come to this house?" Rudi says in an interrogative tone. "The people in the main house told me to come here." Rudi started to scold Charlie, "Well, don't do that again. I don't want my tenants to be bothered like that, understand?" Charlie started to get angry and turned around, then began walking away. Rudi closed the door.

While he was in Italy, Rudi hired William Garretson, a nineteen-year-old who had come to Los Angeles with the hopes of making it big. But after a few months, Garretson already wanted to return home to Ohio. Rudi hired him to stay at the guesthouse and take care of the property for thirty-five dollars a week. Garretson had to take care of both cats, the dog, and the property. He also wasn't allowed to bother the tenants in the main house. When Rudi returned to California, he was going to pay for Garretson's flight home to Ohio.

A month later, in April, Tate asked Frykowski and Folger to move into the main house to keep an eye on their things. She didn't know Garretson and felt more relaxed having their friends stay there while they were gone. Not to mention that when Tate returned home and Polanski was still away working, she would have company and not be alone.

~

Charlie did everything he could to find Melcher. Manson told everyone they both knew that he needed to speak to Melcher.

Meanwhile, he got the Family back on track for getting ready for Helter Skelter to start. Bobby Beausoleil returned to the ranch, accompanied by his new pregnant girlfriend, Kitty Lutesinger. Another new member of the Family was one of Charlie's old prison friends, Bill Vance. He liked having Vance on board, as he was a skilled document forger, and Vance could start creating fake driver's licenses for Family members. The newest female member was Barbara Hoyt, a runaway teenager from Canoga Park.

Beausoleil became a more regular presence at the ranch. Not only was it a better place for Hoyt to have his child, but he also had dreams of becoming a famous rock star. If Charlie got a record deal with Melcher, he thought he could as well.

The Los Angeles Sheriff's office decided to raid Spahn Ranch on April 19th, believing that the hippies who were living there were behind all of the recent vehicle thefts after receiving some reports that some of the stolen vehicles had been seen on the ranch. Several of the stolen cars were recovered, and police arrested the family members present at the time of the incident. They were all charged with grand theft auto.

Charlie didn't appear to be on the ranch at the time of the raid, so he wasn't arrested. After a few days, the police did not have enough evidence to prove that the vehicles found at the ranch had been stolen, so they dropped all charges. Charlie and the family weren't intimidated by the arrests at all. They picked right up where they left off, only now they had to steal some more dune buggies as the police had taken some of them in the raid.

The day after those who were arrested returned to the ranch, Tex Watson was arrested for being under the influence of drugs and alcohol in public while he was in Van Nuys. Somehow, he had eaten some Belladonna root and was found on the sidewalk walking on his hands and knees like a dog, saying "Beep Beep" every time he got behind someone. He was released the next day, appearing to have regained his senses. Someone being high on drugs had become a common thing for police, and they treated them the same as if someone had been drinking too much.

Tex returned to the ranch upon his release, but he seemed different to many of the other Family members. Tex had always been a pretty mild and calm person, but now he was behaving aggressively and even demanding of them. The minute he returned, he began ordering the girls around and telling them what they needed to do. Tex never did this before the Belladonna arrest. Several of the girls thought that maybe the Belladonna had some effect on him, turning him mean. Tex suddenly thought of himself as the second in command. When Charlie wasn't around, he was in charge. Some of the girls became scared of him with his new pushy attitude towards them. When they complained to Charlie, he just put them off and even laughed a little. Inside, he knew that Tex was important to him and his plans, and if anything, perhaps a tougher Tex would be even more useful for him.

At the beginning of May, Manson finally heard back from Melcher, who said that he would visit the ranch to listen to Charlie play his songs for him on May 18th. Even though Melcher didn't show up back in March and he didn't tell him that he was sorry for not showing up then, he guaranteed that he would come this time for sure.

Now, for the second time in as many months, Manson was getting a chance to secure a recording deal, and he told the Family to put the Helter Skelter prep on hold and instead prepare for the Melcher visit, as they had done before. This time, however, there would be many more rehearsals. Almost daily, he and the girls got together and rehearsed all the songs he wanted to play for Melcher. It had to be perfect. Charlie also wanted the girls to wear tight, sexy clothing for the performance, and he ordered them to all strip down when Melcher was here watching them. He was not taking any chances of not getting the record deal.

11

CIELO DRIVE CHANGES RENTERS

In the Summer of 1968, *Rosemary's Baby* became a hit film in the United States, catapulting Roman Polanski—its writer and director—into the spotlight. Roman married Sharon Tate back in January of that same year. Hollywood was noticing Sharon after she starred in the movie *Valley of the Dolls*. She was being courted by several producers and directors, all of whom wanted her to be in their next film.

The couple was looking for a house to live in where they could entertain and impress the Hollywood crowd, rather than the small apartment on Sunset where they had been living since their wedding. In February, the search for a new place became urgent after Tate became pregnant. She knew Terry Melcher, so she called him to find out if Cielo Drive was a good place to live. After he told her how wonderful it was there, she told Roman what Melcher had said, who, in turn, called Rudi Altobelli. Altobelli said he was looking for a new tenant to take over his house since Terry Melcher and Candice Bergen had moved out. He was thrilled to get the call from Polanski. The two men made a deal over the phone, and within three days, the Polanskis moved into the Cielo Drive house.

Altobelli remained on the property, though, living in the guest cottage. He agreed to look after the house when the Polanskis went away to film a movie or go on vacation. If he ever had to travel, then he would have a caretaker stay in the cottage to take care of the property.

1969 continued to be a year of protests and fighting amongst Americans, just as the rest of the sixties were. On January 20th, Richard Nixon was sworn in as president, and one of the first things he did was to try to crack down on the student protesters of the war in Vietnam. He cut financial aid, federal scholarships, and loans to students who were caught protesting.

Also, in January, Alprentice Carter and John Huggins, two of the Black Panther leaders in Los Angeles, were shot on the UCLA campus by gang members of the "United Slaves." The Black Panthers later accused the FBI of being behind the murders of their leaders.

~

Manson used these conspiracies to help convince his followers that the race war was beginning. He started giving survival courses to the Family so they could be ready to live in harsh conditions. He tested them to see how long each member could live without having water or food.

Manson then issued an order that every Family member had to carry a knife with them at all times after training them on using their knives for self-defense. The girls told stories of how he would take turns standing each member in front of a wall so he could throw knives at them. He wanted them not to be scared of knives, so he continued to do this until they no longer flinched.

Manson next began to trade things like dune buggies and drugs for guns. They had to conceal their newfound weapons from the Spahn Ranch owner and employees, knowing that if they were caught, they would be expelled from the ranch. Charlie and some Family members went out into the desert to practice target shooting to become comfortable using the guns.

Manson explained during his nightly talks to the Family that they were never to use the weapons on anyone unless they were attacked. Their training was just for survival. They were to let the Blacks fight their war with the Whites, and the Family was to hide out and not get involved until after it was over.

Manson's plans were so detailed that they had hidden food, water, and other necessities in various locations between Spahn Ranch and Barker Ranch, which were all marked on maps. They did this in case the war began and they had to leave Spahn Ranch quickly, then they would be ready.

Around this time, Tex Watson decided to return to Spahn Ranch and the Family. He didn't like living in the city and didn't feel a connection to the people he encountered. Charlie had no problem with forgiving him and letting him back into the Family, since he was a great mechanic, and that's what was needed. They had been stealing various dune buggies and other desert-useable vehicles and needed someone to get them running properly.

Now that Manson was working to get his Family ready for the civil war, he needed more money. First, he tried having the girls go to Los Angeles and get work as dancers at strip bars. But most of the girls were turned down because they didn't have large breasts. Manson then decided to convert one of the buildings at Spahn Ranch into a bar or nightclub, which he called the "Helter Skelter Bar." They all chipped in to paint and decorate the building to make it look psychedelic. He served beer and allowed underage people to drink there. He also let everyone smoke marijuana freely. Some of the Family girls took turns being go-go dancers at the club to help keep the men there, spending their money. However, the bar didn't last very long after someone reported the activity to the police. Within a week, they fined Spahn Ranch owner George Spahn $1,500 for operating a bar without a license.

The bar closure left Manson yet again seeking another way to generate some quick money. This time, Charlie looked at drug dealing like he had been involved in for a few years in the past. He needed to increase his sales by establishing more connections or bringing in additional salespeople. Manson looked at making deals with the motorcycle gang "Straight Satans" as he had some connection to them already. A few of their members occasionally rode out to the ranch and partied with the Family.

Manson and the bikers worked out a deal where Manson would sell them drugs, and they would sell them to third parties. He also gave the bikers an extra perk by offering them free sex with any of his girls any time they wanted it. Ruth Ann and Leslie Van Houten were the two who went with the bikers the most often, as they genuinely enjoyed spending time with them.

The Straight Satan's Treasurer, Danny DeCarlo, or "Donkey Dan" as the Family called him because he was rather well endowed, was the official contact between the biker gang and the Manson Family. If any deals were to be made between the two groups, he would be the one to make them.

One deal of note was made after Charlie saw and admired a sword carried by the biker gang's leader, George Knoll. DeCarlo struck an agreement between the two men, where Charlie paid off a fine for Knoll in exchange for the sword. The sword would later become one of Manson's favorite tools.

All of the recent activity with the bikers, who were starting to become regulars hanging out at the Spahn Ranch, upset the owner, George. His lead worker, Shorty Shea, who already disliked Manson and the rest of the Family, kept asking George if he could clear them all off the property. Once Charlie caught wind of what Shea was saying about them, he added him to his list of enemies and had Squeaky keep a close eye on everything he was doing or saying, reporting it back to him.

Even though they generally got along, a growing tension between the bikers and several of the Family members was the fact that the bikers hated the Blacks and often called them names or made fun of them. During Charlie's descriptions of how Helter Skelter was going to unfold, he was cautious not to speak ill of Black people. He explained that the Blacks were different from the Whites, and that because they had been oppressed for so long, it was only proper that they rose up and fought back.

But Blacks were never meant to be in charge of the world. That was going to be their job after the race war. During many of his talks to the Family, he said that Blacks had a lesser intellect, but they were still human beings. Some of his Family members challenged Charlie on what he was saying because they had heard him disparage Black people in the bikers' presence. He explained to them that he was only pretending to do this because he needed to keep the bikers happy with him.

One of the best explanations that Charlie gave to fool his Family was to tell them that the races should never mix. Otherwise, they would be left with a garden that had only one type of flower. Instead, we needed a garden full of various beautiful flowers.

By this time, with all of the talking and planning for the race war, Manson and most of his Family were on edge. Several incidents were happening around the ranch, indicating this. On one occasion, while Charlie and Jakobson were walking around and discussing what kind of film should be made about the group, Charlie suddenly got enraged and pulled out a gun and pointed it at Jakobson's head. "What would you do if I pulled the trigger?" he asked in a loud manner. "I guess I'll be dead then," Jakobson answered, hoping it would show him as being brave to Charlie. Manson put away the gun, and his demeanor returned to normal. Then he began talking again about making a movie. Inside Jakobson's mind, he knew right then that Charlie was all about fear and had nothing to do with love.

In another incident, Charlie attacked Little Paul Watkins after Watkins told Charlie about a new guy, Paul Crockett, who had been hanging around the Family members at Barker Ranch, telling them that Charlie was wrong about many things he had said. Charlie's rage came from his desire to be in complete control of the Family, and he didn't want anyone else to take his Family members away from him. Charlie grabbed Watkins, wrapped his hands around his throat, and began to choke him aggressively. Watkins struggled and tried to fight back, but Charlie's grip only became stronger. Knowing that he was going to die, Watkins just gave up and let his body go limp. Almost immediately, Charlie let go of Watkins and allowed his body to fall to the ground. Watkins survived this attack but was now convinced Charlie was about death, not life or love.

This kind of nervous energy was enhanced by several of the Family members as well when Manson started putting together small groups and taking them into the city, where they would do what they called "Creepy Crawling." Each group would break into a person's home as quietly as possible without being noticed. Once they got into the house, they would rearrange their furniture, such as moving a living room recliner into the kitchen. They also moved personal items to places that they knew the owner would notice, such as putting their toothbrush in the fridge. The owners of the home would wake up to realize that someone had been in the house and rearranged their belongings.

To make it even stranger, nothing was stolen. The reason for doing these creepy crawls was to prove to themselves that they could get into any house, anywhere, and anytime they wanted. And it was a fun game to play.

The Family also didn't just pick one particular neighborhood or style of house. It was all done randomly. John and Michelle Phillips, of the famous rock band the Mamas and the Papas, owned one of the houses they hit.

~

In early March, Terry Melcher informed Charlie that he would be visiting. The prospect of getting a record deal got Manson excited. He was sure he was finally going to get to audition for Melcher and secure a record deal. He immediately had Tex Watson and some of the other men in the family make repairs to the buildings to improve their appearance. He also had them clean up all the horse manure that was lying around the ranch's roadways. Manson didn't want anything around that might turn off Melcher. Charlie also had some of the girls make him a new outfit to wear for the audition. He didn't believe in killing animals but wanted some leather in his outfit, so he had the girls order some deer skins to make his new outfit.

The whole family prepared several dishes for Melcher's arrival, including baked cakes and cookies. Manson even bathed, shaved, and cut his hair for the audition. Every detail was seen to and had been completed to perfection. They were all dressed up and ready to perform for Melcher, only he never came.

Manson was downright embarrassed in front of his Family, and his ego was insulted. And all of that upset soon turned to anger. He couldn't understand how Melcher could stand up the most talented musician alive today. Charlie worried about the timing, as Helter Skelter was about to happen, and he needed every member of his Family dedicated to him and the plans. Having Melcher ditch him like this could cause some of his followers to lose faith in him and possibly even leave the ranch.

So Manson now had to make a new plan. He would have to go and get Melcher and make him come out to the ranch immediately, enabling his followers to see how strong and essential he truly was. He was determined to save face by going out and finding him directly and ordering Melcher to attend his audition. Since he was no longer seeing Melcher out at any of the parties around town, he would go directly to Melcher's home on Cielo Drive to confront him.

12

MANSON LIVE

America was in what seemed to be emotional turmoil in 1969. The fighting in Vietnam shaded excitement over the July moon landing, and the new president, Richard Nixon, was attacking the colleges and universities that were allowing student protests over the war. It was angry over the Black riots that continued to happen in major cities. It was obvious that Nixon believed Blacks were inferior to Whites on several levels. He supported Congress by providing them with programs and funding to improve the lives of minorities. He thought it was his duty to make the system appear to help minority communities, even though he did not honestly believe in it himself. All the turmoil gave Manson more proof that the race war was coming.

It was now May 19th, and a nervous Charlie waited for Melcher to arrive. When he finally showed up, Melcher was direct and wanted to get down to business. He had several other plans lined up for the day and didn't want to waste any time eating cookies and chatting with the Manson Family.

Charlie grabbed his guitar and began playing, while some of the girls sang backup for him, and a few others danced and stripped. Melcher sat quietly, focusing on the performance. After a few songs were played, Manson decided to take a break. During that short break, he walked over to Melcher and tried to strike up a casual conversation, but Melcher never engaged him.

After having no luck with Melcher socially, Charlie returned to the stage and continued playing his songs, with the girls performing behind him. After another half hour of playing, Charlie stopped and thanked Melcher for attending. Melcher walked over to Charlie and led him away to have a private conversation. He told Charlie that there were a couple of songs he thought had potential and mentioned that he knew a great guitarist, Mike Deasy, who had also recorded for other bands. He said he would return with Deasy and see if he would be interested in recording some of Manson's music. Melcher gave Charlie a $50 bill and told him to buy whatever he thought the Family might need. He then got back into his car and left.

After Melcher pulled away, most of the Family gathered around Manson to find out what he had said and what had happened. Charlie was smart enough to realize that Melcher wasn't interested in his music, but that would be too embarrassing to admit. So, instead, he told them all that Melcher had given him money as a signing bonus and would be returning with a recording van and engineer. Manson also explained to the Family that because his word was like gold, there was no reason for them to sign a contract. It was just unnecessary.

In reality, Melcher didn't think Manson's music was good. In fact, he felt that it was way below average. He lumped him in with all the other poor hippies out there who were playing on street corners and believed they were going to be the next big rock star, just one of a thousand out there who would never make it. Melcher did want to send Deasy out to the ranch to see if he might like something that Manson was doing. That part was true. But the kind of music that Charlie was doing would be for a small niche audience and wouldn't be worth Melcher's time. Melcher scheduled Deasy to go out to the ranch on June 6th.

While Manson was waiting the three weeks for Melcher to bring Deasy out to the ranch, he began to preach about the coming revolution again. Most of his Family didn't want to have to go back to Barker Ranch again, but those were the plans when the race war started.

On the morning of June 6th, Melcher arrived at the ranch with

Deasy, accompanied by Gregg Jakobson. Like the first performance that Manson and the girls did for Melcher, they went through the same songs. Only this time, someone in the Manson group made a catastrophic move. They decided to drop a hit of acid into Deasy's drink. Deasy was not used to taking drugs like that, and shortly after he drank it down with his drink, he went on a terrible trip where he began screaming and crying out loud.

The performance stopped, and Melcher and Jakobson had to carry Deasy back to their car and take him home. Manson and most of the gang followed them to the car, and one of the Family members, Randy Starr, started talking to Melcher about the movie *Cat Ballou*. Charlie, already on edge, snapped and began to beat Starr up. Charlie began to think that his dreams might be over now.

Not wanting to tell his followers what he thought, because if they lost faith in him becoming a rock star, they might also lose faith in him being their leader during the race war. So, Manson decided he would tell them a lie. He told them that Melcher had promised him a contract, but that he had decided to cancel the deal. Melcher had betrayed him, just as Jesus had been betrayed in the Bible several times.

From this point forward, Manson displayed his anger every day. He was no longer the peaceful individual who frequently spoke about love.

Behind the scenes, Manson continued to reach out to other musical artists about his music and attempted to secure a record deal. He traveled to Cass Elliot's, singer in the band the Mama's and Papas, and played some songs for her, but she passed on them. He also asked Bobby Beausoleil to play Frank Zappa some of Charlie's recordings, but Zappa didn't like them either.

During this time, Manson began to order the Family members to take things when they were out on the creepy crawls. He told them to look for credit cards or items that he could easily sell.

When Charlie found out where Melcher had moved to, he sent out some of his Family members to do a creepy crawl at his new place. When they arrived, they were unable to break into the place. So instead, they stole a telescope that was sitting on his deck. Even though Manson thought this would send a message to Melcher for turning him down, Melcher never associated the theft with Manson.

He never gave him another thought after the acid debacle with Deasy.

Charlie then thought that they should up their creepy crawls even more by confronting and scaring their targets in person after they had broken into their homes. He preached to them that death wasn't any different than life. Therefore, they shouldn't fear death. At the end of every sermon, he asked everyone there if they would die for him. They all responded that they would.

13

THEY COME AND THEY GO

By the Summer of 1969, several of the girls began to tire of living at the ranch and Charlie's constant rants of anger. One of the girls who was complaining the most and openly was Leslie Van Houten. In response, Charlie took her for a ride in one of their dune buggies out to the top of Santa Susanas. After they were parked, he firmly told her that if she wanted to leave him, she would have to jump. She didn't want to jump to her death, so she told Charlie that she wanted to stay with him and that she was going through a bad time.

Another Family member, Patricia Krenwinkel, left with one of the bikers who often visited the ranch. She was not looking forward to making the move to Barker Ranch and would rather live freely, as the family used to before all the Helter-Skelter talk. Charlie, knowing the biker she had left with, found them later at one of his hangouts and told Krenwinkel she had to come back with him, so she did.

Charlie's problem of Family members leaving him also happened with the few members that he had left behind at Barker Ranch. The other ranch was much harder to control, being so far away at Spahn Ranch. Paul Crockett continued to visit the ranch and eventually persuaded Brooks Poston to work with him instead of wasting his time waiting for Charlie. Juanita also left the ranch after meeting and marrying one of Crockett's business partners.

Manson was also frustrated with the Blacks for not being organized enough to start their race war. Charlie began to think that he would have to show them how, as they were just not smart enough to figure it out themselves.

Manson sent Paul Watkins to Barker Ranch to try to restore stability there. Because Watkins thought Charlie was going off the deep end, when he got to the Barker Ranch, instead of setting himself up to stay there for a while and restoring Charlie's control, he also went to Crockett's place and decided to join him.

On top of everything else, Clem "Scramblehead" Grogan, the Spahn Ranch employee who had become another of the Manson Family members, was arrested for exposing himself to a group of children. He was convicted of the crime and was sentenced to spend ninety days at the Camarillo State Mental Institute for observation on June 19, 1969. A month later, on July 19th, Clem suddenly appeared at the ranch, surprising everyone. It seemed that because the mental institute wasn't a secure premise with guards, Clem decided one day to leave and head back to Spahn Ranch.

Manson had lost five members in a very short period and needed to gain some new followers to replace them. He then put the pressure on his primary recruiter, Gypsy, to start finding some more people to join the Family. Even though Gypsy was beginning to think about leaving herself, she agreed to do more. She felt that being at the ranch was no longer about peace and love, but rather about work and anger. Despite this, when it came right down to it, she would never desert Charlie or her obligation to the rest of the Family.

Gypsy was friends with many of the members who lived in other communes nearby and thought that might be a good place to begin her search for recruits. On her travels, she decided to meet up with an old friend, Charlie Melton. At one time, they both lived in the same commune.

Melton had been living in a trailer with his friends, Bob and Linda Kasabian, and her little girl, Tanya, in Topanga Canyon. The Kasabians had recently reconciled after a year-long breakup. But still, they weren't getting along well. Bob wanted to go south and buy a boat so that they could sail around the world. Linda didn't want this. She wanted something more, especially now that she had a young daughter. She didn't think that would be a good upbringing for her.

Shortly after Gypsy arrived at the trailer, the two men went out on a short construction job together, leaving the two ladies at the trailer alone. Linda began to explain her life problems to Gypsy, who was very loving and understanding. It wasn't long before Gypsy told Linda that she had the perfect answer for all of her problems. Charlie Manson was not only a handsome man but also a figure she looked up to, and they had a beautiful Family that all lived at Spahn Ranch. She also told Linda that the Family would be happy to help her care for her daughter, Tanya, and invited her to come out for a short visit. If she wasn't comfortable or didn't like it, she could return to Bob in their trailer.

The following week, after Linda and Bob got into a huge argument, she left to visit her friend Gypsy at Spahn Ranch. After she arrived, Gypsy took her around and introduced her to many of the Family members. While this was happening, a few of the other girls took Tanya to play with the other children living at Spahn Ranch. Linda loved the atmosphere and the Family members.

That night, she met Tex Watson, and an immediate connection was formed. That same night, after the two chatted for hours, they ended up spending the night together. By the next morning, Linda had decided that Spahn Ranch was where she wanted to live.

During their first night together, Tex learned that Linda was living in a trailer with Bob, her husband, and their friend Charlie Melton. She had also told him about their plans to buy a boat and sail around the world. When he asked how they could afford a boat, Linda told them that Bob and Melton had saved around $5,000.

Later that day, both Gypsy and Tex worked on convincing Linda that she should take the five grand when she returned to retrieve her clothing and personal belongings. Gypsy told her that this was sure to impress Charlie and help the Family live better. Even though Linda felt guilty about stealing someone else's money, when Gypsy drove her out to the trailer to get her things, she took the money. Then they returned to the ranch.

After they got back to the ranch, Gypsy took the money and went to find Charlie to give it to him. When he saw the money, he came out and finally met Linda. She became even more desirable to Charlie after he spoke with her for a while and discovered that she had a driver's license. Linda was the perfect candidate to join the Manson Family.

14

LOTSAPOPPA

Manson was determined to keep the Family together. He now believed that if they were all in one place, he could maintain control over everyone. He also thought that the further away from Los Angeles, the easier it would be, with fewer distractions, so Barker Ranch was the ideal place for them to go.

There were two significant problems with the move to Barker Ranch. One was Paul Crockett, but in Charlie's mind, he would take care of him for good. The other was finding enough money to survive in Death Valley. Charlie and Tex Watson devised a plan to gather enough money to make the trip and stay out there for a little while without any problems. One of Watson's drug-dealing ex-girlfriends, Luella, would be part of it.

Tex phoned her up, telling her that he had twenty-five kilos of prime marijuana and wanted her to sell it for him. He wanted $2500 for it, but he needed the cash up front. Luella said that she could sell it easily. She would make a good profit and take some of the pot for herself.

What Tex and Charlie didn't tell her was that they didn't actually have 25 kilos of pot. Instead, they planned to take the $2,500 and let Luella take the fall for not having the pot to give to her buyer. If her buyer believed her story about Tex burning her and showed up at Spahn

Ranch, Manson would tell them that Watson hadn't been there for weeks and that he didn't know where he went.

The plan didn't go as intended. Luella's buyer was Bernard Crowe, otherwise known as "Lotsapoppa," a six-foot-five-inch, three-hundred-pound Black drug dealer who had the reputation of being as bad as you could get. Once he met Luella and she didn't have the weed that was promised, he and his two partners decided that they would hold her until they got the pot they bought.

Luella and Tex were waiting at her apartment for Lotsapoppa. When he finally showed up, he brought two other guys with him, who gave Tex the money. When they realized that Tex didn't have the weed, they told Tex that they were going to stay there with his pretty girlfriend, Luella. If he didn't come back with the weed soon, then he was going to take her apart piece by piece.

Tex swore that the deal was on the level and that he was going to take the money back to Charlie, and they would get their weed. Then he scurried out of Luella's apartment. After a few hours, Lotsapoppa figured that he had been ripped off and decided to call Charlie himself.

When Charlie answered the phone, he acted surprised and said that he didn't know what was going on. Tex was supposed to give them the pot. Lotsapoppa knew then that he had been taken advantage of and demanded to know where Tex was. Charlie told him that Tex wasn't there, and he didn't know where he was or how to find him. Lotsapoppa then described to Charlie how he would cut Luella into tiny pieces and feed them to the dogs, but that didn't faze Manson at all.

Still not getting his way, Lotsapoppa then told Charlie that he was a member of the Black Panthers and that if he didn't give him back his money or bring him the weed he had bought with it, he would get the Panthers to visit Spahn Ranch, and before they left, everyone would be dead. Now, Lotsapoppa was telling Charlie a lie. He never belonged to the Black Panthers. Still, they terrified Manson as he had spent years in prison, and during that time, he was intimidated and harassed by the Black Muslims serving time there, and he believed the two groups to be connected. He also thought that the Panthers would be the leaders during the upcoming race riots. If Manson had been more up-to-date on current events, he would have known that by that time in 1969, the

Panthers were already falling apart and several of their leaders had been killed.

Manson nervously told Lotsapoppa that he would settle things by bringing his money to him at his North Hollywood apartment. After they agreed, he grabbed family member T.J. Walleman and told him in private that they needed to kill Lotsapoppa. T.J. asked him how they were going to do this, and Manson pulled out a gun. He tucked it in the back of his pants and covered it up with his shirt. Charlie told him that when they got to the apartment, he would walk in first. When Charlie gave him the signal, T.J. would pull the gun out from the back of Charlie's pants and shoot Lotsapoppa. He agreed, and they left for the North Hollywood apartment.

After they arrived, they both walked through the front door with Charlie in front of T.J., but they were surprised to find two other men standing beside Lotsapoppa. Once T.J. saw the other men, he started to shake and back away from Manson. Charlie had a streak of anger rising through him when he noticed T.J. walking backwards toward the door, and he just grabbed the gun out from his back himself and aimed it at Lotsapoppa and pulled the trigger. It misfired.

The two men standing beside Lotsapoppa ran towards Charlie, and T.J. ran out the door. Charlie pulled the trigger again, and this time it fired. The bullet went right through the chest of Lotsapoppa, and he collapsed face-first onto the floor. He then turned the gun towards the other two men, who stopped in their tracks. Then Charlie backed out of the front door slowly while aiming his gun at the two men.

Charlie and T.J. drove back to Spahn Ranch recklessly and in a hurry. And the whole time, Manson was so angry at T.J. for getting scared and backing away from the plan that he yelled and slapped him across the face. T.J. had now witnessed Manson murder someone and knew he made him mad, so as soon as they got back to the ranch, he grabbed his bag and ran away.

Charlie initially said nothing to his Family, and early the next morning, he had some of his girls run out to get the newspaper. Charlie grabbed the paper out of their hands as soon as they arrived back at the ranch. He took it to where he could be alone to read through it.

On the front page, he saw the headlines about a Black Panther being shot and killed, and he thought it was Lotsapoppa they were talking about. But it wasn't. Charlie couldn't read very well and didn't realize that it was a completely different shooting that took place in another part of town.

Lotsapoppa wasn't dead and ended up surviving his gunshot wound. He wasn't a Black Panther and never did tell the police who shot him.

Manson told a slightly different story to his Family. He was proud that he had "blown away a Black Panther," as he put it. He told them how easy it was just to shoot the man dead, but it might trigger the Panthers to get a group together and attack them at the ranch. He immediately handed out guns to all the men of the group and posted them on lookouts around the outskirts of the ranch.

Over the following two weeks, no attacks happened. But Charlie would take every opportunity possible to keep his Family on edge. Every time Black tourists came to the ranch for a horse-riding tour, he would tell them to be careful since they might be Panthers instead of tourists. Once, a bus full of Black tourists came to the ranch, and Charlie said they were really with the Panthers, scouting the ranch and trying to figure out what kind of security they had in place.

15

LANDING ON THE MOON

On July 20, 1969, American astronauts Neil Armstrong and Buzz Aldrin landed and walked on the moon. Most of the world watched on television, including Sharon Tate with friends Jay Sebring, Voytek Frykowski, and Abigail Folger.

The only place in the world where they were not watching the moon landing was at Spahn Ranch. Charlie was highly suspicious about the possibility of a moon landing. He said it was all staged by the government. Manson never provided his Family with any reasons why the government might have faked the moon landing, other than the general suspicion that one can't trust anything they say. By this time, many of his followers thought that if Charlie didn't say it was real, then it probably wasn't. After all, nothing was real unless he said it was.

Manson wasn't all that interested in what was going on around the world, especially if it wasn't related to fighting or killing among the races. He was only focused on gathering enough money to not only move to Death Valley but also survive while they were there.

Charlie was still trying to get in touch with Dennis Wilson because he wanted money from him for stealing his song and not giving him any credit. He went to places Wilson hung out and left threatening notes for him. Once, he even left a bullet for him, knowing that he would get the message.

PART II

THE MURDERS

16

GARY HINMAN

Still frantic to find some money, Manson started looking at other acquaintances that he or his Family members had. The situation with Wilson wasn't faring out too well. Gary Hinman may be a better target. Not only did he own a house, but he was a maker and dealer of mescaline. Beausoleil often bought his drugs from Hinman and even bought medicines for others at the ranch, including some from the Straight Satan bikers who hung out there. Charlie figured Hinman must have a nice stash of cash around his house. He thought that it was the perfect time to shake him down when he heard that Beausoleil had just given him a grand in cash that he received from the bikers for a thousand tablets of mescaline.

After Beausoleil got the drugs back to the ranch and the bikers realized they were not real, they got angry with Beausoleil. They said the drugs didn't work correctly and demanded their money back. It was Charlie's way of thinking that not only should Hinman give the bikers back their money, but he should also give Manson some money as well to make up for all the trouble he caused them.

Beausoleil never wanted to join Manson's Family and certainly didn't want to go to Death Valley and take part in any race war stuff. He did, however, want to keep his biker gang friends happy.

A few days later, on July 25th, Bruce Davis drove Bobby Beausoleil, Mary Brunner, and Susan Atkins over to Hinman's house to discuss the bad drug deal and to get their money back from him. Beausoleil had a knife and a gun hidden on his body so that Hinman didn't see them when he invited them into his house.

When Beausoleil confronted Hinman about giving him fake drugs that made the bikers angry, he said that there was nothing wrong with the drugs and insisted they were good. Hinman told Bobby that if the person taking the mescaline didn't have a clean system, they would get sick. So it wasn't the drugs that were bad, it was the person taking them.

Beausoleil got frustrated and yelled for Susan to come into the kitchen and hold the gun on Hinman while he looked around the house for something he could sell or give to the bikers instead of cash.

While he was looking through the house, Hinman jumped on Atkins and tried to wrestle the gun from her. She screamed for Bobby. He ran into the kitchen right away and jumped on Hinman, making the gun fire. The bullet hit the cupboard below the kitchen sink. Once Beausoleil got control over Hinman, he punched him in the face. After a while, Hinman was still claiming that he had no money. So Beausoleil convinced him to sign over the titles to both his cars to him. They weren't worth much—a Volkswagen bus and a Fiat station wagon—but the combined total of both vehicles should be at least a thousand dollars.

He wasn't sure if that would be good enough for Charlie, so he decided to phone him out at the ranch and ask him. Manson told him to wait there, and he would be there soon. Around midnight, Charlie and Bruce Davis showed up at Hinman's house.

Beausoleil let them into the house, and Charlie approached Hinman, who was sitting in a kitchen chair. Manson brought the sword that he was given by the bike gang's leader earlier that year and started waving it around Hinman's head. "I know you have some money for me," Charlie said in a smooth, sinister tone.

Hinman started to beg Charlie, telling him that the drugs were good and that there was nothing wrong with them. Charlie kept waving the sword around his head and began to grin. Hinman then grumbled that he had always been a good friend to the Family, and he didn't understand why Charlie was doing this.

Suddenly, with a quick swipe, Manson whacked off most of Hinman's left ear. Hinman fell to the ground on his knees and began sobbing loudly. Charlie wiped the blood from his sword and, growling, said to Beausoleil, "I expect you to bring me everything he has. You know what needs to be done." Then Charlie and Bruce Davis left, got into the car, and drove back to the ranch.

Saturday night turned into Sunday, and during that time, Beausoleil intermittently kept beating Hinman. When he wasn't hitting him, both Atkins and Brunell pleaded with Hinman to tell them where the money was. If he would just tell them, they could stop his suffering. While the girls were with Hinman, Beausoleil phoned to let Charlie know what was happening.

Sometime in the late afternoon on Sunday, Hinman became angry and aggressive again. He wasn't strong enough to do anything physically to Beausoleil, so he began to threaten that he would go to the police as soon as they left. He threatened to get them all arrested.

Beausoleil phoned Charlie and told him that Hinman was going to the police and intended to have them all arrested. Charlie softly but firmly responded, "You know what to do." With that, Beausoleil hung up the phone and walked over to Hinman, who was now lying on the floor. He jumped on top of him and began stabbing him several times in his chest.

While he was still alive and the blood was flowing out of his chest and stomach onto the floor, he clenched his fist and put it partway into Hinman's stomach just enough to cover his whole hand with blood. He pulled it out and stood up, walking over to the wall and pressing what looked like a paw print with blood on it. Then he drew what looked like four panther nail prints with his finger on the wall. His goal was to make it signify the commonly used Black Panthers marking. Beausoleil walked back to Hinman's body and got some more of his blood on his fingers, then walked back to where he had put the paw print on the wall and wrote "Political Piggy."

The three of them then went through the house quickly, trying to wipe or remove any of their prints and gather everything that belonged to them. Beausoleil also grabbed a set of bagpipes that Hinman often played to entertain his friends and threw them into the Fiat. The girls got on the bus and drove back to Spahn Ranch. There they waited to see if any news had come out about the murder, to see if the Panthers got the blame for it.

Two days passed, and there was no news about the murder at all. Beausoleil started to worry and decided to return to Hinman's house to see if it had been discovered yet. When he got there, he realized that nobody had found Hinman's body yet. While he was there, he got scared that the panther paw print he had made with Hinman's blood on his wall could be traced back to him somehow, so he tried to wipe it off. He couldn't, as it had dried completely after two days.

Later that week, on Thursday, July 31st, a few of Hinman's friends went to his house to see where he had been all week. They usually saw him around the college that they all attended. Hinman wasn't there all week. After getting no answer, they were beginning to leave when they noticed one of his windows was wide open and several flies buzzing around it. So they called the police.

Two police detectives from the Los Angeles Sheriff's Department went into Hinman's house and discovered his dead body. Over the next few days, police were able to obtain some unmistakable fingerprints from the crime scene and issued an all-points bulletin for Hinman's two missing vehicles.

During the first week of August, Beausoleil took off for San Francisco by himself. He was worried about being caught and arrested by the police for the murder of Hinman, so he thought that it would be better if he just went away for a while. His first mistake was that he fled in one of Hinman's cars, the Fiat. The second mistake was that he took the knife he used to murder Hinman and stabbed it into the tire well.

The Fiat was not in the best running condition, and by the time Beausoleil got close to San Luis Obispo, it broke down. Tired from driving for a long time, he decided to take a nap in the car. Two patrolmen happened by the broken-down car, and when they ran the license plates, they found that the vehicle was connected to a murder in Topanga Canyon.

The patrolman approached the car and found Beausoleil asleep in the back seat. They arrested him. After the Fiat was towed back to the police station and a search was done, they discovered the murder weapon lodged in the tire well.

During questioning, Beausoleil claimed that he had just bought the Fiat from a black man he had met. He was hoping now that Hinman's body had been found, police would have also discovered the Panther paw print in Hinman's blood on his wall and think that it was a Black Panther murder.

Instead, the fingerprints police were able to get from the murder scene matched Beausoleil's fingerprints. They confronted him with that evidence, and after hearing that, Beausoleil gave detectives a new story. This time, he said that he went to Hinman's place, along with two of his girlfriends, that he wouldn't name, and they found Hinman badly hurt. He said they tried to help him. After Hinman started to feel better and seemed to be getting back to normal, he signed over his two vehicles to them as a gesture of thanks for their help. Beausoleil said that Hinman was alive and well when they all left his place. Police didn't believe him. He was booked for murder and transferred to the Los Angeles County jail until his trial.

~

On Thursday, August 7th, Beausoleil called Spahn Ranch, looking for Charlie, who wasn't there. Linda Kasabian answered the call. He told her that he had been arrested for murder, and he wanted Charlie to know that everything was okay and that he wasn't talking to the police. They both decided it was best to wait for Charlie to return, as he would know the best course of action.

On the morning of Friday, August 8th, Charlie returned to Spahn Ranch, and Kasabian immediately grabbed him and pulled him away from everyone else.

"What, what is it, my lady?" He calmly asks her as he pulls away from her hold.

"Charlie, Bobby called!" She answered him in a panic as she grabbed hold of him again.

"Yeah, and so what's the problem?" Charlie said with a smile.

"He's been arrested, arrested for murder. He called us from jail."
Kasabian continued with her panicked tone.

"It's all okay, baby, it's okay. What did he tell you?" He was a little
more serious now when he spoke.

"He said for you not to worry. He hasn't said anything to anyone,
and he's not going to. But he needed to know what you wanted him to
do." Kasabian responded with her eyes wide open and intently focused
on Manson's face.

"It's okay, baby. Thank you for telling me, darling. Let me think
about it for a while."

Charlie walked into his shack alone and closed the door behind him.
He needed to figure out how to handle this. Beausoleil's call to the
Family was good, as it meant he had remained silent so far. However,
Charlie was now faced with the task of getting him out of jail. He knew
that if he couldn't get Beausoleil out of jail after a certain amount of
time, he would probably start talking to the police. Not only would that
implicate Charlie in Hinman's murder, but Beausoleil also knew about
him shooting Lotsapoppa.

At first, Manson considered the possibility of going on the run, just
leaving and going somewhere that he had been before. At least long
enough to know where he could hide. Charlie had been to the
Northwest a few times, and it was cool. He also knew Chicago a little.
Charlie also realized that securing a record contract or recording for a
major label was no longer a feasible option. The outside world had
ignored his great talent entirely, and that was one of the primary reasons
he was hanging around in the Los Angeles area.

Of course, fleeing would also mean leaving all his Family members
behind—not taking any of them with him, and not telling them where
he was going. Charlie could trust them. He was sure of it. After all, they
all believed that he was the second coming of Jesus, so they would do
what they were told. However, trying to travel with his followers would
require a lot more time and money. He would have to find ways to
support everyone, not just himself.

Charlie figured that when he settled somewhere new and things
were relatively quiet, he could start over again and begin recruiting
anew. There were always many lost souls out there looking for direction,

and he knew how to find them and lead them. But that thought made Manson angry. Thinking about the last few years and all the work, time, and money he had invested in his followers, and how he had brought them to where he wanted them to be. So maybe he could find another way out of this problem.

Charlie decided to ask his followers what they wanted. When he told them that he might have to leave the ranch and go away out on his own, several of them cried and said to him that they loved him and that he couldn't leave. They wouldn't know what they would do without him. They pleaded with Charlie and told him that they were willing to do whatever he wanted to keep him at the ranch.

The entire group gathered together, and several of them began sharing ideas on how to address the problem they now faced. One of them excitedly suggested they go to the jail and break Beausoleil out. Charlie knew that they didn't have the workforce or strength to pull that off in a prison. Another member said that they should maybe try committing another murder and do it the same way that Hinman had been killed.

Charlie grabbed hold of that idea and ran with it. Manson figured that if they made it look like it was the same murderers who did the new crime, the police would figure that it wasn't Beausoleil who did the Hinman murder, and they would drop the charges and set him free.

They would have to do the same things that Bobby did with the Hinman murder by leaving a panther paw print on the wall and writing stuff like "Political Piggie." Doing it in the same way would surely create the idea in the media that it was a Black Panther murder. Eventually, they would tie it to the Hinman murder since they were similar. Both had panther marks and names written on the walls in the victim's blood.

In Manson's mind, an added perk was that not only should this convince the cops that it wasn't Beausoleil who committed the murder, but it should even cause some Whites to commit crimes and attacks against Blacks, which should instigate even more Blacks to fight back against their attackers, finally starting the race war Charlie had been talking about.

Manson then told his Family that they had to do one significant thing differently. They would have to select their next victim or victims more wisely. They would have to be major people in the community. They would have to be popular and wealthy, and that would keep the murder in the news and on people's minds. Gary Hinman was not an important person. He didn't mean anything to the people of Los Angeles. If anything, because he was a poor drug maker and dealer. He told them that some people were probably happy that he was murdered.

Charlie told Mary Brunner and Sandy Good to use some of the stolen credit cards to buy him the things he needed. Manson required to be left alone. He told his followers that it was time to create a plan—a plan to lead the world to "Helter Skelter."

Around eleven that night, the phone rang, and suddenly Squeaky ran into Charlie's room to tell him that both girls were arrested for using stolen credit cards at Sears. Good and Brunner were locked up in the women's jail called Sybil Brand, which was located in Los Angeles. Squeaky also told Manson that it would cost $600 for each of their bail.

Charlie began to panic. Not only was Beausoleil in jail, but so were Brunner and Good. He wasn't sure how long it would be before any of them broke down and told the police something. He knew that he had to make his move now. Manson needed the planned attack to happen tonight, and he left the ranch quickly to find Tex Watson.

17

PLANNING THE TATE MURDERS

Charlie's teachings to his followers preached that all things were the same. Things were all an illusion, love and hate, or life and death. All of those whom he chose were ordained by both the Bible and the Beatles to rule the world. But they had to be chosen by him. And as the new rulers, they were tasked with making the world a better place for everyone, marking the beginning of a new golden era of life.

Having such high goals to achieve, Charlie told them that they might have to do some things that were not the prettiest. But it was what needed to be done. Whatever sacrifices are required, it would be worth it in the end. What we call murders, the Family called deaths. He said that they wouldn't be killing anyone, but only ending their physical life, not their soul. He told them that their soul would continue and move to a different place.

So, if the Family did a copycat murder of what was done to Gary Hinman, and some deaths had to occur, it would be acceptable. The victims were just sacrificed for the greater good of the world. Manson only told his followers what he needed done when he needed it. He did this because he had to ensure that they perceived him as selfless in all his acts.

In Charlie's mind, it was the perfect plan. Nothing could go wrong.

Firstly, as long as the people who were murdered were prominent people of the city, and the murders were made to look like they were racially motivated, by a group like the Black Panthers, police would have to associate it with the murder of Gary Hinman. Secondly, if the Family did a few more murders in different locations and on other days, it would add to the theory that there was a racially motivated group who were planning attacks on white people regularly. Therefore, police would have to take that seriously, and it kept them busy from investigating Charlie. Thirdly, Manson would select the Family members personally and direct them to the place where the murders would take place. This way, Charlie himself wouldn't be directly involved with any of the killings. He could then say that each of these murders was done entirely by the Family member and it was of their own doing.

Manson knew that on each of the murder rampages that the Family did, there had to be a man to lead the charge. After all, given his Family's structure, the women were always led by the men. He began by selecting Tex Watson as that leader, as Tex was ideally suited for the job. He was a rough-and-tumble guy and a former high school jock who played sports and remained in great shape, despite now being a regular drug user. Tex had wanted to be Charlie's right-hand man for a while and had lately been acting more aggressively with the other Family members, perhaps trying to impress Manson. Charlie was a good judge of character and knew how Tex felt, making it all the easier for Charlie to lay guilt trips on Tex when he had to.

"You remember my boy, Tex, not too long ago," Charlie said just slightly louder than a whisper as he placed his arm around Tex's shoulder.

"Yeah, Charlie, what?"

"You remember, boy, how when you fucked up that drug deal and it nearly got us all killed?" Charlie continued to lead Tex down a gravel pathway on the ranch.

"Oh, I, yeah, I didn't mean to," Tex answered, barely being able to stutter out the words.

"Tex, my boy, it's alright, man. Now, you can make it up to me.

Yeah, you can make it up to all of us, okay?" Charlie answered with a bounce in his voice.

"Sure, yeah, Charlie."

"Yeah, man. Lotsapoppa was going to get his Black Panther brothers to come out to Spahn Ranch and visit us. But it wouldn't have been a regular type of visit, you know, where everyone sits around and has a few drinks and talks about love. They would have killed everyone here, right?" Charlie stopped walking and looked directly into Tex's eyes, and smiled at one of the evilest grins Tex had ever seen from him before.

"Yeah, I guess so," Tex answered as if he were sorry.

"That's okay, Tex. Charlie took over and stopped it all, didn't he?" Charlie continued without moving or changing his smile. "Old Bobby there had to knock off Hinman, didn't he?" Still looking directly into Tex's eyes.

"I guess he did," Tex answered quietly. He was so scared that he couldn't even blink his eyes or break the concentration that Charlie's eyes had on him.

"Bobby made a sacrifice, Tex, didn't he? He made a sacrifice for all of us, right?"

"Yeah, Charlie, I guess he did. What can we do for him now?"

"I'm glad you asked me, brother, because tonight we are going to pay him back for his sacrifice. We are going to help out Bobby. You want to do that, don't you, Tex?" Manson started to move again and took his stare off Tex.

"Yeah, Charlie, anything. You name it, we will do it."

"Tex, would you like to be the leader tonight?"

"Yeah."

"Bobby had selflessly killed for you, Tex. I'd say it was time to return the favor, don't you?"

"Sure, Charlie. What are we doing tonight?"

Charlie now had what he wanted in Tex. A leader. A man who would take up the charge and commit murder for him. For the Family. Now it was time for Charlie to figure out who needed to be killed—who it was that needed to make the sacrifice to free Bobby and the whole Family. If he chose the correct victims, his plan would succeed. Bobby would be freed, and the race war would begin.

"Tex, what rich and famous person's place have you been to before?"

"Umm, I don't know, let me think?"

"Didn't you go to that famous rock producer's house once? What was his name again, Mel..."

"Melcher man. Yeah, I know it. But I don't think he lives there now, Charlie."

"That's okay, Tex. I mean, it doesn't matter if it's Melcher. Whoever is living there now must be rich and probably famous, too. After all, who else could afford to live in a place like that?" Charlie said slyly, knowing that he had just planted the idea for Tex to decide where he needed to go and murder people.

"Yeah, but how does it do it? I don't remember what I'm supposed to write on the walls or anything."

"Hey, relax. I'll have some of the girls go with you, and they'll remember for you. You don't have to worry about any of those details."

Charlie knew that he would have to slowly explain the details of how the murder should happen at Cielo Drive. Instead of telling Tex, he would ask about things to get Tex to come up with the answer on what he should do. This way would work out perfectly if Tex were to be arrested for the crime. Then Charlie could claim that it was all Tex's idea, not his own.

Charlie began by asking Tex, "Is there an electronic gate or fence around that property?"

"Yeah, that's right, Charlie. There is."

"Well, maybe you should climb over it to get in so that they don't know you are coming?"

"Right. I should have some wire cutters to cut the phone line, too, right, Charlie?"

"Now you're thinking. Yes!"

Tex then went and grabbed a rifle, a .22 Buntline, and held it as if he were going to shoot, smiling.

"Hey, boy, you should take a knife. You should only use a knife so that nobody hears you. Only use that rifle if you have to."

"Right on, Charlie!" Tex answered, giddy now like he was a young boy going on a camping trip.

Charlie next had to decide which of the girls would accompany Tex. His first choice would be easy: Susan Atkins. After all, she had been with Beausoleil during the Hinman murder and knew firsthand what was done to him as well as what had been written on the wall with Hinman's blood. She would be able to guide Tex on how they needed to leave the place so that it looked the same as how Hinman's place was left when he was murdered. By this time, Charlie knew the lengths to which Susan would go for him, and he figured this would help during the murders. Whatever Tex couldn't do, Susan would be able to do.

Linda Kasabian was a good second. Not only was she useful because she had a driver's license, but she was also one of the newer Family members and was willing to do almost anything. She was desperately trying to fit in with the Family. She was also very quiet and not aggressive, which would help with Tex taking the lead. The less resistance he had, the better things would turn out.

Patricia Krenwinkel was deeply committed to Charlie and the Family and would do anything that Charlie wanted her to. Not to mention, she was already a cold and distant person who often didn't care about other people's feelings—an excellent characteristic to have when you are going out to hurt and even kill people.

Charlie laid out the rules to each one of them separately. Because he knew who each of them was and what their weaknesses were, he knew how to explain the plans to each one so that they would understand what he needed them to accomplish. Each of them would be dressed in dark, unmarked clothing and carry their knife. They would each bring an extra set of clothes and keep them in the car until the murders were completed. Then they could take off their clothes from the crime, dispose of them, and put on the brand-new clothes.

Charlie repeated one more order to Tex before leaving them to their job. Whatever you do, only use the gun as a last resort. Only if needed. Charlie then sent everyone on their way to get ready.

Tex and Atkins were all excited about their assignment from Charlie and decided they needed to get high before leaving. The two of them ran off alone to do some meth. Both of them liked using meth as it seemed to charge them up or give them the energy to work. Meanwhile, Krenwinkel went back to her room, got dressed, and packed up her extra clothing, but she couldn't find her knife. She didn't want to make Charlie angry at her, so she decided to return and not tell him that she didn't have her knife. Kasabian was nervous, sitting on a bed in the room with Charlie, waiting for everyone else to get ready. Once they were all back, Charlie told them to use the 1959 yellow Ford, which belonged to Johnny Swartz, a young man who worked on the ranch.

Tex returned with the car as ordered, and the girls all got into the car. Kasabian first walked up to the driver's door and looked at Tex, figuring that since she was the only one there with a driver's license, she would be driving. Tex looked at her and told her to get in the car. She slowly got into the front passenger seat without saying a word. As the four of them began to drive away, Charlie yelled out, "Do something witchy!" While he was staring into Atkins' eyes, she began to smile and then laugh. Soon, all four of them were laughing out loud.

Later, after the crimes were committed and they were arrested, all three of the women claimed that in that moment, when the four of them were leaving the ranch, none of them had any idea that they were about to murder some people. They were carrying knives or some weapon, but that was normal given that they were all scared of the impending race war and needed to be able to protect themselves at a moment's notice.

While Tex was in charge and driving, he wasn't telling the women anything about where they were going or what they were about to do. The women were all talking lightly to each other so as not to disturb Tex. They claimed that they thought they were going on another "Creepy Crawl" and were deciding what kind of food to get for dinner.

18

CIELO DRIVE

R udi Altobelli hired William Garretson to look after the Cielo Drive residence and stay in the guest cottage at the back of the property while he was away with Tate in Europe. He was strictly instructed never to interfere with or bother the tenants living in the main house. His job was to maintain the property and keep an eye on things so that nothing got stolen or damaged. Like a security guard but without any weapons. A pair of eyes to keep watch on things and call the police if needed.

A few weeks prior, when Garretson was trying to hitch a ride home, an eighteen-year-old stereo and electronics salesman, Steve Parent, picked him up. The two men got along instantly. They had very similar tastes in music and beer. When they arrived at the Cielo Drive home, Garretson thanked Parent for the ride home and told him to come by and have a beer sometime. Parent probably believed that Garretson had some money because he was living in such a beautiful home in a wealthy neighborhood.

Parent decided to return to the Cielo Drive home on August 8th to visit Garretson, just as he had been invited to do. However, he also decided to bring one of the newest clock radios that the store where he worked had on sale. Parent thought that Garretson was rich, so purchasing just a clock radio should be easy.

Parent arrived at Garretson's place just before midnight. Garretson was surprised when he heard someone knocking on his front door that late. He jumped up and looked out to the driveway, where he saw a Rambler parked there. He opened the front door, and Parent stood there with a big smile on his face.

"Hey, man, do you remember me? I picked you up a couple of weeks ago."

"Oh, yeah, right, man. How are you?" Garretson answered slowly, still trying to figure out who Parent was.

"Great! Great to see you, man!" Parent replied, sounding jubilant as he lightly pushed his way through the front door. He was holding the brand-new clock radio he had brought from the store. After Garretson closed the door and turned around to face him, he began trying to sell it to him right away. "Have you seen one of these babies yet? We just got them in at the store, and they are super. I need to show you what they can do!"

"Oh, okay. Do you want a beer? I'm going to have one." Garretson politely responded, not listening to Parent's sales pitch.

"Yeah, cool." Parent chirped out while plugging in the clock radio and setting it up so he could give a demo of it. Garretson handed him the beer and sat down, listening to Parent give his sales pitch. After it was over, he told him that he didn't want a radio right now. The two continued to sip their beers in silence for a while, and then Parent asked if he could use his phone. The call was short. Parent had to go and help a friend fix his stereo, so he finished his beer, packed up the clock radio, and left around a quarter after midnight. Garretson walked him to his car and said goodbye.

Meanwhile, Tex finally found the house on Cielo Drive. He had been there before, but for some reason, he got lost during the drive over. It could have been from the drugs, the excitement of what they were about to do, or perhaps he just wasn't an excellent navigator. Cielo Drive was a narrow lane surrounded by several wild animals, including deer. He had to drive to the top of the hill to get to the residence.

When Tex arrived at the closed electronic gate that kept the Cielo

Drive home from intruders, he parked the Ford and told the girls to stay in the car. He got out of the car and walked around to the trunk, where he removed the bolt cutters he brought with him. Tex then climbed the telephone pole, which was only a few feet away from the outside gate of the house. He cut all the wires that ran to the house before climbing back down and returning to the car.

Slowly, Tex backed down the hill just until the car was out of sight from the front gate area. He then parked again. Tex took the .22 and stuffed it into the front of his pants. He got out of the car and walked back to the trunk, where he retrieved the rope he had brought and threw it over his shoulder. He then told the girls to get out of the car and follow him.

Tex walked the girls around to the side of the fence, which had a slight incline in the ground, making it easy to climb over. After they all made it over the wall, Tex told them they needed to go into the main house, which was in front of them, and that they were to murder everyone who was in the house. And even though all the girls said they never went to the Cielo Drive house to kill anybody, none of them thought twice about doing it. They were Charlie's orders, and that's what they were going to do.

At that moment, they all noticed a set of car lights heading towards them from the driveway coming from the back of the property. Tex quickly told the girls to get into the bushes and hide. As the girls were running, Tex took the .22 out of his pants and stood waiting for the car that Steve Parent was driving. Just as Parent got close to the gate with the button to open it, he stopped the car.

Parent rolled down the car window to open the gate. That's when Tex walked out of the bush and stood in front of the car holding his .22 in his right hand. Parent jumped when he saw Tex and the gun.

"Hi, please, please don't hurt me. I'm your friend. I won't tell." Parent blurted out while remaining focused on Tex's weapon.

Tex walked over to the driver's side window, which was open, and with his left hand pulled his knife out and slashed Parent across his left arm. Parent quickly grabbed his left arm with his right hand to try to stop the bleeding and began to try to slide over to get out of the passenger car door.

Tex, even though Charlie ordered him not to use the .22 unless he had to, aimed it at Parent and shot him four times, causing Parent to fall over dead onto the front steering wheel. It caused his car horn to go off, but Tex quickly moved Parent's body away so that the noise stopped. Putting the Rambler into neutral, he began pushing it backwards just far enough so that anybody who came to the gate couldn't see the car.

The Cielo Drive private security, who were parked about a block away, thought they heard some noises, like a gunshot or the backfiring of a car. They couldn't tell the direction the noise came from, but they called in a report to the Los Angeles Police Department. The phone officer who took the report joked about a murder in the wealthy neighborhood with the security team, and nobody was sent out to check on the homes in the area.

Mrs. Seymour, who lived next door, was awakened from her sleep by the four gunshots. She sat up in bed and remained quiet, trying to listen for any more sounds coming from outside. After ten minutes of silence, she turned off her bedside lamp and went back to sleep.

Garretson, in the meantime, was in the guesthouse reading and listening to music, so he also didn't hear the gunshots. He also tried to phone a friend, but when he picked up the receiver, there was no dial tone. He thought it was weird, since just fifteen minutes before that, Parent had made a telephone call.

Parent and his Rambler taken care of, Tex then called for the girls. They emerged from the woods, and he led them to the main house. Inside the Cielo Drive home, Abigail Folger was in her bedroom reading a book while her boyfriend, Voytek Frykowski, had gone to sleep on the sofa in the front room. The couple had argued earlier at dinner and were still not speaking to each other.

Sharon Tate and her friend Jay Sebring were trying to avoid the drama of Folger and Frykowski's arguing, so they retired to Tate's bedroom and chatted about some of the celebrities who had been in Sebring's salon the previous week.

Once at the house, Tex instructed Linda to go around the back to check for any open windows or doors. She was now terrified after seeing Tex murder Parent in his car and could hardly move. She finally walked to the back of the house, but claimed that she hadn't checked for anything to be opened. Instead, she just stood there, panicked. After she had herself collected, she returned to the front of the house where Tex and the other girls were. She told them that everything was shut and locked. Tex could tell that Linda was far too scared to be of any use to him, so he instructed her to return to the front gate and keep an eye out for anyone who might approach.

Tex saw that a window next to the front door had been left open and was only covered by a screen. He took his knife and sliced open the screen just enough to grab hold of it with his hand. Next, he pulled it off so that he could fully open up the window.

Tex climbed in through the window and told Susan and Pat to follow him into the house. The three of them slowly crept around the house until they found the front room where Frykowski was sleeping on the couch. Tex whispered to Susan to check around the rest of the house to see who else was there.

Suddenly, Frykowski asks, "What time is it?" He likely heard the voices and thought that it was Tate and Folger. He looked up and saw Tex standing there. "Who are you? What do you want?" he asked, not sounding alarmed, as there were often people around the house whom he didn't know.

Tex slowly walked over to the sofa and kicked him in the head, and he began to laugh. "I'm the devil and I'm here to do the devil's business." Tex continued to laugh, then flicked his head towards the hall as he looked at Susan, as if he wanted her to go there. Frykowski raised his head back up and began to speak when Tex turned back around and looked him in the eyes and threatened, "Say another word and you're dead!"

Susan quickly ran into Patricia, who was still searching the rooms in the house. Patricia told her to keep looking while she went to see Linda. Patricia figured she would need her knife, so she walked down the front driveway to where Linda was standing guard and borrowed hers. Once she got back to the house, she continued searching through the rooms.

Susan entered a room where the door was slightly ajar. When she peeked through, she saw Folger, who must have heard her. She looked up and started smiling when she saw the shadow of a person behind the door. Susan opened the door and smiled back at Folger, waving. Folger waved back and then went back to reading her book.

Susan and Patricia returned to the living room, where Tex was, and told him that they had seen three people in total: a couple in one room and a single woman in another. Tex told her to go and get them and bring them into the front room.

Susan took her knife out of her pants and went back to the room where Folger was reading. This time, she walked in holding the knife up and ordered her to come with her back to the living room. When they returned, Patricia held Folger at knifepoint while Susan went to get the other couple, who were in a different room.

Susan entered Tate's bedroom, again holding her knife out in front of her, and ordered, "Come with me and don't say anything or you're both dead!" They both slowly got up from the bed and walked down the hall to the living room while Susan followed them, holding her knife. When they arrived in the front room and saw Tex and Patricia both standing there, also holding knives, Tate stopped in fear.

Tex got up from the sofa where he had been sitting over Frykowski and walked over to Tate and Sebring, grabbing Tate by the arm and pulling her into the center of the room. Frykowski sat up and made some noise, and Tex yelled to Susan to tie him up. Susan grabbed a small white hand towel and got behind Frykowski, trying to tie his hands behind his back with it.

Meanwhile, Tex took the rope that he had hanging over his shoulder and began to tie up Jay Sebring's hands. When Sebring started to ask what was going on, Tex told him to shut up now or he'd kill him. Just then, Frykowski yells out, "He means it!"

After Tex tied Sebring's hand together, he grabbed another rope. Only this time, he looped it around his neck and flipped the end of the rope up over a beam in the ceiling of the room. "Stop it. What are you doing?" Sebring complained. "One more word from you and you'll be dead!" Tex shouted back so loud that spit came out of his mouth and into Sebring's face.

Tex then took the end of the rope that was now hanging down from the beam in the ceiling and tied it around Tate's neck, who yelled out and began to cry. Tex made fun of her by making some fake crying noises, and Sebring yelled out, "Can't you see that she's pregnant?" Tex turned around, grabbed his firearm, and then shot Sebring in the stomach. He fell to the ground. Tate screamed as she continued to cry.

Tex then demanded, "I want all the money you've got here!" as he turned his head around and looked at Folger and Frykowski. "I have some money in my room," Folger answered. Susan grabbed her by the arm and led her to the bedroom, where she had found her. Folger took the money from her purse and gave it to Susan. They both went back to the living room, and Susan gave the cash to Tex, who looked up at Folger and, with a look of nonbelief, said, "That's all you've got?"

Tate then interrupted by saying, "We don't ever keep very much money here at the house. But I have money, and I can get it for you."

"Do you think I'm kidding you?" Tex snarled back at Tate.

"No," Tate answered softly.

Tate's response enraged Tex, thinking that he was ordered to go and murder some rich people and bring back money, and seventy dollars was all that they had. He began to believe that they were trying to play games with him. Maybe they figured if they could stall him long enough, they could somehow get away. The more he thought about it, the angrier he got.

About this time, Sebring regained consciousness and moaned from the gunshot wound in his stomach. It was just enough to set Tex off. He stood up and walked over to Sebring, kneeled over him, pulled out his knife, and stabbed him wildly several times until Sebring was out again. Both Tate and Folger screamed and cried the whole time Tex was stabbing Sebring. "What are you doing? What are you going to do with us?" Tate cried out. Tex looked up at her and pointed his knife, which was now dripping blood all over the floor. "You're all going to die!"

During the commotion, Frykowski had regained enough sense to realize what was going on. He began to work his hands free from the towel that Susan had tied his hands up with. When Tex noticed Frykowski trying to get loose, he told Susan to kill him. By the time Susan got to him, his hands were free. She began to stab at him, but he was able to get hold of her, and the two began wrestling for control of the knife. They both fell onto the floor.

Susan yelled for Tex to come and help her. Tex grabbed his .22 and shot at Frykowski a few times. Even though he got hit with a couple of the bullets, Frykowski was still able to get away from Susan and stood up. He ran out the front door onto the lawn, where he ran into Linda, who, because of all the noise coming from the house, decided to walk back to see what was going on.

Both Frykowski and Linda fell to the ground when he ran into her. Tex caught up with him and jumped on top of him. He began stabbing Frykowski rapidly several times and didn't stop until he appeared dead and no longer struggling. Linda couldn't stop staring at the stabbing and seemed to go into shock. "Please, make it stop. Make it stop!" she yelled out in terror while staring at the blood splashing out from Frykowski's body as Tex continued to stab him.

Susan approached Linda and grabbed hold of her, "There's nothing I can do, honey," she said softly to her.

"But people are coming. We have to stop. We have to go!" Linda said with a hint of fear in her tone.

"Sorry, but we can't stop now." Susan kept trying to calm her, but Linda shook and began to run. She left the house, ran to the electronic gate, climbed over it, and when she reached their car, she stopped.

While Susan was preoccupied with Linda, it allowed Folger a chance to get away. But Patricia saw Folger run outside and in the opposite direction from where Tex had been stabbing Frykowski. She began chasing her. When she caught up with her, Patricia started stabbing at Folger, hitting her a few times, but not enough to slow her down.

Patricia began to scream out of frustration for trying to stop and stab Folger, and not succeeding. Tex looked up when he heard her scream and began to run towards the two women. Once he caught them, he pushed Folger to the ground, jumped on her, and started to stab her. He looked up at Patricia and pointed toward the guesthouse and told her to kill whoever was in that house. Then he continued to stab Folger until he heard her say, "I give up, you got me."

Patricia was now so scared that she had gone into shock. She shook her head to indicate yes and began to walk down the alley towards the guesthouse until Tex couldn't see her anymore. She stood between the two houses for about five minutes, just shaking and crying. Then she headed back to the front lawn, where Tex was, and told him that there wasn't anybody in the house, and he believed her.

Tex rose from Folger's dead body and walked with Patricia back into the living room, where Susan had been watching Tate—the last one still alive. Once they arrived, Tate began to plead, "You don't have to kill me. I can go with you. At least keep me alive until my baby is born, then you can kill me if you still want to."

Tex knew that Charlie wouldn't want him to bring someone from the house who was still alive. He tried to get the most attention from the media and public that he could, so she had to die. As Susan held her, Tex stabbed her until she died.

Now they had to ensure that they left the crime scene in a sufficiently disturbing state to capture the world's attention. The three of them looked over the living room where both Tate and Sebring lay dead. Both of them had the rope, which hung from a beam in the ceiling, wrapped around their necks.

Frykowski lay dead on the front lawn with his face so cut up and bloody that he couldn't be recognized. And not far from his body was Folger, whose white nightgown was now completely blood red. Tex figured this should be bad enough.

They began to look for things that might be worth some money. Tex knew that the seventy dollars they got from Tate wouldn't be enough to make Charlie happy. They found some more money in Tate's nightstand by her bed. Tex stole Sebring's watch from his wrist.

Just before they left, Tex reminded the girls that they had to write things on the walls to make it look similar to the Hinman murder. Tex ordered Susan to make the bloody writings on the walls.

Susan didn't want to use her hands or fingers in case she accidentally left some fingerprints behind. She grabbed a towel from the bathroom and then dipped it into Tate's wounds to get them all bloody. She went to the front door and opened it, then bent down and wrote "Pig" on the outside with the bloody towel.

By the time it was all over, the three of them were covered in blood. They had all gotten blood on their hands during the different stabbings, and each had wiped their hands on their clothing and even faces. They were all exhausted now as they left the house and walked to the electronic gate. Instead of climbing over the gate like they did when they arrived, Tex pushed the button to open it, using only his index finger, which also had blood on it, leaving an excellent print of his finger on the gate.

When they arrived at the car, Linda was still waiting there, looking terrified. None of them said a word to her. They were still mad with her for leaving, and they just got into the car and drove away. During the trip back to Spahn Ranch, the girls changed into their clean clothing, which they had brought with them, as instructed by Charlie. When Tex went to change his clothes, instead of letting someone else drive or stop, he just kept moving and told Linda to take the wheel when he couldn't. Linda rolled all of the dirty crime clothing into a large ball, and she threw them out of the window as they drove past a cliff.

Next, Tex told them that they all had to throw out their knives and his .22 off another cliff, just a few miles past where they dumped the clothing. Susan realized that she didn't have her knife and must have left it back at the house. When Linda picked up the .22, she was surprised to see that a lot of its handle had been broken off. Tex figured it must have broken off when he hit Frykowski over his head a few times. They dumped the weapons and decided it wasn't worth going back to try to find the knife or pieces of the gun that were left behind.

Next, Tex wanted to wash the car. It was well past midnight, so they took a side street in a suburban area until he saw a house that had left its water hose out in the front yard. He pulled over and snuck up to the house, turning on the water tap while Susan and Patricia used the hose to wash down the car.

Even though they were trying to be quiet, the owner of the house, Rudolf Weber, heard the water running and decided to investigate for a leak. He approached Tex and asked him what he was doing on his property. Tex told him that they had been walking and were thirsty, so when they saw the hose, they figured the owner wouldn't mind. Weber noticed the car parked there, and Linda was still in the front seat, so he didn't believe the story being told.

Once Tex realized that Weber wasn't believing his story, he yelled to Susan and Patricia to get into the car. Weber ran for the car on the passenger side and reached over Linda's lap to grab the keys, which were left in the ignition. But Tex beat him to it. The car started, and they took off. Only Weber was able to remember the license plate number of GYY 435.

They finally arrived back at the gate at Spahn Ranch, and Charlie was sitting there with Nancy Pitman, another Family member. Tex pulled up to Charlie, who asked him, "Why are you back so soon?"

Tex now had to tell Charlie that things were just really messy at the house, but everyone there was dead. Susan had to interrupt so that she could tell Charlie how much she enjoyed killing for him. Charlie responded with no tone in his voice, "You didn't kill for me. You did it for yourself."

"Tex, how much money did you bring home?" Charlie asked with some excitement in his voice.

"Charlie, we only found seventy dollars. That's all they had there." Tex said real timidly.

"If that's all they had, then you should have kept going to each house on that road until you found more," Charlie answered, sounding annoyed. "How did you leave the house? Was it like Hinman's? Did you write the witchy words?"

Susan piped up again, "I wrote 'Pig' where you walk in on the front door."

Charlie was starting to get upset as he wasn't getting any good answers. "Do you feel any remorse?"

Each one of them tried to assure Charlie that they felt nothing, but he didn't believe them. "Now wipe off the goblets of blood that are all over this car, now!" he demanded angrily before going back and sitting with Pitman to wait for them to finish. When they were finished, Charlie got into the driver's seat and told them to get in. Then he drove back to Cielo Drive.

Once Charlie walked into the house, he grabbed a clean towel and began wiping all the surfaces to remove any prints. After the mistakes that Beausoleil made during the Hinman murder, he no longer trusted his Family members one hundred percent. Tex and Susan kept saying things to Charlie, but he wasn't listening and didn't answer them. His mind was racing as he tried to think of how he should leave the scene.

He was so preoccupied the whole time they were at Cielo Drive that he forgot to search for any money or valuables.

"Let's move these trunks out into the hall," Charlie ordered Tex just as they entered Tate's bedroom. Two trunks had been dropped off at the house earlier that day, and she had them placed in her room. After that, Charlie threw the towel that he was using to wipe off fingerprints over Sebring's face.

Manson found a large American flag folded and sitting on a table in the living room. He opened it up, laying it over the sofa right beside Tate's body. Charlie thought that having an American flag laid out beside a murdered pregnant woman's body would attract the media and shock people who would see a picture and read about it in a newspaper.

Once Charlie was sure everything was just right, he ordered everyone back into the car, and they returned to Spahn Ranch. They never checked the guesthouse or the property for anything that Tex and the girls might have dropped or left behind.

19

THE MORNING AFTER THE TATE MURDERS

The first sign of life at the Cielo Drive house was around five in the morning. Every morning at this time, the Polanskis had the *Los Angeles Times* newspaper delivered to the front mailbox just outside the electronic gate that surrounded the house. Today, something was different, which made the delivery boy stop and take notice. Some wires had been cut, and they were hanging down from the telephone pole right in front of the gate. He stopped and got off his bike, put the paper in the box, and stared at the cut wires. He had never seen that before.

One of Polanski's neighbors, Seymour Kott, also noticed the cut wires hanging down from the telephone pole when he walked out front to retrieve his newspaper at about half past seven that same morning. But neither Kott nor the paper delivery boy reported it to anyone.

The Polanskis had a regular housekeeper, Winifred Chapman, who came by five days a week at around eight in the morning. This morning, she also noticed the cut-down wires hanging from the telephone pole, and her first thought was that perhaps the gate wouldn't open. She always gauged how her day was going to go by things like this—things that we had no control over. If they went wrong, then you know that it was going to be one of those days.

Winifred pressed the gate button, and it opened. She was relieved and thought maybe it would be a good day after all. As she walked up the driveway towards the front door of the main house, she passed by the Rambler parked on the grass beside the driveway. By now, she was so accustomed to the Polanskis having people stay all night after partying at the house that she never bothered to look inside the car. Often, she saw cars parked all over the property.

This morning, Winifred decided to go into the house through the back door instead of the front, as she figured that there would be overnight guests sleeping in the living room on the sofa, so this way she wouldn't disturb them.

She removed her coat and put it down in the kitchen, then decided to walk quietly down the main hallway to see which bedrooms were occupied and if anyone was sleeping in the living room. As she started down the hall, she saw the two large trunks sitting in the way. She knew she would have to squeeze by them to get past. Just as she approached the first one, she noticed what looked like smeared blood on the top of it.

After squeezing by both trunks, Winifred saw what looked like a puddle of something, maybe blood as well. Then another one. Starting to be alarmed, she looked into the living room and noticed that the front sliding glass door was wide open. And then, suddenly, a body lying on the lawn came into focus.

Winifred was in shock and couldn't believe what she was seeing. She began to walk slowly backward down the hall. When she ran into the trunk, she jumped in fear and began to scream. She turned around and left by the same door through which she had entered.

As she ran down the driveway, heading toward the main gate, she passed the Rambler again. This time, she decided to look inside. When she saw the bloody body of Steve Parent lying over in the front seat, she lost control and started yelling for help at the top of her lungs, "Murder, death, bodies, blood, murder!"

The neighbors of the Polanskis heard the screaming and decided to call the police. Two squad cars responded to their call around a quarter after nine. One of the officers, Jerry Joe DeRosa, pulled up to the front gate at the Cielo Drive home. Standing there, crying more than screaming, was Winifred. She told him what she had seen and then opened the gate for him.

DeRosa walked down the driveway slowly until he reached the parked Rambler. When he looked in the car and saw Parent's body, he pulled his weapon and stopped walking any further. He decided to wait for backup to arrive first.

Shortly after, Officer William Whisenhunt arrived. Winifred directed him to the gate. He pulled out his weapon and slowly walked down the driveway until he met up with DeRosa at the Rambler. After a brief conversation, the two officers slowly approached the main house.

As they were examining the cars parked outside the main house, a third officer, Robert Burbridge, arrived at the scene and caught up with them. After another brief conversation, the three officers started to cross the front lawn where the bodies of Folger and Frykowski were lying dead. They all spotted the sliced-up screen and the open window and thought that the assailants could still be in the house.

They slowly entered the house and cautiously scanned the surroundings. When they entered the living room, they spotted the bodies of Sharon Tate and Jay Sebring. There was a rope that had been tied to a beam in the ceiling, with both ends extending down to each of the bodies. Each rope end was tied into a noose and placed around the necks of the victims.

The officers approached the bodies slowly and carefully, as there were several puddles of blood around them on the floor. After they cleared the house of any other potential victims, DeRosa and Whisenhunt headed to the guesthouse located at the back of the main house.

Whisenhunt walked around the back while DeRosa and Burbridge went up the front stairs and approached the front door. They heard a dog barking from inside the house and heard a muffled voice of a man telling the dog to shut up. Both officers pulled out their weapons again before kicking in the front door. Just then, the dog started to run at the officers, growling and barking. Whisenhunt managed to push the broken door on top of the dog, preventing it from reaching the officers.

Garretson walked out of his bedroom and called for the dog. Both officers grabbed him and threw him to the ground, then cuffed his hands behind him. They stood him up, and while Whisenhunt questioned him about who he was, DeRosa asked him if he knew what had happened. Garretson seemed confused and couldn't seem to answer any of the questions, leading both officers to think that he was probably on drugs.

Each officer grabbed one of Garretson's arms, and they dragged him out of the guesthouse and first took him to the front lawn where two of the bodies were, and stopped in front of Folger and asked him who it was. Garretson, now beginning to wake up, looked down at the body, which was cut up and covered in blood, and he didn't know who she was. Both officers kept screaming at him, wanting to know who it was. Not knowing anyone who was in the main house except for the maid, he said he thought it was Winifred Chapman. Next, they hauled him, still cuffed, over to Frykowski's body and asked who the body was, to which he claimed that it was Polanski's younger brother.

DeRosa asked Garretson where he was, and he claimed that he had been in the guesthouse sleeping all night and hadn't heard anything. Neither officer believed anything he was saying, as the guesthouse was no more than one hundred feet from the main house. Whisenhunt read Garretson his rights and placed him under arrest for murder.

DeRosa led him down the main driveway towards his police car, and when they passed the parked Rambler, he briefly stopped and asked him if he could identify the body in the front seat, but he couldn't. When they approached the front gate, DeRosa pushed the button, which accidentally opened the gate, wiping away the bloody fingerprint that Tex Watson had left earlier that night.

When DeRosa got back to his police car, he placed Garretson in the back seat, keeping him in handcuffs. Then he went around to the front, where he picked up his radio and called in the five murders that happened at the Cielo Drive residence they were at and reported that he had the suspect in custody. In the 1960s, the press monitored police frequencies, and within a few minutes, they arrived at the Cielo Drive home. Within half an hour, numerous media vehicles were lined up from the bottom of Celio Drive to the top, where the Polanskis' house was.

Along with the media trucks came several other detectives and police, but most of them were able to drive right onto the property. The forensic officer for the Los Angeles Police Department, Joe Granado, ultimately collected forty-five samples of blood to be analyzed. The property was covered with blood, but much of it had been tracked throughout the house by different police officers attending the scene.

Detectives got hold of Polanski's press agent, William Tennant, and told him about what happened at Cielo Drive and asked him to come by and try to identify each of the victims. He was able to name everyone except for the man who was found in the Rambler parked by the driveway of the house.

Police then made their first statement to the public and press about the murders and told them that the families of the victims were all being notified. After that, police would release the names of the victims. The body found in the parked Rambler, Steve Parent, still had not been identified. Detectives must have been preoccupied with the surroundings enough that they didn't even think to check the plates on the car to see who it belonged to. Parent's mother and father were beginning to worry as he had not returned home the night before.

That afternoon, the homicide detectives arrived at the house. Sgt. Michael McGann was the first to arrive, and even after five years on the job, he hadn't seen anything this bad before. Police had left all the bodies in place for the detectives for their investigation.

The detective in charge of the evidence found at the crime scene was Danny Galindo. It wasn't long before the knife that Susan Atkins lost was found under one of the sofa pillows. Police were stunned by the amount of drugs found throughout the house. There were at least thirty grams of hashish, seven grams of marijuana, and ten MDA pills, and most of it was left in the open for anybody to see. Nothing was hidden.

Detectives also discovered both marijuana and cocaine in Sebring's car, which made the stories that he was a drug supplier for many celebrities even more true to the police. The drugs found were an essential component to detectives at the time, as they immediately suspected that the murders must have resulted from a drug deal that went bad.

During the sixties, most police, politicians, and even regular families saw that drugs like marijuana were ruining the country. It was taking their children away and killing them. So, it wasn't that hard to understand why detectives directed their focus on the drugs found around the house.

Before detectives were able to release the names of the victims officially, the press started reporting the names of four of them: Sharon Tate, a movie star; Abigail Folger of the Folger's Coffee family; Jay Sebring, hairstylist for the stars; and Voytek Frykowski, a Polish screenwriter for films. What should have been news reports on the five murders and how they were committed instead became a sensational story about the murder of a movie actress, Sharon Tate. Before the day ended, the titles of the stories had changed from "Five Slain at Cielo Drive" to "Tate Murders."

Los Angeles Police Chief Ed Davis demanded that this case receive the full attention of the most senior detectives available and wanted the case to be solved as soon as possible. He did not want people to be scared of there being murderers on the loose. Davis also knew that the longer the case dragged on, the more stories that would emerge. And that would ultimately cause more panic in the city. So Detectives McGann and Galindo were assigned to the case, along with Sergeants Jess Buckles and Lt. Robert Helder, the supervisor of investigations for the LAPD.

Galindo was ordered to stay at the murder scene all night to protect any evidence there. Later, he talked about how unnerving it was for him and that he had no place to sit or lie down, as everything seemed to be covered with blood. Garretson was their only suspect and remained their prime suspect.

～

Charlie, Tex, and the girls didn't return to Spahn Ranch until shortly before sunrise. They all went to bed without talking much. While Charlie slept, the rest of them got up early, having only a couple of hours of sleep. Tex, Susan, Patricia, and Linda were unsure of what was going to happen. They all had mixed feelings, a combination of excitement and fear about what they were doing.

They turned on the television and all sat around waiting for some news to come on. When the first broadcast about the murders came on,

Susan Atkins got a massive smile on her face and became super excited as if she had been given a gift. The rest of the Family members hadn't known any of the details of what happened the previous night at Cielo Drive. The only two members who committed the murder, Tex and Susan Atkins, were both very proud of what they did, and wanted it to be known by everyone that they had accomplished this all for Charlie.

But Tex and Atkins knew they couldn't say too much, as that might upset Charlie. They would wait for him to make any announcements to the Family. Everyone was very excited that what they had done was so important that it was all the news shows were talking about. What they had failed to realize was that throughout all of the reports they watched, not one of them mentioned any connection between the Black Panthers or the Gary Hinman murders and these new killings on Cielo Drive.

∾

The detective's attention remained on suspect Garretson. After he was assigned a legal aid lawyer, he made an official statement regarding what had happened that evening. Garretson stated that he didn't know any of the people who lived in the main house and that he was only hired recently by the owner of the house to take care of the property while he was away in Europe. The only person he had met was the maid, Winifred Chapman, a few times, as she came and went.

The evening of the murders, Garretson said that he had watched some television until a guy he had recently met, Steve Parent, dropped by to see if he would be interested in buying a clock radio from him. After Parent left, Garretson turned on some music, read, and wrote letters to friends. He didn't hear anything out of the ordinary.

The attention of the murder victims was still on Sharon Tate, and Steve Parent had still not been identified, even after Garretson's statement mentioning him dropping by the house to see him that night. It wasn't until a reporter who had taken down the license plate number of the Rambler while police were towing it off the property that the discovery was made. He checked with one of his sources, who worked at the Department of Motor Vehicles, and found out that the car was owned by a couple, Wilfred and Juanita Parent, in the Los Angeles suburb of El Monte. The next day, the reporter visited their house, where he discovered that their son, Steve Parent, a stereo salesman, had been missing for a few days. After the name was publicized through the press and the police became aware of it, they initiated their investigation by visiting the parents' residence. Soon, Steve's mother and father went to the coroner's office and identified their son's body.

~

Charlie didn't rise until late afternoon, around four, and began watching the news broadcast about the murders. He was distressed right away as none of them were mentioning the connection of these murders with the Black Panthers or calling it a copycat murder by comparing it with Gary Hinman's murder.

It wasn't what Charlie had expected, and Beausoleil wasn't going to be released as he had hoped. It also didn't help start any kind of race war like Helter Skelter. Charlie began to think more about the situation. He figured that it couldn't be his idea, as it was a good one. Perhaps it was only because Gary Hinman wasn't anybody essential, and most people had forgotten all about his murder by now. Charlie realized that the murder of Sharon Tate completely overshadowed Hinman, so the best thing for him to do next was to commit a copycat murder of Tate instead of ending with the Tate murders. He had to make that the start of them. Nobody was going to look back at the Hinman murder and compare it to how Tate was murdered. She was far too big. So tonight, he would have to set up a copycat murder of the Cielo Drive murders and again have it look like the Black Panthers were behind the murders. It would at least solidify that the Panthers were out murdering rich white people and at least get Helter Skelter started.

20

THE LABIANCA MURDERS

E ven though the Family members were all celebrating the Tate murders and not realizing that the news media had completely missed the connection to the Hinman murders and the Black Panthers, he needed his people to feel good. He got his guitar and began to sing for them while everyone smoked weed. After a fun evening, most of them had crashed or gone to bed.

Charlie then gathered Tex, Susan, Patricia, Linda, Clem, and Leslie. While they were all sitting around, Charlie began to tell them what had gone wrong the night before during the attack. "There was far too much panic, too much turmoil. We need to go out again tonight, and this time we do it right." This time, Charlie decided to go along with them and show them how to do it. Charlie told them all to get ready, just as they had the night before, and he would wait for them by the Ford.

Charlie had no plans to take part in any of the murders that would happen tonight, just as with the Cielo Drive murders the previous evening. But tonight, he was planning two separate murders at two different locations, and each was done by a different three-person team whom Charlie himself picked. Having two more murder scenes that were done in the same manner as the Tate murders, just one day later, should make the police connect them all.

Charlie chose Leslie Van Houten because she was smart, probably the smartest Family member that he had. She also took orders well, and he could depend on her to ensure everything was done perfectly. He could count on her not to leave any evidence or fingerprints at the scene.

Choosing Clem was for completely the opposite reason, as he was not very smart. He was probably the dumbest Family member Charlie had, but he would do whatever he was told to do and had no problem with murder.

Tex, Susan, Linda, and Patricia were quiet during the drive, as they each had gone through this exact scenario the night before. They knew what was about to happen. And this time, they were worried. They knew they had disappointed Charlie with their performance the night before at Cielo Drive.

The only person talking in the car was Charlie, who was giving orders to Linda. He would yell out to her to turn right or left, just as they were at the road. Often, she would miss the turn, then have to stop the car and turn around. Charlie kept telling her that she was stupid, but it was more a matter of his not telling them where they were headed. He might have wanted to keep their destination secret, or maybe he wasn't sure where he wanted to go because he kept telling Linda to stop so that he could get out and look around. There were times when Charlie told Linda to follow a car for a while, then they would go and check out a church, watching the priest for about half an hour.

After a few hours of what Linda thought was aimless driving, Charlie suddenly became serious and seemed to know where he wanted to go. He directed her to the Los Feliz part of town and instructed her to drive slowly up Waverly Drive. Tex Watson, Susan Atkins, and Patricia Krenwinkel all perked up in the back seat as they all knew this part of town. They had partied around here before. It was where Harold True had lived many months before but had since moved away.

As they arrived at True's former home, Charlie told Linda to park on the curb in front of the house. He then ordered everyone to remain in the car, and he got out and walked away. Charlie first looked around the house where True lived and saw that it was still empty. He noticed lights coming from the neighbors and thought whoever lived next to True would be good enough to kill. Tex and Atkins couldn't think of a reason that they would be at True's old house because they all liked him, so why would he want to kill True?

Finally, Charlie returned to the car, and he told Tex to get out and follow him. They walked back to True's neighbor's house and slowly snuck up to the living room window. Charlie told Tex to look inside and report back to him what he saw. Tex said that he saw a man who must have been sleeping on the couch, as he had a newspaper open, covering his face.

Charlie took the lead and went to the back door, which wasn't locked. They went inside the house and quietly approached the sleeping man, Leno LaBianca. Charlie bent down and began to poke Leno's chest with the barrel of his gun. Leno slowly woke up, and when he saw Charlie and Tex, he quietly asked, "Who are you?"

Charlie softly spoke and informed Leno that they were going to rob him, and nobody was going to be hurt. He then told Leno to roll over onto his stomach while staying on the couch, and then he took a leather thong that he had wrapped around his neck. And he handed it to Tex and told him to tie Leno up.

Leno began to move around and say that it was too tight, and asked Tex to loosen it up. Charlie asked him who else was in the house. Leno said his wife was somewhere upstairs, probably in the bedroom. Charlie quickly left to go upstairs and returned with Rosemary LaBianca a few minutes later, and he pushed her onto the sofa.

Leno began to complain again about how tightly his hands had been tied, and Rosemary looked at him, asking if she could help him sit up so that he was more comfortable. Instead of Tex or Charlie answering her, Charlie blurts out, "Do you have any money around here?" Leno stopped his complaining and muttered, "Her wallet should be in our bedroom." Charlie looked over at Tex, who said, "I got it," before running up the stairs.

Tex ran back down to the living room and gave Charlie the wallet. "Watch them!" Charlie demanded, and he took the wallet and left to go outside, where the car was parked. There, he told Leslie and Patricia to get out of the car and follow him into the house. When the three of them returned to the house, Charlie told the girls to take Rosemary back upstairs to the bedroom, and they did.

Charlie looked directly into Tex's eyes and sternly ordered, "Make sure that everybody here does something!" Charlie nodded his head up and down until Tex agreed, making sure Tex understood what he meant. Charlie left the LaBianca household and went back to the car. He opened the driver's side door and told Linda to move over. He got behind the wheel and began driving, while Clem and Susan remained quiet in the back seat.

After Charlie left, Tex ran upstairs to the bedroom and grabbed the two pillowcases off the pillows that were on their bed. First, he took one of them and placed it over Rosemary's head, telling her not to make any noise. Then he ran back down to the living room, where he put the second pillowcase over Leno's head. He grabbed the lamp from the end table, tying the cord around his neck.

Patricia went into the kitchen and searched through all the drawers until she found the knives. She took some with her back out into the living room. Tex got excited when he saw her carrying the knives, as he realized that he wouldn't have to kill everyone himself. Patricia was scared since she didn't want to hurt anyone. But she knew that if she didn't follow Tex's orders, Charlie might kill her.

Leno tried to get free and started yelling, even though his head was covered with the pillowcase and the lamp cord was tied around his neck. His screaming stunned Tex, who didn't think he would be able to make any noise. So he grabbed his bayonet and stabbed at Leno, piercing him in his throat. Tex kept stabbing him until he stopped making any noise and fell to the ground.

Both Patricia and Leslie went upstairs and entered the bedroom, where Rosemary was. She had her hands tied, and a pillowcase was over her head. They could all hear Tex attacking Leno, and Rosemary screamed, "What are you doing to my husband?" She stood up and tried to get free, running for the bedroom door.

Tex had also wrapped her bedside lamp cord around her neck, just like he had with Leno, and tied it to the pillowcase. Another cord connected both lamps in the bedroom, so when she stood up to run, it made the second lamp crash to the floor. Trying to drag two lamps behind her slowed her down enough for Patricia to catch up and start stabbing her. Because she was flailing around trying to get free, Patricia missed several times. Finally, Tex appeared and stabbed Rosemary with his bayonet through her stomach.

Tex and Patricia returned downstairs, and unbelievably, Leno was still moving. So Tex stabbed him a few more times. He ordered Patricia to carve some words in his stomach. She carved "War" on his lower abdomen with her knife. She then took a carving fork that she had found in the kitchen earlier and stabbed it into his belly, leaving it there. After that, she took a smaller knife that she had on her and stabbed Leno through his lower chin again, leaving it there.

Tex now needed Leslie to participate in the murders, so he ordered her to come upstairs with him into Rosemary's bedroom. Rosemary was lying dead on her stomach. While Tex pulled her nightgown up to expose her buttocks and legs, he looked at Leslie and nodded his head. Leslie knew what he meant and responded by stabbing Rosemary's legs and buttocks several times.

The three of them now had to make the scene resemble the Tate murder scene. They began to write words on the walls using the blood of their victims. "Rise" and "Death" were written on the walls, and "Helter Skelter" was written on the refrigerator door by Patricia, not realizing that she had misspelled "Helter."

They then searched the house for any additional money or valuables. Tex found a bag of coins, which they took with them when they left. Leno was a coin collector, so it was probably some that he had bought for his collection.

When they were finished, they took towels and wiped down every room that any of them were in to ensure no evidence was left behind for the police to find. They must have stopped to eat some food, too, as there were several watermelon rinds left in the kitchen sink along with empty milk cartons.

∽

Charlie gave Linda the wallet he had taken from the LaBiancas' house and told her to wipe it clean after she removed the money from it. There weren't any bills in the wallet, only a few coins. So after she removed those and cleaned off the wallet with a cloth, she placed it on the seat beside her, waiting for Charlie to tell her what to do next.

Charlie intended to drive into one of the black parts of town and toss the wallet. He figured some black person would find it and try to use the credit cards or something, thereby tying them to the murders. For some reason, Charlie changed his mind. He drove them to a gas station that was right beside a Denny's restaurant in Sylmar and ordered Linda to go into the women's bathroom and leave the wallet there. While Linda took the wallet into the bathroom, Charlie went to Denny's and bought four milkshakes to go for everyone.

Now that they were all back together, Charlie told Linda to drive them to the beach. All four of them got out of the car and walked along the waterfront, talking about life in the sand. None of the murders from the last couple of nights were mentioned at all. The main topic became Linda's pregnancy. During their walk along the beach, two officers approached them and inquired about their activities. Charlie told them that they were just out for a walk and enjoying themselves. The cops didn't feel anything suspicious was going on and left them alone.

After their walk, they all got back in the car, and this time Charlie told Linda to drive them to Venice. While they were traveling, Charlie casually asked if any of them knew somebody who lived in Venice. All of them said no, which gave Charlie a surprised look. Charlie then looked at Linda while she was driving, "Didn't you and Sandy meet some guy out there when you were panhandling for some money once?" Linda began to think and moaned. "It wasn't that long ago," Charlie added. "Oh, Yeah! Now I remember. A guy named Saladin Nader asked us to go back to his apartment with him and hang out for a while. I think he was an actor or something like that."

Charlie put a grin on his face. "Do you remember where this actor lived?" Linda thought for a moment, then said, "Yes, Charlie. Did you want me to take you there now?" Charlie nodded his head yes.

Linda pulled up to Nader's apartment and parked the car. "Would this actor let you back in?" Linda nodded her head yes. "How about letting you and Clem in?" Charlie asked Linda. "Sure, he would. He was friendly." Charlie then pulled out a knife and handed it to her. "You are to slit this actor's throat!"

Linda took the knife from Charlie and slowly looked down at it. "I just couldn't. I'm not you, Charlie." "No? Which apartment does this actor live in?" They all got out of the car with Linda in the lead. She went up the stairs and walked to the end of the hall with everyone following her just a few feet behind. Linda then raised her arm and pointed towards one of the apartment doors, knowing that it wasn't the apartment that belonged to Nader. Charlie smiled, then told them all to follow him. He walked back down the stairs and to the car.

He turned and looked at them, then began to give his instructions on what they needed to do. Just as he did with the LaBiancas murders, he would tell them what to do and then leave. "Linda, I want you to go to the door and knock. When the actor lets you, Clem, and Susan into his apartment and everything is going well, Linda, that's when you slit his throat. Then, Clem, you need to shoot him." Just then, Charlie removed a gun that was stuffed down the front of his pants and handed it to Clem. "While you guys are busy doing that, I will drive back to Spahn Ranch. "I want you three to hitchhike back to the ranch when you are finished."

After they watched Charlie drive away, Linda led the other two up the stairs in the apartment building and approached one of the apartment doors that she knew didn't belong to the actor, knocking on it. The door opened just a crack, and a man asked what they wanted. Linda shook her head no as she looked at Susan and Clem. Linda apologized for knocking on the wrong door.

Linda then told them that she didn't remember where the actor lived. The three of them walked down to the beach to figure out what to do next. Should they find someone else to kill, or do they just go back to the ranch? After an hour of discussion, they decided to bury the gun in the sand and hitchhike back home.

By the time they got back to the ranch, everyone else was already home. Tex, Patricia, and Leslie were picked up by a man who had previously visited Spahn Ranch and had also been with Leslie before. Tex, Patricia, and Leslie had also bought the guy breakfast at a restaurant on the way back, paying for it with some of the coins they had stolen from Leno LaBianca. Everyone was exhausted, so after a brief chat, they all went to bed. Linda, Clem, and Susan didn't want to run into Charlie as he'd probably be angry that they didn't murder the actor.

The following morning, someone had retrieved a copy of the *Sunday Times*, and the complete first couple of pages were all stories about the Tate murders, and that a suspect, Garretson, had been arrested and charged. Most of the speculation in the paper was about the murders being some ritual, perhaps even satanic. There were also rumors about Roman Polanski and Sharon Tate not getting along, and that she was partying at the house in just her panties and bra on the night she was murdered.

When Charlie finally got up, he was going around to the different Family members who had been involved in the LaBianca murders on the previous evening and barraging them with questions about whether they had made sure to wipe any surface where they might have touched and make sure that they had disposed of everything they had worn during the murders. Tex kept on telling Charlie that everything was good.

Frank Struthers, Rosemary LaBianca's son, returned home on Sunday night. Just after eight, his friends' family, with whom he had been camping all week, dropped him off at his home on Waverly Drive. As Frank was walking up the driveway, he saw that the speedboat Leno had picked up the day before was still sitting outside, which was not normal for Leno. He walked around the back door and knocked, but got no answer. He couldn't see in the house as all the blinds had been pulled down, so he walked back down the driveway and down the road a few blocks to where there was a payphone. He called his older sister, Suzanne, who had a spare key.

Suzanne, along with her boyfriend, Joe Dorgan, picked Frank up at the payphone, and the three of them returned to the LaBiancas' Waverly Drive home. All three of them entered the house through the back door and into the kitchen with Suzanne's key. The two men left Suzanne in the kitchen because she was scared, and then they walked into the living room.

They saw Leno lying face up on the floor with something

protruding from his stomach. Both were shocked. They returned to the kitchen immediately and grabbed Suzanne, leading her out the back door of the house. "Everything is okay," Frank hurriedly said. "We need to leave now!" Suzanne had been looking at some writing that was put on the refrigerator using red paint, but didn't have enough time to read what it said.

21

LENO & ROSEMARY LABIANCA

Leno and Rosemary LaBianca resided in the upper-middle-class neighborhood of Los Feliz, located on Waverly Drive. They had been married about ten years and were very close. Previously, they both had been married and had children from those relationships. Both had worked their entire lives to afford their lifestyle, with Leno managing a chain of grocery stores and Rosemary owning a clothing boutique.

Early on the morning of Saturday, August 9th, the LaBiancas, along with Rosemary's twenty-one-year-old daughter, Suzanne, had travelled over one hundred and fifty miles to Lake Isabella to pick up her fifteen-year-old son, Frank, and their speedboat, which they had let him use since the previous Tuesday. When they arrived, her son Frank, who was there with his best friend and his family, wanted to stay until Sunday night. They both thought that was fine, and they hitched up their speedboat and headed for home.

By the time they got back to Los Angeles, it was late at night. They dropped Suzanne off at her apartment after midnight, then stopped at their local all-night newsstand for Leno to get a newspaper to check the sports section. He was a regular gambler at the racetracks and needed to see how his horses did, which he did almost every night.

The newsstand was owned by John Fokianos, who happened to be on duty when the LaBiancas picked up the paper that night. He liked talking with the couple as he thought they were entertaining people. They spoke of the Sharon Tate murders, and he was surprised that they hadn't heard about them up to that point, since it seemed like it was all everyone was talking about. After their conversation with Fokianos, around 2 a.m., the couple headed home. The bars were closing and their customers were flooding out onto the streets.

When the couple arrived home, they were both exhausted. They went up to their bedroom, changed into their sleeping clothes, and Rosemary went into the bathroom. Leno went back down the stairs and into the living room to read the sports section of the newspaper. Neither of them had to get up early the next day, as they were taking the day off.

22

AFTER THE LABIANCA MURDERS

After seeing Leno on the floor, Joe Dorgan, Frank, and Suzanne ran over to the next-door neighbor and called the police. The police arrived and entered the house on Waverly Drive around 10:30 that morning. They found Leno's body upon entry and, a few minutes later, discovered Rosemary's body upstairs in one of the bedrooms. Both victims were dead and had sustained injuries that looked like several stab wounds. On Leno's body, it looked like the word "WAR" was carved on his lower stomach. The walls appeared to be covered in blood. The words written there were "Rise" and "Death to Pigs." And written on the refrigerator was "Healter Skelter."

Detective Galindo was instructed to visit the Waverly Drive residence without speaking to anyone, especially the press. But the media already knew from listening in that there was a murder there. By the time Galindo arrived at the crime scene, a large group of reporters was already gathered outside on the curb. They all began to shout out different questions to Galindo as he got out of his car and headed for the house. "Do these murders have anything to do with the Tate murders?" Galindo instinctively answered, "I don't think so. If anything, they are a copycat type of murders." In the minds of cops, they thought that some insane person had heard about the murders at the Tate residence and wanted to do the same thing.

The following day, Monday, August 11th, all the press led with stories about another set of bizarre murders that also had words written in blood on the walls. Only these murders happened in the Los Feliz part of town, and with two people who were not celebrities. Some of the media were suggesting that there might be a connection. But police still believed that the Tate murders were somehow drug-related and the LaBianca murders had something to do with Leno's gambling issues. Leno had owed racetrack bets in the area of two hundred and fifty thousand dollars in total, which surely must have had some Mafia ties to it.

∼

A significant problem among police departments in the 1960s was that they all worked independently. There were no computer systems or the internet back then. Each city would police itself, and they rarely sought help from other city law enforcement. The standard protocol for police if they were dealing with a murder that crossed state lines was that they would contact the FBI, since the crime was considered federal. All three of these murder cases were within California and really in the Los Angeles metro area, so there was no immediate need to bring in the feds.

In addition to the standard issues between city police forces not working together, the two sets of detectives assigned to each case had very different personalities. The detectives working the Cielo Drive murders were much older and had gained their expertise from working in the field for years. The LaBianca detective team was a younger group with minimal real-life experience, but they had more education and studied the latest techniques in technology.

The bottom line was that both groups of detectives didn't believe that these cases were connected, and the murderers were not the same people. They thought that the Tate murders might have influenced the LaBianca murders, but that was about as close together as they got.

As expected, having two high-profile murders in the city created a lot of talk, and with that, fear. The residents of Beverly Hills, as well as other high-end communities, didn't know how to react to the Tate murders. After all, she was a celebrity who had the basic security around her home and in a nice neighborhood. At the same time, the LaBianca murders hit closer to home with the working-class people. Nobody could be considered safe.

Sales of guns skyrocketed by over one hundred percent. The demand for trained guard dogs also rose, and with it, so did the prices. The average cost was around two hundred dollars before the murders, and fifteen hundred after.

23

TIME TO GET OUT OF DODGE

M anson was growing increasingly frustrated with each of the news reports he either read or heard on TV or the radio. Nothing was mentioned about these murders being racially motivated. Charlie couldn't understand why. The race issues were running high in most major American cities, including LA, especially after the Watts riot. There were obvious signs of the Black Panthers left on the walls using the victim's blood. Why were neither the detectives nor the press picking up on this?

What Manson didn't understand was how the city of Los Angeles was different from the other major cities in America, and why this made a difference. Los Angeles was spread out over a considerable distance, and each area was separated from the others by highways and interstates. So, unlike a city like New York, where both Blacks and Whites walked the streets, took the buses and subways, and shopped in grocery stores together, in Los Angeles, they were still very much segregated from each other. So if a van full of Black Panthers drove through the streets of Los Feliz, police would have been notified by residents via the phone several times. At that time, most people who were living in communities like Los Feliz would never see or interact with a person of color. After the fear that was created after the recent Watts riots, the moment any of them saw a black person in their community, they called the police. It was the primary reason behind the detectives' not thinking the murders were racially motivated.

On top of all the other worries that Manson had, he now had to worry about Beausoleil keeping quiet since it was now apparent he wasn't going to be set free because of the copycat killings. Manson needed more time to relocate himself and his family to Death Valley, where they could be well hidden. He figured he would send Linda Kasabian to jail to visit Beausoleil and give him a message from Charlie. He wanted him to know that things were going as planned, and he should remain quiet.

～

When Linda arrived at the prison, she realized that she hadn't brought any identification. So the prison wouldn't let her see Beausoleil. After leaving the jail, instead of returning to Spahn Ranch, she drove to New Mexico to visit her ex-husband.

Linda told Bob all about the murders that Manson and other Family members had committed and what she had seen. Bob demanded that the two of them go back to the ranch and get their daughter, Tanya, who Linda had left behind. She refused, saying that if they showed up at the ranch asking for Tanya, Charlie would find out that she had told Bob about the murders. Manson would kill them both. It would be best if she just went back and acted normally.

～

Charlie realized that it was best to get Tex away from the ranch and the possibility of the police finding and questioning him. He told him to go to Barker Ranch. Tex left, taking Dianne "Snake" Lane with him. Now was the time to start planning to move the Family.

～

The following day, Tuesday, August 12th, Sharon Tate's movie, *Valley of the Dolls*, was rereleased in theaters nationally. In a way, this served as a tribute to her.

≈

Also on August 12th, a Straight Satan biker, Al Springer, showed up at Spahn Ranch to talk with DeCarlo, who was still living at the ranch. Springer wanted to convince DeCarlo that he should return to living with the Straight Satan's. But DeCarlo told him that if he left, Manson would find him and kill him because that's what he did to those who left the group. DeCarlo also told Springer about how Charlie was responsible for a murder where he had sliced a guy's ear off with a sword.

To make things more tense while DeCarlo and Springer were talking, Springer asked Charlie what he did to support all of his girls at the ranch. Charlie responded that he liked to go out at night to the swankiest parts of town, where he'd knock on the door and kill and cut up the people who lived there. He bragged about just cutting up five people in one house the other night.

Springer wasn't buying everything Charlie was telling him. But he also knew Charlie was dangerously on the edge, so he didn't challenge him on any of it. He hung around a bit longer after Manson left, and he told DeCarlo that he'd be back to get him.

Most of the Straight Satans had not been going out to the ranch since the bad drug deal that happened with Beausoleil and Hinman. So when Springer returned to their clubhouse and told everyone what was going on with DeCarlo, most of them were enraged. It was now time to go and get DeCarlo, even if they had to kill anyone who got in their way.

≈

The country's attention soon shifted from all of the murders in Los Angeles and the race riots throughout the country when the Woodstock four-day music festival began on Friday, August 15th. Over four hundred thousand people made their way to upstate New York. It was the ultimate party for the hippie generation to let loose of all of their anger and disappointment with their country for being involved in the Vietnam War without having to protest. It was where they could get together with other like-minded people and embrace love.

~

At the same time, people were gathering for Woodstock, about a dozen Straight Satan bikers showed up at the ranch. They had every intention of beating up Charlie and bringing their biker gang member, DeCarlo, back with them. Instead of Manson being confrontational with he bikers, he instead offered them food and drinks. Even when they were yelling and saying that they should burn down the ranch, Charlie responded by asking some of his girls to come and please these fine men. Several of the bikers took him up on his offer, and they began to party with the women.

After a while, when the bikers all got back together and asked to see DeCarlo, Charlie told them that he had several of his men on the rooftops, aiming their guns at them. He advised them to leave if they didn't want to die, and so they did. Only now, Springer and the rest of them were angrier than they were before.

24

ARREST AT SPAHN RANCH

On Saturday, August 16th, police decided to conduct another raid on the Spahn Ranch. Despite their first raid that had taken place just over four months earlier being somewhat successful, this time, the police were going to use all the resources they could manage, including several helicopters and over one hundred officers, some of whom were on horseback. They didn't want anyone getting away or them missing any evidence.

Minutes before sunrise, the sounds of the helicopters and the yelling of orders, such as "Raise your hands" or "Freeze," fell upon everyone at Spahn Ranch. For several hours, the chaos continued until police were able to round everybody up and locate all the stolen vehicles.

Detectives had everything that they wanted except for the man who ran the show, Charles Manson. He had escaped capture again, or so it seemed. Finally, just before sunset, one of the officers discovered Charlie hidden underneath one of the shacks that some of the girls used for living quarters. That day, they arrested a total of twenty-six people, including Charlie, and took them off to jail.

In the Sunday newspapers around LA the next day, the Manson and Family arrest at Spahn Ranch was only given a small article listed on page three, right beside the mention of the LaBianca funeral. The first two pages were littered with Sharon Tate and the Cielo Drive murders.

Everyone was still fascinated with what could have been going on at the Tate residence. Wild stories such as the bodies had cuts on their sex organs, and that there were several types of drugs there as well. Was it some wild, ritual sex party gone wrong? Another mistaken theory was that the word written on the wall in blood was "PIC" and not "PIG", which they thought must have been the initials of the murderer's name. Police were constantly releasing statements with the actual facts, but people preferred to run with the fantasy. It must have been more fun.

When Monday, August 18th, came around, the police dropped all charges against Manson and his followers and let them go. Apparently, when the police obtained the search warrant for the ranch, it was dated for August 13, 2023. So, they needed to reschedule it for Saturday due to logistical issues in obtaining all the necessary support to complete the search. They had forgotten, or just didn't bother, to get the warrant dates changed, ultimately making the raid illegal.

Even though several of the vehicles the police had found were stolen, they were unable to use any of the evidence they had collected during the search. There was no way to prove who, among the Family, was involved in any of the thefts. Police would not let any of the children return to Spahn Ranch and instead moved them to child welfare, as they considered the living conditions at the ranch to be unfit. It allowed Linda Kasabian to contact the child welfare service and retrieve her daughter, Tanya.

After their release and return to the ranch, Charlie was on high alert and more scared of something happening than ever before. He had Family members in jail: Beausoleil, who had run away from Spahn Ranch, and Linda, who could talk to the police. Either the Black Panthers or Straight Satan's could come back for revenge and attack him and the Family at any time. And the police were onto them. Obviously, after two raids in four months, the police were watching them to see if they would steal any more cars and drugs. He wondered if maybe the FBI was involved as well. He had to do something and do it fast, as he was running out of time.

Charlie was now angry at anyone who wasn't being real and caused him problems. The first person who came to mind was DeCarlo, whom he had recruited to leverage his ties to the biker gang, but that didn't go so well. DeCarlo was arrested with the rest of the Family, but when they all returned, Charlie decided that DeCarlo was no longer welcome. He told the rest of the Family, and everyone at the ranch began to ignore him, and none of them would have sex with DeCarlo anymore.

Charlie needed to find out why the cops had raided the ranch again so soon. There must have been a stool pigeon, someone who was talking to detectives. Why else would they have raided the ranch again after only four months? There had to be a leak. The only person at the ranch who was very upfront about not liking Charlie or his followers was ranch employee Shorty Shea. After all, it was Shorty who was constantly telling George Spahn that he should get rid of Charlie and his group, and he would be more than glad to do it for him.

Manson's plans to move the Family from Spahn to Death Valley were now delayed again. The police had confiscated all of their dune buggies because they had been stolen, so now Charlie had no way of moving them. They would have to start all over, stealing new vehicles to take them to the desert. And that would take time. The only thing was, Charlie knew they didn't have enough time, as it seemed the walls were all starting to cave in around them.

The date isn't precisely known, but somewhere near the end of August, Barbara Hoyt, who often slept in her trailer parked on a hill just outside the movie set part of the ranch, was woken up by what she thought was a scream. Hoyt went back to sleep, only to start hearing more screams. After they continued, she decided to get up.

That same night, Charlie, Clem, and Bruce Davis persuaded Shea to go for a ride with them in one of the few cars they had left around 10 p.m. They must have told him that they needed help fixing something out there. Later, Bruce Davis told other Family members about how he, Clem, and Charlie had taken their bayonets out with them on the night they gave Shea a ride. When they got far enough away from where most of the shacks were that they lived in, they carved him up like a Christmas turkey. Davis laughed about it because it took so long for Shea to die, and he took pleasure in it. Each time they carved a piece of his flesh off, he screamed.

After they buried all of Shea's cut-up body parts in several spots around where they murdered him, Davis returned to Shea's shack and placed all of his possessions into a trunk, which he put in Shea's car. He then grabbed Gypsy, and they drove the vehicle into the desert, leaving it there.

When other workers noticed that Shea was missing, they started asking around. Charlie told everyone that Shea had left to go to San Francisco to work at a new job he had gotten there.

25

THE NEXT MORNING AFTER

Meanwhile, at the Hall of Justice in Los Angeles, everyone who had a press pass was cramming into the building. The Tate autopsies were being performed today, and police officials assured the media that a press conference would be held there as soon as the results were received.

Thomas Noguchi was the forensic examiner who performed the autopsies on all five of the murdered bodies from the Tate house. Everyone involved knew that this would take longer than usual because there had been so much damage done to the bodies. The autopsy reports were released to the media late that afternoon.

The examination showed that Sharon Tate had been stabbed a total of sixteen times. Five of them could have been the fatal blow. Jay Sebring had been stabbed seven times and shot once. Abigail Folger had been stabbed twenty-eight times. Voytek Frykowski was stabbed a total of fifty-one times and shot two times, but was also hit on his head with blunt force a total of thirteen times. Steve Parent was shot four times and had a cut wound on his left arm. All the gunshot wounds were from the same weapon, all .22 caliber.

～

That same Sunday morning, two Los Angeles County detectives tried to contact Detective McGann or any other detective who was working the Tate murder case, but they couldn't get hold of any of them. They were all at the Hall of Justice awaiting the autopsy reports. Instead, they spoke to one of their temporary detectives, James Buckles. They explained that they, too, were working on a murder case that showed some similarities to the Tate case. Their case was the murder of a man named Gary Hinman. He, too, was stabbed several times in his home, and the murderer had also written on his wall in his blood, "Political Piggie."

The L.A. County detectives further explained that their primary suspect was Bobby Beausoleil, and he had been arrested and charged with the murder. They had him in custody. Beausoleil had lived on an old movie set ranch just outside of the city with a commune that had a leader, Charles Manson, who they believed was Jesus.

The L.A. County detectives wanted to set up a meeting with the Tate murder case detectives to compare notes and see if there was any connection between these two murder cases. But Detective Buckles told them that that would just be wasting everybody's time and that they were far too busy at the moment. He also said that the Tate case was almost certainly a drug-related murder.

Later, when McGann returned to the office, he saw the note about the phone call from the county detectives, so he asked Buckles what it was about. Buckles told McGann that it was nothing, just a waste of time. So McGann didn't bother following up on it. Buckles had unknowingly set back the solving of the Tate murders. He also angered Charlie in the midst of it all because if the police weren't connecting the two murder cases and not promoting the copycat murder to the press, then they were also not going to help start Charlie's race war either.

~

McGann and the other LAPD detectives continued on the drug-deal-gone-wrong theory as the motivation behind the Cielo Drive murders. Not that they thought there was too much marijuana found at the house for personal consumption. The amount found was typical of what was found in most Hollywood homes. Instead, Frykowski was the center of attention for the detectives as he was already under investigation for dealing harder drugs such as heroin. There were also FBI-authorized investigations on some of the shipments received at the Tate household, which came from England. The police had to look at every possibility.

∾

Later that same Sunday, the police were disappointed when they received the results of the lie detector test administered to their key suspect: William Garretson passed with flying colors. But even though he passed the test, the police still didn't trust him. They just couldn't believe that he didn't hear any noise coming from the main house or out on the front lawn when these brutal murders occurred.

Detectives couldn't decide whether Garretson hid in fear, knowing the murders were happening, or if he knew who they were. They were confident that he didn't commit any of the murders, though. Police had to tell everyone in the Justice Hall that their main suspect was being released after passing his lie detector test.

∾

When the detectives arrived at the Tate murder scene, they found out who owned the houses and property, Rudi Altobelli, and where he was at the time. Once they contacted him, he got on the next plane, arriving back in Los Angeles on Sunday night.

Instead of returning home at Cielo Drive, he went and stayed with his friend, Terry Melcher, who was living at his mother's beach house with his girlfriend, Candace Bergen. Altobelli was worried about fans and perhaps some weirdos trying to get souvenirs from the crime scene, so he called Gregg Jakobson and asked him to stay at his Cielo Drive home to keep an eye on things for him. He said he didn't want even to go there, let alone return to live there.

∾

Roman Polanski also flew back to Los Angeles and arrived on Sunday night. The first thing that he had to do was make a statement to the press and let them know that there was no truth about it being a drug deal that had gone bad or any ritual. He, too, was asked to take a lie detector test by the police, which he agreed to do. When the test was completed, the police also eliminated him as a suspect. Basically, in hiding from the press, Polanski stayed in a private apartment on the Paramount movie studio to avoid being disturbed.

26

THE WEATHERMEN UNDERGROUND

Both the Tate and LaBianca murder cases kept police working hard without much progress being made. The press continued to run many of the wild stories and rumors that had inundated the people of Los Angeles. Roman Polanski was offering a $25,000 reward for help to catch the murderers of his wife, Sharon Tate, and their unborn child. All the attention led to several anonymous leads being given to the police, but all of them ultimately went nowhere.

~

Los Angeles had one of its most violent years on record in 1969: there were three hundred and eighty-eight homicides, which was almost ten percent higher than in 1968. Police officers and detectives were overwhelmed by the over 169,000 crimes reported that year.

From the race riots of the '60s came the Student Democratic Society (SDS), which mainly protested the treatment of Blacks in society and the Vietnam War. By the late 1960s, a subgroup of the SDS, called "The Weathermen," broke off, taking several SDS members with them. The Weathermen thought that the SDS was too soft. When they protested, they did so in the Martin Luther King Jr. (MLK) method—making speeches, holding rallies, and avoiding violence. The Weathermen thought that the MLK method had accomplished nothing. They wanted to take a more extreme approach to the protests, similar to the Black Panthers and many other more aggressive, and sometimes violent, groups that were active at this time.

Over the next six months, the Weathermen became the "Weathermen Underground" and started planning a series of bombings, numbering around two hundred, targeting different government buildings and businesses. The bombings soon took over the news spotlight.

The night of October 8th began calmly, with several group members delivering speeches to the public in Chicago. Anger led to the events getting out of control. Several followers ran through the business district, breaking the glass windows of many of the businesses, which led to looting.

The violence only escalated. As the night turned into morning, six of the Weathermen Underground were shot by police, and sixty-eight were arrested. Twenty-eight police officers were injured.

The following day, the riots seemed to be the only topic being covered in every newspaper and press outlet. For the first time since they happened, the Tate murders were not mentioned. Before anyone had a chance to analyze what led to the riots, they happened again, not even forty-eight hours later, on the evening of October 10th. This time, twice the number of protesters were arrested, and thirty-six police officers were injured.

The Weathermen Underground had the exact makings of what Manson had with his followers. They both lived similar lifestyles, doing LSD while having sex orgies. They lived just like most people in those days, in an apartment or house where they cooked dinners and bought food in grocery stores.

On October 15th, more than one million protesters packed the streets and sidewalks in every major city, including New York, Boston, and Washington, D.C. This was known as the "National Moratorium Day," a protest against the undeclared war in Vietnam. President Nixon appeared not to care about the protests that day and instead decided to watch a football game between the university teams of Texas and Arkansas, ensuring that all the press knew he was doing it too.

The Chicago 8

The trial of the group known as the Chicago 8—David Dellinger, Rennie Davis, Tom Hayden, Abbie Hoffman, Jerry Rubin, Lee Weiner, John Froines, and Bobby Seale—began around the same time in Chicago on September 24, 1969. The trial captured the full attention of America from the very first moment, as the charges were being read aloud. One of the defendants, Abbie Hoffman, stood up in front of the judge and blew him a kiss.

27

DEATH VALLEY

The move to Death Valley for Manson and his followers began on September 1st and took more than a week to complete. After the last police raid had taken away most of their dune buggies, they had to make several trips between Spahn Ranch and Death Valley to retrieve their belongings. Just as Manson had done when he moved most of his followers back to Spahn Ranch, where he left a couple of them to stay at Death Valley, he also left a couple of his girls at Spahn Ranch. He knew the owner, George Spahn, certainly wouldn't mind having some of the girls there full-time to keep him company. And they could let Charlie know if anything happened at the ranch that he should be aware of, such as if the police returned to the ranch asking questions or conducting a search.

The Barker Ranch in Death Valley had fewer buildings for his followers to live in, so they had to live outside on the land of their new neighbors—the Myers' Ranch. The owner of that ranch, Cathy Gilles' grandmother, never lived on the ranch or visited there, so she wouldn't know who lived there or not.

～

Ten-year-old Steven Weiss, living near the corner of Cielo Drive and Benedict Canyon Road, was playing in their sprinkler on the morning of September 1st when he noticed a gun lying on the grass in his backyard. Steven often watched the popular police shows on television, such as *Dragnet*, so he knew he shouldn't touch the gun. He might leave his fingerprints on it. So, he carefully picked up the weapon by its barrel, using a pencil, and gave it to his parents. His parents later gave it to the police.

The officer who picked up the gun from the Weisses noted that it was a .22 caliber that was missing its right-hand grip. It had a nine-cartridge chamber with two live rounds and seven empty casings in it.

~

After everyone had moved into their new homes, Charlie assigned jobs to everyone to prepare for the upcoming race war, instead of having them build and fix what they needed to support all the new residents. He had everyone scared that the police were looking for them, and they would have to fight back if that happened. Charlie had them dig large pits to hide weapons and food. He also had bunkers constructed on the sides of nearby mountains.

While it was mostly the men who did the more challenging digging work, he created smaller teams of women who each took turns going out to search for the bottomless pit where they would live during the war. They all still believed that after the battles ended, the Blacks would then ask Charlie and his followers to come out and lead the new world.

Charlie often described to them what they would see in this bottomless pit. After traveling through the upper tunnel, they would reach a magical city hidden below. In this new city, everyone would be able to transform themselves into any being they wanted. During the entire time they lived in this new city, none of them would age. It would be as if the world outside would move on without them. When it was time for them to return to the world to help the Blacks figure out how to run things, they would still be young and who they are today.

Manson's followers all seemed to believe what he was telling them, perhaps at different levels, depending on how devout each was to him.

The bottom line was that none of them questioned Charlie on anything, no matter how fantastically it sounded. They were in deeper than they ever were. Perhaps it was that they were so exhausted from doing all the heavy labor of getting the ranch ready for the war, and enduring the hot temperatures with little food and water. But even if a member didn't like or believe in what Charlie was saying all the time, they were far too weary to question him on anything. A few of his members even ran with the fantasy of living in an underground magical city where they could turn themselves into anything that they desired. Leslie Van Houten often dreamed and talked about what she would do when she got there. She said she would transform herself into an elf with wings and have the ability to fly.

Every night, the Family got together and did LSD just as they had at Spahn Ranch. Only in Death Valley, they didn't follow their drugs with singing, dancing, and group sex. Instead, they all sat around and listened to Charlie tell them stories of what was to come. His stories had now taken on a much more serious tone. They had to survive and find the bottomless pit where their new home awaited them.

Also, in their group get-togethers, Charlie told everyone about the murders he had committed in detail. He described graphically the murders of Lotsapoppa and Shorty Shea. He used them as examples of those who opposed him and his Family. Lotsapoppa tried to threaten Charlie, so he had to die. Shea was the one who informed the police about the Family and their intentions, so Shea also had to die. Death was the fate of anyone who tried to betray Charlie. It was a subtle warning to any Family members who were considering leaving.

Charlie had all of the men working in shifts around the ranch as guards. They patrolled the outer edges of the ranch, carrying weapons and keeping a watchful eye out for anyone approaching. The women had to do more laborious work, such as cutting wood for the stoves and fires at night, as well as cooking and serving the men's meals and caring for the children. The women were always the last to eat. After the men finished their dinner, the women had to feed the kids, and then they would eat whatever was left. On top of all of this, if any of the men wanted to have sex, they could choose any of the women they wanted to. The woman had to have sex with the man who asked.

When they first arrived in the desert, both Straight Satan DeCarlo and ranch worker Juan Flynn decided to join the Family in Death Valley. DeCarlo probably went with them because he was still in fear of Charlie, and he didn't want to do anything wrong that would get him kicked out of the Family again. Juan was searching for his friend Shorty Shea, who had suddenly disappeared. It was believed that he moved to San Francisco to take a new job. Juan didn't believe that story and figured that if he went with the Family, he would eventually learn the truth.

In only a month, both DeCarlo and Juan learned what they needed to know to plan out their futures. Both men did LSD and sat around the campfire with the others at night and listened to Charlie tell his stories. Soon enough, they both heard about how Shorty was a rat fink and needed to be murdered, so Charlie and a few others killed him, cut up his body into pieces, and buried the pieces around the outskirts of the Spahn Ranch.

DeCarlo was scared after hearing this story, and a few nights later, he packed up and snuck away from the desert. He ended up going back to one of the Straight Satan branches and hiding out there. In his mind, Charlie was going to come after him and kill him. Juan didn't run, but instead decided to hang out longer, as he had nowhere else to go and nothing else to do.

Now that Charlie was back in Death Valley, he was reminded of how one of the neighbors, Crockett, had managed to take away two of his Family members. He had left them behind at Barker Ranch to take care of it when Charlie and the rest of the Family returned to Spahn Ranch. Charlie first approached Crockett to see if he could convert him into a follower and convince him to join his Family. Crockett didn't like Charlie very much and didn't believe in any of his prophecies about a coming race war. Charlie also tried to win back his two lost Family members, Poston and Watkins, but neither of them returned to him.

Manson then allowed Juan to become a full member of his Family if he did something for him. He told Juan that he had to kill Crockett. Instead of carrying out the murder, Juan took his stuff and moved in with Crockett at his place. Charlie was angry and embarrassed when

Juan defected to Crockett's group, and now felt that Crockett intended to take all of Charlie's Family members away from him.

Charlie ordered some of his Family members to do a creepy crawl at Crockett's house, not only to freak him out by moving his things around, but to scout out his location for an upcoming attack on him.

Crockett became suspicious of Manson's intentions and started preparing for an attack. Crockett didn't want to show the others that he was scared of Manson, but he knew that Manson was capable of anything.

Charlie had other problems now that they were at Barker Ranch. The Family was running out of food, drugs, and other supplies. They were down to just a couple of sacks of rice, some powdered milk, and cinnamon. Charlie had run out of LSD, too, so they were no longer able to have their group get-togethers like they used to. When they did, it just wasn't the same atmosphere as it used to be.

Charlie took a trip back to Los Angeles and had some of his girls go out and beg for money. He also started approaching his wealthier friends to ask them for some cash. One of those friends was Dennis Wilson, who gave him enough money to fill his bus with food and supplies to take back to Barker Ranch. However, this pattern continued every month. As soon as they ran out of supplies, Charlie had to return to the city to obtain money for new supplies.

When the Family had food and supplies, Manson sent several small groups, typically three or four, out to search for the bottomless pit— each group going out three or four times a day. Even with all the issues and extra work they had in Death Valley, his followers still believed in the impending race war.

When Family members got close to Death Valley National Park, Charlie told them to be careful of the park rangers who were patrolling the park. He told them the rangers were not to be trusted, as they were the same as the cops and therefore couldn't be trusted.

During one of the Family members' outings near the state park, while searching for the bottomless pit, they discovered a large excavator. They didn't like the look of it. So, as with most things they didn't like, they had to destroy it. They completely stripped the machine of any removable parts, and then poured gas all over it and set it on fire.

A few days later, park rangers discovered the burnt-out vehicle and investigated the area. From the tire tracks left behind at the scene of the crime, rangers were able to determine that the vandalizers drove what was likely a Toyota with four-wheel drive. They began asking around the rural areas for anyone who knew of such a vehicle, and often they were told that the hippies living out near the Barker Ranch drove a red four-wheel-drive car.

A few days later, Tex Watson was out driving with a few of the girls. They spotted a park ranger, Dick Powell, so they sped away into a rougher, busier area and managed to evade him. Powell was able to obtain the license plate number from the car, though, and, after running a check on it, found that it belonged to a different vehicle. It indicated that the plates were probably stolen. They reported the incident to the California Highway Patrol, who issued an APB for the car and joined the search for it in the desert.

Ranger Powell, along with Officer James Pursell, decided they'd go out to the Barker Ranch area on September 29th to try to find the hippies who were supposed to be living out there and question them about the burned-out excavator. When they arrived at the ranch, there were only two female Family members there. Manson had everyone else out searching for the bottomless pit that day. Whenever they asked the two women any questions, they received no real answers. Not that the women were refusing to answer, but rather their answers made no sense.

After Powell and Pursell left the ranch, they were heading back to the ranger station when they approached a truck. They pulled the car over and found it being driven by Paul Crockett and Brooks Poston on the passenger side. The first question Powell asked Crockett was whether he knew of any hippies in the area who were driving a red four-wheel drive car. It was the perfect opportunity for Crockett to exact revenge on Charlie.

Crockett informed the officers that a group of hippies was staying at the Barker Ranch. It was led by a crazy drug addict named Charlie. The group was also known for having large sex parties and doing lots of drugs. He also told them that this Charlie fellow thought he was Jesus, and his followers believed him.

The next thing Powell and Pursell were told by Crockett was that Charlie often talked about killing different people. He even bragged about the murders that he got away with. The information alarmed both rangers, and although they suspected the report was probably exaggerated, they still needed to investigate. But instead of going to Barker Ranch, they would search the area surrounding it.

~

Meanwhile, the conversation with the officers scared Crockett because he knew neither officer believed his stories. Therefore, if Charlie didn't get arrested and if he found out that Crockett told the police these stories, he would surely come after him. So, Crockett and his small group of cohabitants decided to move away from the area.

Crockett and his group all ended up in Wyoming to set up their new home. By the beginning of October, once Crockett and his group were established, Crockett decided to try reporting Charlie again. He went to the local sheriff, Don Ward, who recorded their conversation. He again went over the crazy stories about Manson and his Family and the murders that they had bragged about.

~

The two officers who were searching the area around the ranch came across seven women who were all naked, and Pursell asked them what they were all up to. Squeaky was among the women there, and she took the lead and approached the officers and, with a sexual flirtation, replied, "We are a Girl Scout troop from the Bay Area. Would you like to be our scoutmasters?" Both Pursell and Powell tried to keep asking them serious questions about who they were and what they were doing there, but all of the women just gave silly, sexual answers to everything they asked.

Realizing that they wouldn't get anything serious out of the women, and none of them were committing any crimes, they decided to leave them and continued searching the area. About an hour later, they discovered two different vehicles covered with tarps. When they removed the tarps, they found that one of the vehicles was the red Toyota four-wheel-drive car they had been looking for. Inside both vehicles, they found leather rifle and gun cases. They then decided to turn off the cars by removing a couple of leads from the spark plugs while they drove back to headquarters to run checks on them. Once they returned, they learned that both vehicles had been reported stolen from a used car lot.

Even though they didn't fully buy into the story they heard about Manson from Crockett, they now knew that, at the very least, there were stolen cars there. After the highway patrol learned about the stolen vehicles, they began to plan the raid on Barker Ranch.

～

Just after the officers left the scene to drive back to police headquarters, Tex Watson, who had been secretly watching them from a bush on a hill behind the cars, immediately returned to the scene. He was a skilled mechanic, so he knew how to replace the spark plug, which allowed the vehicle to start. He then moved the Toyota far away into the hills, so that they couldn't find it when they returned.

Manson returned to the ranch, and the women told him about their encounter with two cops, which freaked Charlie out. Watson then said to him that they had found the Toyota and tried to disable it by messing with the spark plug, but Tex was able to get it started and moved it in the mountains behind the ranch. Charlie told Tex that they would have to go out that evening and scout the property to see if they noticed anything suspicious.

While the two of them drove around in the dark, Charlie was positive that he had seen what looked like several car headlights glowing in the distance. It had to be the police searching the area. It was time for them to take control of the situation. When they returned to the ranch, Charlie gave Tex one of their shotguns and told him to go to the main building of the ranch, where he was to sit and wait patiently for the two cops to arrive. Charlie told Tex that he wasn't even supposed to give them a chance. As soon as he saw the officers coming down their driveway, he was to kill them both.

During his time alone, waiting in the hot ranch building for the two officers to arrive, Tex began to rethink everything he had learned from Charlie. Could Charlie be wrong about everything? Or maybe just some things. The doubt started to set in. What if there is no bottomless pit out in the desert? What would they all do?

That day, Tex decided that he no longer wanted to take orders from Charlie. He no longer wanted to spend all of his waking hours in pursuit of this bottomless pit. So, he waited until the following night, and he quietly got into a stolen station wagon parked on the ranch and drove away.

Tex traveled until he arrived in San Bernardino, where he phoned his parents in Texas and asked them if he could come home. They wired him enough money to buy an airplane ticket home. Before leaving to fly home, he cut his hair short to fit in better in small-town Texas.

Tex's stay at his parents' place wasn't a long one. In fact, it only took an hour for him to remember why he hated them so much, and so he retreated to his bedroom. A week later, he asked them for more money. And with that, he flew to Mexico, where he began to reconsider his options. By this time, he was starting to think he had acted too hastily by leaving, and he began to believe in all the stories he had been told about Helter Skelter again.

Meanwhile, back at Barker Ranch, Charlie was angry with Tex for deserting him. So, he had two of his most devoted girls, Squeaky and Sandy, watching and reporting directly to Charlie any dissenting talk from anyone. He wasn't going to tolerate another member leaving the group. With Tex gone, Charlie decided to promote Clem to the position of his right-hand man. But Clem was ordered by Charlie to always carry a rifle. Charlie wanted his followers to be scared that if any of them ever talked against him, then Clem would shoot them dead.

The California Highway Patrol had set the date for the raid on the Barker and Myers ranches for October 10th at 4:00 a.m. The raid would be more challenging to accomplish than the police raid on Spahn Ranch. Not only were the Barker and Myers ranches in a much more desolate area, but they were also harder to access. They were surrounded by rough mountain roads that were difficult to navigate, even with four-wheel drive trucks.

Once they had both ranches surrounded, they slowly advanced toward the main buildings. The first people the police came across were Clem and a new Family member, who had both fallen asleep while on guard duty. Both men were arrested without incident. Even though they had their rifles with them, they were caught by surprise and captured before they could respond.

After arresting a third man who was also on night watch, the officers proceeded directly to the main buildings on the Barker Ranch. There, they detained Family members Leslie, Patricia, Gypsy, Susan, Squeaky, and Little Patty.

When the officers arrived at the Myers Ranch, they found Sandy, Ruth Ann, and Nancy Pitman. They were all arrested without incident. Police also discovered Susan's young boy, Ze Zo Ze, and Sandy's one-month-old Ivan, and had them both sent to child protective services in Los Angeles. Officer Powell decided to bring his wife along with him for the raid, just in case they found some children, so that she could look after them until everything was settled.

During the raid, police found several weapons and eleven vehicles, eight of which were reported as stolen. All of the people who were arrested that night were taken to Independence, where they were formally charged with arson, theft, and having stolen property in their possession.

After all of the occupants of both ranches were taken away, two of the Family members who had decided to run away from Charlie earlier that day, Kitty Lutesinger and Stephanie Schram, came out of hiding and turned themselves in to the police. During their interrogation, both women admitted to being part of the group and some of the crimes of theft, but no longer wanted to be there. They were both scared of Charlie.

Lutesinger and Schram were both held in the Independence jail, separated from the rest of the Family members. They were expected to cooperate with the police and likely testify in court for the prosecution. Just after they arrived, Lutesinger called her mother, who told her that Bobby Beausoleil, her boyfriend and father of her unborn child, was on trial for murder, which she didn't know anything about. She was told that Beausoleil was only in jail for theft, not murder.

Another Family member who was also at Barker Ranch that night was out back and escaped, even though she was very near Clem when police were apprehending him. Everyone was so focused on taking Clem and the other guard, who both had rifles without incident, that they didn't notice her slowly creeping behind them on her way out of the ranch.

She immediately called Charlie, who was at Spahn Ranch at the same time, as soon as she could get to a phone. She told Charlie that there was another police raid and that everyone had been taken to jail. Even though Charlie had been worried about being arrested for the murders that they were involved with, he now had plenty of experience with these police raids. He always managed to evade arrest and was never charged with any crime. It gave him the courage to continue searching for food and money and not to be overly concerned about these arrests.

Charlie returned to the Barker Ranch, where he met up with Bruce Davis, Dianne Lake, and John Philip Haught. They were away from the ranch at the time of the raid, looking for the bottomless pit for Charlie. They all decided to remain at the ranch until they determined the fate of the Family members who had been arrested. They had to decide what their next steps would be. But it would end up being the decision that Manson would regret forever. Only two days after the original raid, the police decided to return to the ranch and conduct a second raid. They were hoping that this time, the group's leader, Charlie Manson, would be there.

The raid began just before dusk when the officers had the ranch surrounded. Before they were about to make their move, they saw several men walking outside, coming from one building and all going into another. A few minutes after the officers entered the same building behind the men, they surprised them. All seven were arrested without any problem.

As in the first raid, Pursell felt frustrated because again they had arrested everyone who was there except for Charlie. He always seemed lucky and evaded capture. After the people detained, Dianne Lake, Bruce Davis, John Philip Haught, and four other members, were placed in a van that would take them all to jail, Pursell decided that he would take one last look around.

Pursell was using a candle to find his way around the house, and when he walked into the bathroom, the light from the candle cast a shadow from some long hair on the cupboard doors below the sink. It looked like a relatively small cupboard that wouldn't hold very many things, let alone a large male body. As he stared at the shadow, and before he could even open the cupboard door to take a look, it popped open, and a man fell out. Pursell jumped back quickly, and he pulled out his revolver. "Don't Move! If you make one false move, I'll blow your head off!"

A short man worked his way out of the cupboard under the sink. When he finally got himself balanced enough to stand up straight, with a smile, he said, "Hi!"

"What's your name?" Pursell demanded.

"Charlie Manson." The man replied, still speaking in a lighthearted tone. Pursell then cuffed Charlie's hands behind his back before walking him out to the truck, where he had the other prisoners lying in the bed. A few more officers came over and helped Charlie into the back of the truck bed with he others.

While they were riding back to Independence to be arrested, officers had another truck follow the prisoner truck closely enough that its headlights kept the prisoners visible to the guards. Pursell rode with Charlie and the other Family members. He noticed that the women were all acting as if they were going on a trip or something fun, rather than being arrested. The whole time, they were all talking and laughing back and forth with each other. When Charlie noticed that it was annoying Pursell, he began staring at them with one of his looks, which they all knew, and they all went quiet. Charlie then looked up at Pursell and started to inform him about the Blacks' uprising against the Whites, which was about to happen any day now. He also explained how, because Pursell was a cop, he would be a primary target for the Blacks because not only was he white, but he was a cop as well. He went on to explain how it would be very dangerous because the Black people were going to win the war. Charlie then explained that time was short and that Pursell would be far better off not wasting any more time on Charlie and his Family, but instead should let them all go and spend what time they had left on getting away and saving their own lives.

Pursell answered with a laugh and a broad smile across his face, while he shook his head no.

Even after everyone from the Family had been arrested and were in custody, most of Charlie's followers were still utterly devoted to him. The police raid and arrests had made them one hundred percent behind Manson, with no doubt in anything he said.

Unlike before, though, this current raid had pushed a few of his followers the other way. Lutesinger, who never really completely fit in with the Family or their lifestyle, was now completely over all of the moves, being raided and arrested all the time, having her boyfriend facing trial for murder, and even the day-to-day life of living in the desert heat with no food, no water, or anything to do while six months pregnant. As soon as the Los Angeles detectives running the Hinman murder case learned of Lutesinger's arrest, they went to see her in jail as soon as they could. After striking a deal with them, she was moved into protective custody and made a written statement to the police.

Lutesinger said that Bobby Beausoleil was instructed to visit Gary Hinman's house to retrieve some money that Hinman owed Charlie. Beausoleil brought along two of Charlie's girls with him: Susan and a red-haired girl she didn't know much about, except that she was extremely slim. After they arrived at Hinman's, they all got into a large brawl where Hinman was killed.

Lutesinger said that Susan later told her about some of what happened that night. According to Susan, Hinman began to pull her hair so forcefully that it was coming out of her head. She said that's why she had to stab him a few times to get him to stop. After they completed their interview with Lutesinger, the following morning, they took Susan from her cell to question her about the events at Hinman's house the night he was murdered.

As soon as Susan sat down in the interrogation room, the officers started by telling her that they now had a witness who claimed that Susan was involved in the Hinman murder and wanted her response. Even after several warnings from Charlie to never talk to the cops, Susan believed that Bobby Beausoleil must have finally given in and told the detectives what had happened that night.

Susan explained the story to the detectives with an almost proud tone as if she had just accomplished something great. Her story was much the same as what Lutesinger had told them the prior day. Susan had gone with Beausoleil to see Hinman at his house to obtain the money from him. When Hinman refused to give him any of the funds, Beausoleil sliced his face with a knife.

She then claimed that they spent two days there trying to get the money from him, and finally, when she wasn't in the room, she heard Hinman scream, "Don't, Bobby!" The next time she saw Hinman, he had a large wound in his chest that was bleeding badly. Susan said that Bobby wouldn't let her leave until Hinman was dead. And after that, the two of them had to go around the house and clean up everything. She added that it was while they were cleaning up the home that they both heard Hinman making some gargling noises. So Bobby went back into his room and finished him off. They then left and drove back to the Spahn Ranch using one of Hinman's cars.

What Susan didn't mention throughout her interview with detectives was the fact that they went to Hinman's house for Charlie, or that the money they were trying to get from him was owed to Charlie. She also didn't mention having her hair pulled or stabbing Hinman herself.

The only two redheads in custody were Squeaky and Patricia, so they were taken in for questioning by the detectives. But they both claimed not to have been at Hinman's house when he was murdered, and neither of them had heard anything about it, so they knew nothing. After that, they were both released from jail. While Squeaky returned to Independence to be near Charlie and the rest of the Family, who were also in jail, Patricia decided to travel to Alabama to stay with her mother. It turned out that Mary Brunner was the other woman who went with Beausoleil to Hinman's house.

Police in Independence, California, had the same set of problems with the Manson Family after they raided his ranch as the Los Angeles police had after they raided Spahn Ranch. They couldn't tie any one particular person to any of the car thefts. None of the Family members would speak to detectives about how the stolen vehicles ended up at the ranch. They also couldn't get any of them to talk about how the excavator got burned.

On the first court date, Sandy, Bruce Davis, Cathy Gilles, and Philip were all released due to a lack of evidence. Once released, everyone, except Sandy and her baby, moved back to Spahn Ranch. Sandy ended up staying with Squeaky, who had a motel room in Independence.

Both Sandy and Squeaky visited Charlie in jail several times every day. They were trying to keep Charlie up to date on what the other Family members, now free, were doing. They would also receive messages from Charlie to pass on to the other Family members, gather their answers, and then give them back to Charlie.

∾

Susan was transferred to the Sybil Brand Institute for female prisoners in downtown Los Angeles, so Sandy or Squeaky were unable to contact her. She hated being in this prison because the women inmates there were tough and loved to get into fights.

Shortly after she arrived at the prison, two of her friends, Ronnie and Virginia, were placed in the same dorm that she was in. The three of them all worked as prostitutes, where they got to know each other very well. It was a big break for Susan, as she was already being called "Crazy Sadie" by the other inmates, who wanted to beat her up. Now she had some friends to help her out. Susan and Virginia were assigned to the same job of running messages for the hospital staff members. They often told each other different stories about the things that had happened throughout their lives.

∾

The weeks went by, and the detectives were not coming up with any answers about the Tate or LaBianca murders. As the LAPD administration faced intense pressure from both politicians and the press, they felt even more pressure to solve the cases. Soon, they realized that the murder weapon used and being looked for by the police was a .22 caliber rifle with a broken handle.

When Bernard Weiss read the news, he was confused. It was a couple of weeks before this when he had found a .22 caliber, also with a broken handle, and had turned it into the police. Weiss wondered why they were still searching for that rifle. Perhaps he turned in the wrong weapon.

~

After the detectives who were working on the LaBianca murder case heard about the interviews that were done on the three Manson women about the Hinman Murder case, they created a file on Manson. They began to look for any possible connection there. One thing that the LaBianca detectives were stuck on was why Susan Atkins had told everyone about stabbing her victim in the leg, yet when she made her confession to the police about being part of the Hinman murder, she never mentioned it to them.

When they were looking over the Tate murder files, they noticed that one of the Cielo Drive victims was stabbed in the leg. Maybe this is the stabbing that Susan was telling her friends at Spahn Ranch about, and not the Hinman murder. The LaBianca investigators contacted the Tate detectives to inquire about it.

The Los Angeles Tate investigators held a press conference to ask for the public's help in identifying a pair of glasses that they had found at the Tate house while investigating the murders. Police were hoping that someone in the public could identify those glasses.

Along with the press conference, the police had created thousands of flyers and distributed them to businesses that dealt with eyes, ranging from doctors to eyewear stores. They hoped that the doctor who prescribed the glasses or the person who made them for the customer would remember the customer.

~

Meanwhile, Tex Watson had finally decided to return to Charli. He couldn't handle living in society anymore. But he had to figure out how to make Charlie forgive him and take him back into the family. Charlie was always talking about never letting defectors come back, as it would only cause problems within the Family, and how could Charlie ever trust them again? In Tex's mind, he had done more good than bad for Charlie, after all he had done for him. How much more devotion could he ask for? Not to mention how valuable Tex was at fixing their cars at the ranch, they had no other mechanical people living there with them.

Tex made his way out to Barker Ranch only to find that everybody had been arrested and taken to jail in Independence, California. There was nobody left at the ranch. Scared of being arrested himself, Tex worked his way back to Los Angeles, only to call his parents again, asking for money and a plane ticket to return home and live with them once more. Both parents said that they would pay for his way home, but only if he stayed this time. Tex convinced his parents that this time he meant it and would come home to stay.

PART III

ARREST & TRIAL

28

IT ALL BEGINS AGAIN WHEN IT ENDS

As November began, everything was about to change for the investigators of both the Tate and LaBianca murders. What started as an ordinary conversation between inmates Susan Atkins and Virginia Graham was about to be the grounds for the first significant breakthrough in the investigation for the police.

November 3rd started like every other day for the two women in the Sybil Brand Women's Prison. Both had reported to their assigned jobs at the message center, but that day, for some reason, it was prolonged. The two sat for over an hour, waiting for their first delivery job. While they waited, they did what they always did: tell each other stories.

Virginia started the conversation, "What are you in here for?"

"First-degree murder," Susan replied, keeping her usual big smile that she was known for. "Yeah, a guy I knew well snitched on me." In Susan's mind, it was Bobby Beausoleil who had informed the police. She didn't realize that it was Kitty Lutesinger.

Shocked by the answer, Virginia decided not to pursue her questions further. Most inmates didn't want to get into the details anyway, so she tried to change the subject. "Why is it so slow around here? Haven't any of these workers got messages to send?" Just then, they both got assignments and had to go to work. Nothing more was said about the murder that day.

The next day, they both returned to the message center for work. Susan started right in about her arrest. "Yeah, me, my girlfriend, and Bobby Beausoleil killed a guy called Gary Hinman." Virginia didn't say a word. She was surprised that Susan had even mentioned it. However, she then continued with her story. "The cops are stupid, man. They thought that I held this Hinman while Bobby murdered him." She then let out a cackling laugh. "It was the other way around. He held the guy, and I stabbed him."

Virginia was shocked and couldn't think of anything to say in response. "But it's great the cops are dumb, cause then they'll never be able to prove anything." Susan continued to laugh, hoping that Virginia would find what she was saying funny and begin to laugh along with her, but she didn't. Instead, she continued to have a shocked look on her face and remained quiet.

Susan then began to tell Virginia about their commune leader, Charlie Manson. About how he was Jesus Christ, and how he was getting them ready to face the upcoming race war between the Blacks and Whites. She described how they were all living in a great place out in the desert and how they were going to move to the bottomless pit once the war began. After the war was over, the Family would come back out so that Charlie could lead the new Black rulers of the world. Eventually, Susan ran out of things to say about the Hinman murder, but enjoyed talking about murder in general, especially if she was in on it. It felt like bragging, and she loved to brag. So, now it was time to talk about some more murders, much bigger ones.

"Hey, there was a popular murder where the cops were even stupider than the Hinman case," Susan said, beginning her irritating cackle again. "Yeah, what one was that?" Virginia questioned. "You know, the one out in Benedict Canyon, Cielo Drive?" Susan answered.

Virginia only knew about the Sharon Tate murder that happened out there, but maybe there was another one, as she didn't think there was any way Susan was behind the Tate murders. "You don't mean that movie star one, Sharon Tate, do you?" Virginia hesitantly asked.

Susan stopped laughing but kept the large grin on her face. "Yep, that one!"

Virginia sat up suddenly and looked at Susan directly in her eyes. "You know who did it?"

"You are looking at her!" Susan replied before letting out a loud, belly-laugh that everyone in the room could hear. Virginia remained silent, shocked again at what Susan had told her.

After Susan stopped laughing, she began to randomly spew out information about the murder case without making much sense. She blurted out one sentence after another about how they wanted to kill the people at Cielo Drive because they wanted to commit a crime that would shock and scare everyone. Susan then threw something else in there, making it even more confusing to Virginia. "They just picked that house because they knew a guy who used to live there."

Susan went into more detail when she began talking about Charlie. She explained how he had taught them everything. Charlie told them what kind of clothing to wear and to bring backup clothing to change into after the murders. He also told them where they should park the car and how to get past the gate.

As Susan went on and on about the murders, it was apparent that she was particularly proud of the fact that it only took four of them to kill everyone in the house, and three of them were women. The man, Charles, she said, shot the first victim to death. Virginia thought that Susan was speaking of Charles Manson, as she had never heard of Charles "Tex" Watson during the story.

Susan got more excited with each story that she told Virginia about that night. She could hardly wait to tell her about how both Jay Sebring and Sharon Tate each had one end of a rope tied into a noose around their necks.

The story Susan seemed to be most proud of was the fact that she was able to fight off a big Polish guy called Vic Frykowski and stab him several times all over his body. He was able to escape for a few minutes before Susan and Tex caught up with him on the lawn, where they finished him off.

Virginia was a tough woman and had been around the block a few times, so most of these stories didn't faze her. But eventually, Susan came up with something that even made Virginia cringe. Susan told her how Sharon Tate was the last one in the house to die. She was particularly proud that, as Tate was begging for her life and the life of her unborn baby. But Susan just laughed at her. According to Susan, after she murdered Tate, she began to taste her blood, which she described as warm, delicious, and pleasant, except it was very sticky.

Virginia was now completely freaked out by what she had been told. She quietly got up and said that she had to go and shower, then left the room. As she was leaving the room, Susan told her that there were more things that she could tell Virginia about the following night, and two more murders.

Over the next couple of days, Susan went on to talk not only to Virginia but also to her other friend in jail, Ronnie. After explaining what happened during both the Tate and LaBianca murders, she also told them about her experiences with the Beach Boy Dennis Wilson and rock producer Terry Melcher.

The following week, both Ronnie and Virginia made an effort to avoid Susan as much as possible. They began to share what they had heard from Susan, and then tried to determine what, if anything, was true. Could Susan just be crazy? How could they have gone and murdered all of these people, celebrities included, and not have been caught?

Susan's stories continued to come in every day. She had told so many stories that she couldn't remember what she had told them, and began repeating them. She also began to give them more details of the murders, such as writing words, such as "Pig," on walls and doors of the houses, using the victim's blood.

It also became evident to both Virginia and Ronnie that even if these tales were the truth, Susan must have exaggerated her part in each of the murders. She always seemed to be the star. The way it had been explained, Susan was the one in charge, committing the murders and creating the bizarre scenes that had been left at both of the murder houses.

One thing that Susan kept telling the women that resonated as true with them was when Susan guaranteed that this was only the beginning and that there were many more murders to come. She also claimed that they had created a celebrity list of names of their future victims, which included stars like Elizabeth Taylor and Frank Sinatra.

～

Susan went to her preliminary hearing for the Hinman murder trial in Los Angeles, and there she learned that it wasn't Bobby Beausoleil who had told the police about her. Instead, it was Kitty Lutesinger, a female Family member. After the hearing, she returned to Sybil Brand jail. She immediately went to Virginia and Ronnie to tell them about Kitty's betrayal of her and the Family, and then said to them that Kitty would die next.

Virginia and Ronnie began to have serious discussions about whether they should inform the prison administration about what Susan had been saying. It was a real struggle for them, as anyone who had ever been to jail before knew that the worst thing anyone could do was snitch on another inmate. You would be marked forever, and in any prison that you were in, you would not be accepted, and there would be plenty of other prisoners who would try to kill you. So, if they did end up telling, it could mean the end for both of them.

Virginia felt a sudden sense of relief when she was told that she was being sent to Corona, California's central state prison for women, which was forty miles away from downtown, to serve out the rest of her sentence. She began packing up her things and started to smile for the first time in weeks, knowing that this would take the pressure off of having to tell authorities about Susan, as well as off not having to listen to any more of Susan's stories.

After Virginia was taken away and on her way to Corona, Ronnie began the process of freeing her mind of this knowledge by approaching one of the guards with whom she got along well and telling her that she knew who had committed both the Sharon Tate and LaBianca murders. She asked for permission to use the phone to call the Los Angeles detectives who were working on those cases. The guard informed Ronnie that she needed permission from her superiors for her to make such a call.

On the morning of November 17th, Ronnie was being taken to a court hearing in Santa Monica by bus. While waiting for the bus, the female prisoners were allowed to use the payphone. Ronnie decided that she would call the detectives who were working on the Tate and LaBianca murder cases to tell them what she had found out from Susan Atkins.

Ever since the murders had hit all the newspapers, the police started receiving phone calls daily from individuals who claimed to have either known who the killers were, or they were confessing to the crimes themselves. So, when they received the call from Ronnie, to them, it was just another one of those calls, nothing to take seriously. The police told her that they would send someone to talk to her, but they never did. Ronnie attended her hearing and was brought back to prison.

In a few days, however, two detectives working on the LaBianca case showed up at Corona prison to speak with Ronnie. The prison provided one of its meeting rooms for the interview, and after introductions and seating, Ronnie began to recount what Susan Atkins had told her. She wasn't very far into her story before the detectives started to believe what she was saying. Especially when Ronnie told them about Susan having lost her knife at the Cielo Drive house, which clinched it for them, as that information had never been released to the press or public. They asked the prison administration to move Ronnie into a solitary confinement unit for protection. Then they returned to the department to tell the rest of the investigators that they had just gotten a big break in the Tate murder case.

As soon as Virginia got settled into her new prison, she too decided that she would tell the authorities about the things Susan Atkins had told her about all of these murders. The prison psychologist, Vera Dreiser, whom Virginia had known for several years, felt that she could trust her. The meeting request was approved, but it did not take place for a few weeks.

In early December, Virginia was finally able to meet with Dreiser, and she was finally able to tell her what she knew about the Tate and LaBianca murders from Susan Atkins. The information was passed on to Bugliosi's team, and they found it to match what they had heard from Ronnie, which further strengthened their case.

29

DANNY DECARLO

On Friday, November 14th, the LaBianca investigators also brought in Manson Family regular and Straight Satan biker and treasurer Danny DeCarlo for an interview. During his question, DeCarlo would only discuss how everyone lived out on Spahn Ranch—the weird rituals, the orgies, and how every night they would all get high and listen to Charlie preach about life and death.

For DeCarlo, the weekend flew by. On Monday, November 17th, he was supposed to meet the LaBianca investigators at 8:30 a.m. to give a recorded statement, but he didn't arrive on time. Instead, he finally showed up around five that evening, telling the detectives that he had been arrested that morning. He was pulled over for speeding, and when the officer ran a check on DeCarlo, it was discovered that he had several outstanding tickets, so he was arrested. Once released from jail, he went to the detective's office as soon as he could.

During the recorded interview, DeCarlo discussed the things that he could remember during his five months living with the Manson Family. After about an hour of listening to his descriptions of the lifestyle at Spahn Ranch, the detectives stopped him and began to ask more specific questions.

"Do you know who murdered Gary Hinman?"

"Yes, Bobby Beausoleil did."

"How do you know this?"

"He told me about the murder himself."

"Were there other people who were involved with the murder or were at the murder scene when it happened?"

"Yes. Beausoleil brought Susan Atkins, Mary Brunner, and Bruce Davis with him to Hinman's house."

"How was Charlie involved, or was he?"

"Yes. As with everything that happened with the Family, Charlie was behind everything."

"How did it all go down?"

"Charlie called Beausoleil and told him to kill Hinman. Bobby and the girls were following Charlie's orders. He also told them to write things on the walls with blood because he wanted it to look like the murder was done by the Panthers."

DeCarlo suddenly took a turn in his direction of conversation away from the Hinman murder. "Charlie used the .22 caliber Buntline to murder a Black Panther once. It was some drug deal that didn't go well."

"Really? Who was that?"

"I don't know the guy's name or anything. I just heard that Charlie shot the guy because he was hassling him about the price or something like that."

Detectives then brought up the ranch hand, Shorty Shea. He told them that he did know what happened to Shea, but suddenly changed his direction again. "Charlie did Tate, you know!"

"Really?"

"What am I going to get from you guys for talking?"

"What do you mean?"

"Fuck, you know what I mean. I have charges pending against me. What are you going to do about them?"

"Listen, if what you tell us turns out to be true, then we're with you one hundred percent. And I guarantee you that you won't do any time."

DeCarlo let out a sigh of relief, relaxed in his chair, and took a moment before he continued talking.

A significant difference in the telling of the Hinman murder story from DeCarlo was that he told detectives that Charlie had shown up at

Hinman's house after Tex called him and said to him that he wasn't getting any cooperation from Hinman. Charlie used the sword that he received from the Straight Satan biker gang to slice off Hinman's ear as soon as he arrived at Hinman's house.

DeCarlo also told them that the biker gang took the sword back and smashed it in half because they were mad at Manson. When DeCarlo was explaining about the fight that had been going on between Manson and the Straight Satan biker gang, they were interrupted by a police officer, and they all left the room. The detectives who had just interviewed Ronnie at the prison returned and wanted to bring the DeCarlo interviewers up to date on the information they had just learned.

Once they returned to DeCarlo, the questions became more precise and focused. They wanted to know precisely what DeCarlo knew about the murder of Sharon Tate and her friends. But most of the information DeCarlo knew was secondhand, so there would be some holes in what he told them. He thought that it was Charlie, Tex, and Clem who went out to do the murders. Clem later said to him that they had got five piggies, and this was around the time of the murders in early August.

DeCarlo was interrogated for over seven hours that night, and when they finished, he brought up the $25,000 reward that Polanski had offered and told them that he should get it, or at least some of it. DeCarlo also told the detectives that he wouldn't testify against Charlie or any of the Family members regarding the Tate or LaBianca case because he knew Charlie would retaliate against him for it. He did agree to testify in the Beausoleil trial in exchange for his outstanding charges being dropped.

30

BOBBY BEAUSOLEIL TRIAL

Also on Friday, November 14th, the trial for the murder of Gary Hinman against Bobby Beausoleil began. Prosecutors didn't have a slam-dunk case, but they did have several pieces of evidence that could convince a jury.

Detectives had found and positively identified Beausoleil's palm prints in Hinman's house. When they arrested Beausoleil, he was sleeping in the dead man's car. Also in the car was the murder weapon with Hinman's blood still on it. But their only witness was Susan Atkins, who told police that she was in another room when she thought she heard Beausoleil kill Hinman.

In less than two weeks, on November 26th, the trial ended in a hung jury. The prosecutor's star witness, Danny DeCarlo, had so alienated four of the jurors that they voted to convict Beausoleil. Yet the other jury members didn't want to convict based solely on the little evidence presented. The prosecutors for the case immediately responded by telling the court that they would retry the case.

The second trial also began with Judge Keene presiding over the case. Bugliosi was excused from this murder trial so that he could focus on the Tate and LaBianca trials. Mary Brunner had made a deal with the prosecution to testify, and in exchange, she would be granted complete immunity. After Brunner took the stand and told the tale of how Beausoleil murdered Hinman, he believed that Manson was out to get him. After all, Brunner would only testify against him if Manson told her to. Beausoleil decided to testify as well. He claimed that Charlie came to the house and murdered Hinman, and he saw it.

The trial ended with Beausoleil being found guilty of murder. The jury didn't believe what Beausoleil had said. He was then sentenced to death.

After the trial, the District Attorney also issued arrest warrants for Charles Manson, Susan Atkins, and Bruce Davis for the murder of Gary Hinman. By that time, Bruce Davis had disappeared.

Later, Brunner came forward saying that she lied on the stand during the trial of Bobby Beausoleil and that she had not seen him commit the murder after all. Beausoleil's lawyer then filed a petition to have his conviction overturned. Presiding over this trial was also Judge Keene, who, after reading the petition, ruled against it and stated that there would be no retrial. Keene believed that there was sufficient evidence, even without Brunner's testimony, to carry the conviction of murder.

The prosecutors then decided to press charges against Mary Brunner, as her deal was contingent upon her providing testimony against Beausoleil. They felt that she violated the agreement by recanting her testimony after the conviction. Brunner's lawyer filed an appeal, which was heard by a higher court. The court decided to overturn her indictment because the deal did not specify what would happen if she recanted her testimony. Brunner was freed from jail and not charged again. She returned to the Spahn Ranch to live.

31

SATURDAY, NOVEMBER 15 PROTEST

On Saturday, November 15th, a quarter of a million protesters marched through the streets of Washington, eventually reaching the White House, where they held a candlelight vigil.

Nixon wasn't concerned about any of the protests, nor did he care about them. Instead, he had devised a plan for some of his helicopter pilots to fly over the candlelight vigil, so that nobody could hear them talk. He was hoping that they would blow out the candles that people were holding as well.

Before his plan was executed, Nixon was talked out of it by some of his closest advisors.

32

DEPUTY D.A. VINCENT BUGLIOSI

For Deputy District Attorney Vincent Bugliosi, the day started like every other day. But before the workday ended, things changed drastically for him and District Attorney Aaron Stovitz. The Los Angeles District Attorney's office was led by Evelle J. Younger, who called both men to tell them that they were getting enough information together to prosecute the Sharon Tate murder case. He selected Stovitz to be the lead prosecutor on the case and assigned Bugliosi as his co-counsel.

The duo was told about the new developments and what the detectives had uncovered from their interviews with Ronnie Howard and Danny DeCarlo. It was now Bugliosi's job to work with the detectives on both cases, Tate and LaBianca, and verify the validity of the information they gathered.

Bugliosi was a very aggressive attorney, or as some called him, a real go-getter. He would dedicate as much time as was required to a case. Once he had been assigned to a case, it would be not only his top priority, but the only thing he did until the trial was over.

When the Manson trial started, he had 103 successful felony jury trials to one loss. He was very proud of his successes and took every opportunity he could to ensure everyone knew about them as well. It caused several of his coworkers in the District Attorney's office to give him a hard time whenever they could. Bugliosi was often called nicknames like "Buggy" or "Bugsy," which bothered him. They would all mispronounce his name so that they could laugh at his expense. Quite often, anyone who didn't know Bugliosi would pronounce his name using the hard G, but in fact, it was silent. It should have been pronounced as BOO-LEE-OSI.

Bugliosi accompanied the investigators of the Tate case wherever they went. George Spahn had no issues with the police and allowed them to visit the ranch at any time and search any area they wanted. Bugliosi was careful to make sure that whenever they had one of their informants with them at the ranch, such as DeCarlo, they would handcuff his hands behind his back, giving anyone who might be watching the belief that he was being forced to be there with the police.

During one of their searches of Spahn Ranch, police were able to find more than sixty slug fragments and twenty casings from where the Family always practiced with not only the 22 caliber but several other weapons as well. Bugliosi wanted to find matching shell casings for the casings they had found at Cielo Drive after the murders had happened.

Bugliosi's primary problem with the Tate murder case was that Chief Davis wanted it to happen right away. He believed that every day that went by without the case being solved and tried reflected poorly on the LAPD. And the longer it went on, the longer it would take for them to recover from their negative reputation.

Davis decided to offer Susan Atkins a plea deal and offer her complete immunity for testifying against Manson. Bugliosi flew off the handle at Davis because he thought it was too soon to offer a deal that they might not need to make. If he had enough time, Bugliosi could put together a solid case that would convict every single one of them.

Bugliosi and his team also visited Barker Ranch and examined all the evidence that the police had collected there. He also interviewed all five of the major female family members: Leslie, Gypsy, Ruth Ann, Dianne Lake, and Nancy Pitman. However, he couldn't get anything meaningful out of them and considered it a big waste of time.

Next, he sat down with both Squeaky and Sandy, which frustrated him the most. The two of them would just ramble about things that had no meaning, certainly nothing to do with Charlie or the murders. He later said that they were all like little girls who were playing little girl games. He even went as far as to say that he thought they were "retarded."

The only two men who were still being held in jail were Charlie and Clem. The District Attorney of the Barker Ranch cases told Bugliosi that Clem had an attorney who had insisted on Clem being examined by a psychologist. Clem was assessed by two of them, and both deemed him insane. Bugliosi then stalled any legal action against Clem for the time being.

Later that same day, Bugliosi watched as Manson pleaded not guilty to the arson charges in court. The judge set his bail at $25,000. It worried Bugliosi, as he wasn't ready to arrest Manson for the Tate murders yet. He needed some more time. He went back to the District Attorney, who was prosecuting the Manson arson case, and asked him to call if anyone attempted to pay Charlie's bail. Bugliosi thought it would be better to let him go free on bail, where he might vanish, than arrest him for the murders, even if he wasn't ready. There was also the possibility that the arson charges would be dropped, as there wasn't enough evidence to secure a conviction, so Bugliosi had to work quickly.

Squeaky and Sandy followed all the moves that Bugliosi and the detectives were making, keeping Charlie up to date on everything. As long as nobody broke down and talked to the cops, things could still work out. At least that's what Charlie thought. He needed the girls to find out what had happened to Tex and Patricia so he could ensure they didn't tell anyone anything. Charlie also knew that he had to get an alibi for the night of the murders, and it wasn't long before he got one. Soon, he had all of his Family members saying the same thing: that Charlie wasn't in California at the time of the murders. This detail put even more pressure on Bugliosi, who ordered his team of detectives to find some evidence to prove that Manson was, in fact, in the area on the two nights of the murders.

Bugliosi had a warrant issued for Charles "Tex" Watson so that he could question him about his involvement with the Tate and LaBianca murders. He also ordered the women's prison to keep all of the Manson

Family members separate from each other so that they couldn't talk about the cases.

Detective Sgt. McGann went to question Leslie Van Houten in prison, who had remained silent up to that point. He told her that her friend Zero was dead and that he had committed suicide. Leslie was stunned. She knew that he wouldn't kill himself and that someone had murdered him. It must have been Charlie.

McGann could see that Leslie was devastated, and instead of remaining quiet for her, he began his questioning immediately.

"We know that Charlie was one of the five people who murdered Tate!"

Leslie was staring down at her feet, which she was swinging back and forth, letting out what sounded like a quiet moan.

"What?" McGann almost shouted out.

Leslie immediately lifted her head and looked towards McGann. She was avoiding eye contact with him, still scared, and then she mumbled something that he couldn't understand.

"What? Will you speak up, please?" Again, he spoke, almost yelling.

"Charlie wasn't in on any of them. There weren't five, there were only four of them there."

"Oh yeah, well, who were they then?"

"Three of them were girls, and Linda was one of them. But she didn't kill anyone. She wouldn't."

This revelation was great. It was what he needed to hear, as it matched exactly what Ronnie and Virginia had said, as told to them by Susan Atkins. But McGann now had to find out who this Linda was, especially if she didn't murder anyone. She was there, so she was a witness. "So, Linda wasn't involved in the murders? Tell me Linda's last name."

Leslie became quiet again and began to look down at her feet. After a few minutes of nothing, she began to mumble something again.

"What?! I can't hear you again!"

Leslie then began discussing the eleven murders she was aware of. McGann started trying to add up the murders that they knew about quickly in his head. Let's see, there were five at Tate's house, two at the

LaBianca's place, Gary Hinman, and then Shorty Shea, but who were the other two?

McGann figured that he could make up things, too, and maybe that would get Leslie to open up more and talk. "We know that Susan was at both the Tate murders and the LaBiancas, too. She bragged about how the day after she murdered Tate, she went to another place and killed two more." With hearing that, Leslie clammed right up. Her whole-body language changed, and she curled her body into a tight circle, never saying a word. McGann then assured her that she would be safe and that they would provide her with complete protection twenty-four hours a day. Leslie began to slowly rock back and forth in her chair, never looking up at McGann or making a noise.

The interview with Leslie had both positive and negative consequences. The good news was that they had another confirmation that the three female family members who were at Tate's house during the murders were Susan, Patricia, and Linda. That left them with still having to find out who this Linda was and where she was located.

The dire consequence of this interview was that Leslie was sure to tell Squeaky or Sandy when they came to visit her that Susan Atkins was now a snitch and was telling the cops everything. They, in turn, would tell Charlie when they visited him in prison. Susan would now have to watch out for Charlie's retribution.

Susan had now appointed a lawyer who, after reviewing her case and the evidence of her involvement, advised her that if she cooperated with the police, he might be able to negotiate a favorable deal for her. At the very least, he could save her from the death penalty.

It wasn't long before detectives learned that Linda's last name was Kasabian and that the woman called "Katie" was Patricia Krenwinkel. Police soon tracked Patricia down at her mother's home in Alabama, but they had no trace of Linda and still hadn't found Tex yet.

The next step for Bugliosi was to have detectives interview anyone who had ever been involved with Charlie and his Family to see if there was anything else they could learn. The first person they were able to locate was Gregg Jakobson, who willingly agreed to talk with them. He told them that Charlie had approached him because he wanted to get into the music business and make records, but Jakobson didn't think very much of his music. Instead, he thought Charlie would be better suited for a movie.

Jakobson's friend, Terry Melcher, was also shopping around for new artists and listened to Charlie's demo recording, as well as visiting the ranch to watch him perform. Melcher also wasn't sold on Charlie or his music.

Jakobson also told investigators that he didn't think Charlie would have gone to where Melcher used to live on Cielo Drive to kill him, as he already knew that Melcher had moved away from there. Instead, Jakobson wanted to describe how Charlie and his Family lived and the unusual things they believed. But the detectives cut him short, since they had already heard about all of those things before.

The important thing that came out of their interview with Jakobson was learning that Charles "Tex" Montgomery's real last name was Watson, which would allow police to run further background checks on Tex. They found his police record, which included drug arrests from that same year, from April in the Van Nuys part of town. Later, they got copies of Tex Watson's fingerprints from his earlier arrests and compared them with the prints that were taken at the Tate murder scene. They discovered that one of his prints was found on the front door of the Cielo Drive house.

Further background checks on Tex revealed that he was originally from a small town in Collin County, Texas. They phoned the Sheriff of Collin County, Tom Montgomery, to obtain the names of any possible friends that Tex might have. It turned out to be far better than they expected when Montgomery told them that Tex was living back at his parents' place now, and he could go and pick him up for them if they'd like.

Montgomery phoned the Watson home and asked for Tex. His father answered and told the Sheriff that Tex was out with an old girlfriend, and he could have him call him when he got back. Tex's dad asked the Sheriff why he was looking for Tex. Montgomery explained that it wasn't he who was looking for his son, but the LAPD who wanted to question Tex about some murders that happened back in California.

A few hours later, when Tex returned home, his father demanded to know what had happened in California because the cops were looking for him about some murders that had happened there. Tex denied knowing anything about any murders. His father dragged him into his car and, along with his brother, took Tex to the Sheriff's office.

When the three men walked into the jailhouse, they immediately saw the Sheriff, who was seated at his desk. "Well, Sheriff, here he is," Tex's dad said with an angry tone. Montgomery answered in a soft, nonaggressive tone. "Oh, I'm sure that it's all just a big misunderstanding, son, and we will get this cleared up right away. We know that you wouldn't commit any murders. One thing is for sure: Tex was well-liked in this community, and as the gossip began to get around about him being arrested for murder, people responded with shock. There is no way Tex would kill anybody.

After their interview with Jakobson, investigators wanted to speak with both Melcher and Dennis Wilson. Both of them tried to avoid any contact with the police. Wilson was terrified of being connected to Manson if he was a killer. The rest of the Beach Boys hated Manson and had no desire to be associated with him. If Manson got in trouble for murder, their link to him would be through Dennis, and it could ruin the band's reputation.

Detectives began by inquiring about why Manson had stayed with him at his house, and whether the two of them were close friends. Dennis told them that Manson was only an acquaintance, but he had lots of people who stayed at his house. Dennis liked to party, and Charlie was just another one of the partiers. They then wanted to know about Manson's music. Dennis claimed that Charlie did audition for the Brothers Record company, but again, so did several other acts. They would give anyone a chance, but if they didn't have the talent, they wouldn't sign them. Charlie was one of those who didn't have it.

Getting Terry Melcher to come to the police precinct for an interview was like pulling teeth. Between him and Columbia Records, they delayed the meeting in every way possible. It wouldn't be suitable for the record company or Melcher himself if he were connected to Manson and the murders. They knew that far too many people had seen Melcher and Manson together and not just once, but many times. It made it hard for Melcher to downplay how well he knew Manson, but he was going to try.

When detectives finally got Melcher in for the interview, he played it cool. Melcher claimed that he didn't really know Manson and that he only met him a couple of times. He said that an agent, Gregg Jakobson, had asked him to go to Spahn Ranch and listen to this guy who had written some pretty cool songs, so he did.

Melcher said that when he heard Manson, he wasn't impressed with either his songs or his performance. He said that he gave Manson some money that same night when he watched him play, because everyone at the ranch seemed to be living in squalor, and he felt sorry for the kids who were there.

When detectives asked Melcher about breaking his promise to give Manson a recording contract, he said that it never happened and that it was the first he had heard of such a thing. He was also surprised that the investigators would suggest that Manson only went to the Cielo Drive home to get revenge against Melcher.

"So, did you like to hang around at the ranch with Charlie and his girls?"

"No, not really, just the regular chit chat, you know. Trying to be cool."

"We have heard from witnesses that you had slept with some of Charlie's female members at the ranch?"

Melcher grabbed his wallet from his back pocket and fumbled through it for a few minutes before he pulled out five or six small pictures of different women. "Here, have a look at these. When I have got these kinds of beauties to sleep with any time that I want, why would I want to screw any of the clap-ridden unwashed dogs that belonged to Manson?"

Just as it had always been in Hollywood during that time, the police never rode celebrities too hard. They had the backing of most of the politicians in town, and with the politicians came the police administration.

The detectives knew that Melcher was lying about almost everything he said. They already knew that Melcher had introduced Jakobson to Manson, not the other way around, as Melcher claimed.

By this time, Melcher had become so scared of Manson that he had hired a full-time bodyguard as well as bought himself a shotgun, which he began carrying everywhere he went. He knew that the Family members were capable of anything, and the hard part was that Melcher only knew a few of them. It meant that whenever he made an appearance or was out somewhere in public, he wouldn't be able to tell the difference between a regular kid and a Manson Family member.

33

ARRAIGNMENT

On December 11th, Charlie appeared in court to be arraigned by Judge William B. Keene. He wore his casual best and looked thrilled to have such a large audience watching.

Paul Fitzgerald, a public defender, was assigned by the Judge, despite his also being part of the Bobby Beausoleil defense team. When Fitzgerald walked out of the courtroom afterwards, he was swarmed by the media, who asked him various questions. Seeming to take everything in stride, he began his statement with a casual tone. "I feel very confident that my client will win the case. All the prosecution has is a couple of fingerprints and Vince Bugliosi."

Meanwhile, back at the prison, Charlie was meeting with several lawyers, all of whom were vying to represent him as his defense lawyer in the murder case. Throughout December and January, he met with enough lawyers to have a total of 139 visits.

∽

On Sunday, December 14th, Susan Atkins was driven around by detectives so she could show them where she figured Kasabian had thrown out the clothes they were all wearing during the murders. She also showed them where the knives and guns were tossed.

Judge Keene had placed a gag order, prohibiting all evidence and witnesses from discussing it with the media. Atkins' lawyer, Richard Caballero, had made a deal in Europe with the press to publish Atkins' personal story on December 16th. The next day, the *Los Angeles Times* had somehow obtained a copy of the upcoming Atkins book and had now printed it for everyone to read, including Manson. After reading everything she said, Manson knew that Atkins still believed in him and followed his ideas. So, if he had a chance to talk to her, he could probably get back on her side and not testify against him.

A positive outcome of the *Times'* story about Atkins was that it prompted people who read it to look for the lost evidence themselves, and eventually, two local television crews found the tossed-out bloody clothes and handed them in to the police. When detectives did forensics on the clothing, they were able to match the blood on them to the Cielo Drive victims. They even matched the hair that had been stuck to the blood on the clothes to Atkins.

Another piece of evidence that reached Bugliosi's attention was a note that Atkins had sent through prison channels to Ronnie Howard. In the note, Atkins expressed that she wasn't angry that Howard went to the police with her story, but she was hurt. Atkins was happy that the world got to see who Manson was and what their beliefs were, and why those people had to die. Bugliosi was able to use this note in court. Letters sent in prison, even if they incriminate the sender, were legal to use in California.

~

While Manson was awaiting his trial, he began to plan his strategy for the court. He was fixated on defending himself. Not so much because his legal aid lawyer wasn't capable of doing a decent job, but more because of what Manson was able to give to the jury. He knew he was capable of manipulating and controlling people. He just needed a platform and time. What could be more perfect than a jury in court?

Manson also knew that if lawyers represented each of the girls, they would probably separate each of their murder cases from his. None of them would be tried together, and each of the girls' lawyers would get them examined by a psychiatrist and try to prove that they were somehow brainwashed by Manson or mentally incapable of being held responsible. Manson was sure he would be able to convince the jury that he wasn't involved with any of the murders. He wasn't at any of the murder scenes when the killings happened, and he didn't kill anybody. If Manson let the other girls, like Atkins did, get their lawyers, he wouldn't be able to get them to plead guilty.

Manson needed to get some money, and he had a plan to do so. He had several recordings of his songs made at Dennis Wilson's studio, so all he had to do was call up Wilson and have him give the tapes to his girls, and they could have them made into vinyl records. He figured they would sell off the shelves because everyone would want to listen to a Manson album.

When Manson called Wilson's house, collect from the prison, the man who answered the phone kept saying no to accepting the charges. The last time Manson called, he screamed out, "You're going to be fucking sorry!"

Manson got hold of Squeaky and ordered her to find Wilson. When she finally found him, he was hiding out at Gregg Jakobson's house. She told him that she needed the recordings, and if he didn't give them to her, he would be killed. Wilson told her that he no longer had the tapes and had to give them to the police. Squeaky then turned to Jakobson and asked him for the recordings that he had made with Charlie. He gave them to her.

Squeaky took them and gave them to Phil Kaufman. Manson phoned Kaufman and instructed him to release his music to the public. Kaufman believed that Manson and his Family were innocent of all charges, so he used his own money to make two thousand vinyl copies of the recordings they obtained from Jakobson. He also created an album cover using one of Manson's pictures, which had recently been featured on the cover of *Life* magazine, and named the album *LIE*. Once everything was completed, Kaufman and Squeaky held a press conference to announce the release of Manson's new album.

If the fact that he was already receiving lots of attention, having his music released on vinyl to the public, and being on the cover of *Life* magazine hadn't gone to his head, the fact that Judge Keene approved Manson's request to defend himself at trial certainly did. The trial was going to be a three-ring circus for everyone to watch, and Charlie was at the center of the stage, ready to perform.

On January 17, 1970, Manson's first request for the Judge was to demand the court release him because being in jail deprived him of his spiritual, mental, and physical liberty. He argued that it was unconstitutional and not in harmony with either God's law or man's law. Despite being rejected by the Judge, Manson remained invigorated since he was getting more attention from the press.

On January 27th, the circus continued when Manson returned to court. This time, he was refusing to enter a plea to any of the charges – neither guilty nor not guilty. Judge Keene said that Manson's failure to make a plea in either direction would be equivalent to pleading not guilty. Keene then set a tentative trial date for February 9th, but they were still waiting on the court's ability to extradite Tex Watson and Patricia Krenwinkel to California in time.

Behind the scenes for the prosecution, a split emerged on how to try the case. Stovitz wanted to play it safe and go after Manson and the Family members who were involved in the murders. He reasoned that they should argue they were doing it for money because they required the funds to pay for the move to the desert. However, Bugliosi was dead set against this. He thought that it was foolish to think that the jury would believe they did it for the money since all they managed to get on the night of the Tate murders was seventy dollars, and a bag full of coins from the LaBianca murders. In both houses, they never took any of the real valuables that they would have if they were just there for the money.

Bugliosi wanted to go all in with Manson, focusing on the plan to start the race war, "Helter Skelter." Because they left Black Panther marks at the scenes, Bugliosi argued it demonstrated their motives. But Stovitz figured the Helter Skelter theory would be too hard to convince a jury of. It was too wild a story.

Stovitz was also able to interview Harold True, a former and brief next-door neighbor of the LaBiancas on Waverly Drive. True told

Stovitz that while he was living there, Charlie and the Family often came by and partied together. He moved in November 1968, only two months after the LaBiancas moved in, so he didn't know them. Stovitz figured that True's testimony would be perfect for tying Manson to Waverly Drive.

At the same time, Bugliosi was able to interview both Shahrokh Hatami, Tate's photographer, and Altobelli, the owner of the Cielo Drive property, who had been living in the guesthouse the day Manson showed up looking for Terry Melcher, who had already moved out at the time.

It gave the prosecution at least two witnesses who saw Manson not only at the Tate house and inside the property behind the gate, but also meeting Tate, who would later be one of his victims.

Another problem to come along for the prosecution was when the *Los Angeles Times* did a story on February 6th, "Theory Links Beatles Album to Murders." Even though the Judge had placed a gag order on the case, this story was published, listing the source as an unidentified investigator. In the report, it claimed that Manson believed that the Beatles were prophets and their *White Album* gave the reasons in their song lyrics for both the Tate and LaBianca murders. Manson wanted the police to think that the murders were committed by Blacks, which would start the beginning of the race war, which was one of the songs on the *White Album*, "Helter Skelter."

On that same date, Manson gave an interview to two reporters from *Rolling Stone Magazine*. He discussed the same things: the Blacks were going to take over the world, and the Beatles and the Bible both said this. He instructed the reporters to visit the Spahn Ranch and speak with the rest of the Family. When they arrived, they were informed that a story would cost them money if they wanted it. Some of the Family even asked the reporters to give the Beatles their phone number and tell them that they need to call us, as Charlie needs their help. Little did they know that the Beatles were going through turmoil, and the band would break up before Manson's trial started. Just before the trial was to begin, Manson's lawyer sent each of the four Beatles a letter requesting that they come and testify on Charlie's behalf. Manson believed that if they did testify, they would support everything he was saying. Kanarek did not receive any response to his letters.

~

Patricia Krenwinkel allowed police to extradite her after she was told that it was okay by Manson, through a message from Squeaky. Krenwinkel's first appearance was on February 24th for her arraignment in a Los Angeles courtroom. She was assigned a public defender in Alabama, Paul Fitzgerald, whom Manson liked so much that Fitzgerald quit his job as public defender and followed her to Los Angeles to become her full-time lawyer. This high-profile case could have given him a promising career.

~

Behind the scenes, Squeaky, along with a few of Charlie's other girls, was working on Atkins by visiting her every day. They were all telling her that Charlie still loved her, and that she should dismiss her lawyer and say to the court that she had lied during her testimony. Atkins didn't want to make any decisions until she could talk to Charlie herself. The prosecutors didn't want to let her see Manson, as they knew he would talk her out of testifying in court against him. Atkins' lawyer, Richard Caballero, advised her to stick with he deal and cooperate with the prosecutors.

Atkins had a tough choice to make. If she went against her deal with the prosecution, they would surely seek the death penalty. Whereas if she went against Manson, he would surely have her murdered.

Atkins ended up getting her meeting with Manson on March 5th, and after that, she returned to her prison and fired her attorney. It was now apparent that Atkins feared Manson more than a death penalty decision. The meeting between Manson and Atkins captured the headlines of all the newspapers, even over the story about three famed bombers of the Weathermen Underground blowing themselves up in an apartment while trying to construct a new bomb.

~

On the same day, Kaufman took Manson's *Lie* albums to the smaller record shops around town. He knew that once he got them out there, they would sell quickly, thereby making the larger chain record stores want to order them, and Manson would ultimately become the rock star he wanted to be. Instead, the small record stores didn't want them. They all believed that if they took these albums and sold them, they would be helping out a murderer. And that was something they didn't want to do.

When Kaufman told Manson that he hadn't had any success in selling his albums in small record stores, Manson didn't believe him. Instead, Manson supposed Kaufman was selling the albums and pocketing the money he was making from them. It wasn't long before things escalated into a minor conflict between the two.

Manson instructed some of his Family to go to Kaufman's and retrieve the money. But when they arrived, Kaufman informed them that he hadn't received any money for the albums, so they left. They all returned the following day, and this time they carried knives with them. Kaufman surprised them by pulling out a shotgun from his closet, scaring them away. The very next morning, they showed up again. Only this time, they all sat around the house in a circle and began chanting and singing about the money. Kaufman got angry and retrieved his .357 Magnum. He flew out of the house, waving it in the air and firing some rounds. They all scrambled and ran away as fast as they could. It wouldn't have mattered anyway. The court had placed an injunction against any money made from the albums, stipulating that it would go to Voytek Frykowski's surviving son. So Kaufman was stuck with the albums and unable to sell them.

~

Bugliosi decided that he needed to secure a backup plan in case Atkins didn't come through for him before she had her meeting with Manson. He went to Linda Kasabian's lawyer and scheduled a meeting with her. During their meeting on February 28th, Bugliosi agreed to give

Kasabian complete immunity for her testimony. She decided to do it. By this time, she was almost due to give birth, and this would give her a chance at a life with her child.

Less than a week later, Atkins's new lawyer, Daye Shinn, held a press conference to announce that his client, Susan Atkins, was now recanting the testimony she gave to the Grand Jury because she had been threatened and pressured by the prosecutors. She felt compelled to make up a story. In response, Bugliosi and Stovitz told the press that they were not surprised by this and knew Atkins would change her story as soon as she met with Manson. They added that even with Atkins' new direction, they still had more than enough evidence to convict all of them, including Charles "Tex" Watson once he was extradited. They ended their response by saying they would also be seeking the death penalty for all five defendants.

However, there was another surprise in store for Manson when they returned to court: Judge Keene had reversed his previous decision allowing him to defend himself at trial. Keene had decided that because of Manson's earlier behavior during the preliminary hearings, he was not capable of defending himself. Several Family members attending the hearing jumped up and began yelling out names at the Judge, who responded by holding them all in contempt of court and sending them to jail for five days.

At first, attorney Charles Hollopeter was appointed to defend Manson, and the first thing he asked for was to have a psychological evaluation done on Charlie. Manson became angered by this and asked the Judge for the right to choose his lawyer, which was granted.

Manson asked Ronald Hughes, the lawyer who had transferred his music rights to Phil Kaufman so he could have records of his music made, to take over the defense of his case. Hughes had never worked on a criminal case or been in a trial before. It was the perfect background for a lawyer to have, as it allowed Manson to control his case. He had no problem telling Hughes what to do. Of course, the choice got no objection from the prosecution team, as they viewed Hughes as an easy attorney to handle in court.

What Manson did next took everyone by surprise. He hired a second lawyer, Irving Kanarek, who was well known for attempting to create judicial mistakes that would result in a mistrial. Kanarek took to the press and bragged about how Manson came to him, and that he didn't need to try to beg to get the case. It certainly seemed to be the correct choice of a lawyer for Manson.

But Bugliosi had a surprise of his own. During their investigation, Bernard "Lotsapoppa" Crowe, who Manson shot a while back, contacted him. Manson believed that Lotsapoppa was a Black Panther Party member whom he had killed in a shooting. Only Lotsapoppa didn't die, but the .22 caliber slug was recovered from him, which matched the bullets used in the Tate murders. It was significant evidence to show that Manson was willing and able to kill someone.

As strange luck would have it, Lotsapoppa was arrested for having drugs on him and brought to court to face his charges just at the time when Manson was coming from a court hearing, and the two would pass each other in the hallway. Manson was finally aware that Lotsapoppa was still alive.

Kanarek filed an affidavit of prejudice against Judge Keene and requested that he be removed from the case. Under California law, defendants were allowed to do this. The reason Manson felt prejudiced by Keene was that he refused Manson the right to act as his own defense attorney. Judge Charles H. Older was assigned to the trial after Keene stepped down. Judge Older set June 15th as the start of the trial.

Next, Manson requested to change the venue of the trial. He wanted it moved from Los Angeles, saying that he couldn't get a fair trial there. However, Judge Older denied the request. When Older gave his decision, Manson stood up and turned around so his back was facing the Judge. After several appeals by the Judge to have Manson turn around and be seated were refused, he was taken from the courtroom and placed in a lockup room. Then Susan Atkins, Patricia Krenwinkel, and Leslie Van Houten all stood up and turned around just as Manson had. Judge Older, growing increasingly frustrated, instructed each of the girls' lawyers to have their clients behave accordingly in court. After several pleas by their lawyers didn't work, the Judge had them removed and also placed them in lockup rooms.

Three days later, on June 12th, he had all four of them brought back into the courtroom and had them stand in front of him, facing them while he spoke to them. "Do you have any idea what you are doing when you cause such a scene? Do you understand exactly how much you could affect your case if you were to pull off such stunts in front of a jury? Do you want to jeopardize your chances by doing this?"

"You leave me nothing. You can kill me now!" Manson responded as he stretched his arms high towards the ceiling, slightly bending his wrists to try to look like he was Jesus at the crucifixion. Then all three women copied him by raising their arms.

Judge Older, now visibly frustrated, told the bailiff to remove them and lock them up again. Manson went down on his knees and sat on his feet. Two bailiffs came over to lift him and drag him out of the courtroom. As the bailiffs pulled Manson to where the exit door to the courtroom was, they seemed to purposely push his head into the door without opening it first. Suan Atkins began screaming in an awful pitch, "You might as well kill us all now! We are not going to be tried fairly!" Krenwinkel and Van Houten began singing "Kill us." Right away, the women bailiffs ran over and began to drag the women out of the courtroom as well.

It left only Kanarek standing and facing the Judge, who then asked him in a somber tone what else he had for the court to address. After Kanarek read off a series of requests, and with each one of them denied sternly, he said that was it. Judge Older looked up, smiled, then said the trial would start on time as planned on Monday, June 15th, at 9 a.m. sharp. He slammed his hammer, got up, and left.

34

TRIAL

When the Court came into order, they began with the jury selection process. It took almost five weeks to complete this part of the process, partly because Manson's growing popularity was becoming a problem for the Court, as it made it challenging to select a jury that hadn't heard or read some of these reports about him. Additionally, the Judge had stated his intention to sequester the selected jury members for the entire trial, estimated to last around six months. When potential jurors heard about being sequestered, they suddenly came up with reasons why they couldn't sit on the jury. Most of them said that they couldn't be away from their families for that long.

The Court finally selected eighteen people for the jury on July 21st, six of whom would be the alternates. The trial of evidence was officially scheduled to begin on Friday, July 24th.

∼

What started as an excellent thing for Manson was now beginning to anger him. The press was starting to paint him as an angry cult leader who was just out to kill the good citizens of the city, as witnessed in the twenty-page *Rolling Stone Magazine* story on Manson. Throughout the story, many wild stories Charlie told to his followers while on acid were recounted. The Family was described as being from the *Village of the Damned*, a popular horror film of the time, where the children all looked, talked, and believed in the same things.

Manson had to keep the remaining members under his control. Bugliosi had several of his members ready to testify against Charlie, including Linda Kasabian, Dianne Lake, Barbara Hoyt, and Stephanie Schram. So Manson ordered Squeaky to visit the jail every day to speak with Susan Atkins, Patricia Krenwinkel, and Leslie Van Houten. He couldn't afford to have any of them turn against him, too.

～

Before the trial began, the prosecutors subpoenaed all of the Manson Family members they were aware of as a way to prevent them from entering the courtroom during the trial and causing a disturbance. California law prohibited potential witnesses from being present in the courtroom to observe other witnesses testify.

The most crucial rule that Stovitz and Bugliosi had to face during the trial was to keep the jury focused on the rule of conspiracy throughout, which simply meant that each person involved in these murders, even if they weren't in the room when a murder happened, was responsible for all of the acts done by the others.

Even with the prosecution having a tight and precise plan for convincing the jury of their case against Manson and his followers, including strong witnesses, the moment Manson walked into the courtroom, he stole the show away from them. He had taken an item with a sharp side to it and carved a large X in the middle of his forehead above his eyebrows sometime during the night. He had let it dry overnight, creating a large bloody scab. The courtroom erupted in chatter, and the Judge had to call everyone to order.

Suddenly, a handwritten statement that everyone who entered the courtroom received made sense.

"You have created a monster. I am not from you. I have checked myself out of your world. No one, nor any lawyer, is speaking on my behalf. I speak for myself. I am not allowed to speak with words, so I have spoken with the mark I will be wearing on my forehead."

The note was signed, Charles Manson.

To further emphasize Manson's X on his forehead, the following day, Atkins, Krenwinkel, and Van Houten each showed up with an X written on their foreheads with a felt-tip pen. Many of his Family members, who weren't allowed into the courtroom, roamed the streets outside the courthouse, also marked with an X on their foreheads.

~

Bugliosi began with a strong opening statement, captivating the jury with his youthful and dynamic appeal. Kanarek started a long series of objections, at least a dozen, which were all overruled by the Judge. After Bugliosi completed his opening statement and returned to his chair, Kanarek asked for a mistrial, but Judge Older denied that as well.

During the first day of the trial, Manson asked the bailiff who was standing beside him the whole time he was in Court, "Can you set me free, brother? I can get you some bread, man, one hundred grand?" Some of the other bailiffs who were on duty that day reported that Susan Atkins, Patricia Krenwinkel, and Leslie Van Houten had all offered them sexual favors if they would let them go.

Early each morning, Manson, Kanarek, Atkins, Van Houten, and Krenwinkel were all allowed to meet in the same room they were placed in before during pretrial when they refused to face the Judge. During those meetings, Manson told the girls what he wanted them to do and showed them a signal for when he wanted them to carry out the act.

One of Manson's signals was to tug on his ear when a person on the stand started talking. When he did that, the girls were to cover their mouths with their fingers and say "Blah Blah Blah." Another time when Manson pulled on his earlobe, all three girls stood up, turned their backs on the Judge, and laughed.

During the first few days at these meetings, when the defense lawyers began to say that they didn't like what Manson was telling everyone to do, Manson responded with a serious threat, including him mentioning their home address and saying how nice it would be if they got some visitors from his followers. Fitzgerald, the lawyer who challenged Manson the most, received a threat. One day, after he returned to his home, he found Squeaky naked in his bed, telling him that he had a choice: to either have fun with her in bed and listen to whatever Charlie told him, or, the next time he returned home, instead of her being in his bed, there would be some of the more aggressive Family members waiting for him.

∾

Manson was not the only Family member who was fighting for his life at this time. Back at Spahn's ranch, the remaining followers were constantly being attacked or shot at during the night, most nights after the trial started. People would drive out to the ranch, park on one of the hills overlooking the ranch, and sporadically take shots at them.

When the police raided the ranch, they confiscated all of their weapons, so none of them had any guns to return fire. They also knew that with all of the trial publicity, the police were not going to come out and protect them or even try to stop the night attacks from happening. They were forced to defend themselves by any means possible.

The only thing they could get their hands on was slingshots. They found some metal ball bearings and, at sunset, they would head into the hills to wait for their attackers to arrive. Whenever any car or truck drove by them, they all fired the ball bearings through the vehicle's windshield. Eventually, the attacks slowed and nearly ceased to occur.

∾

The court bailiffs were under intense pressure. They had to take Manson from his jail cell, strip search him, which couldn't have been pleasant, as they had to do a cavity search, and prisoners only got to shower once a week. Then they had to walk him down the main court hallway into the courtroom, passing by all the press and photographers who would shout out questions to him. And Charlie loved the attention and was very unpredictable. In Court, during the proceedings, they had to keep him and all his girls in line, as well as watch over the courtroom to ensure none of his followers sneaked in and began to cause trouble.

Oden Skupen, a senior bailiff and war veteran, took Manson aside only once. He sternly told Manson that if he ever did anything to embarrass him, he would take him into the locker room and beat the shit out of him. The warning kept Manson in line whenever Skupen was on the job.

~

On the sixth day of trial, July 27th, Linda Kasabian took the stand. Hers was the most critical testimony so far. Up to this point, the witnesses included those who created the setting, explained who the victims were, such as the parents of the victims, Winifred Chapman, the housekeeper who discovered the murder scene, and William Garretson, the groundskeeper who was staying in the guesthouse on the property on the night of the murders.

Of course, it wouldn't be a Manson trial if things didn't go off the rails somewhat. As Kasabian was trying to get into the courthouse, Sandy Good and some other followers were waiting for her and began yelling things like "You'll kill us all!" When Linda raised her hand and the court clerk swore her in, Kanarek stood and objected to Kasabian testifying because of her heavy drug use.

Bugliosi stood and began asking his first question of Kasabian, and Kanarek objected again, this time much louder. During questioning, he ended up objecting close to fifty times. Each time, the Judge overruled it, but this process took a significant amount of time because each objection required the Court to spend anywhere from two to ten minutes addressing it. The numerous delays between questions disrupted the flow of the testimony and the direction Bugliosi was trying to convey.

Linda Kasabian was on the stand testifying for four days, which should have taken, at most, one day total. Over this time, Kasabian described how she found the Family and why she joined. She talked about everything right up until the night the murders happened.

Kanarek had raised over two hundred objections to her testimony, and the Judge became so frustrated with them that he ultimately placed Kanarek in jail for a day for contempt of Court. When the testimony got to the murders, Kasabian often had to stop and cry. Manson also began making slashing-like motions with his fingers, running them across his neck.

When the prosecution was finished, it was time for the defense lawyers to cross-examine Kasabian. The first was Fitzgerald, who went after her for saying that she followed Charlie because she was afraid of him. He tried to embarrass her by asking her about all of the sex orgies she had been involved in at Spahn Ranch. Throughout it all, she remained calm and admitted to everything she had done without any shame. It boded well for Bugliosi, since no matter what the jury members thought of her, she was at least honest.

~

At this time in history, President Nixon was always in a constant battle with various groups: the Vietnam War protesters, the college and university protestors, and the various groups involved in the race riots. He seized any chance he could to make the young long-haired hippies and the press who supported them look bad.

In Denver, Colorado, Nixon was giving a speech when he thought it would be a good idea to take a minute to criticize the press because every day over the last week or so, the newspapers reported on Linda Kasabian's testimony.

"I couldn't help but notice the coverage of the Charles Manson case. Front page coverage every day in all of the papers. It usually gets a couple of minutes on the evening news. Here is a man who was guilty, directly or indirectly, of eight murders without reason. Here is a man, yet, who, as far as the coverage was concerned, appeared to be a rather glamorous figure, a glamorous figure to the young people whom he had brought into his operations, and the Judge seemed to be the villain. All this proves is that the American press set out to glorify and make heroes out of those engaged in criminal activities."

Of course, it wasn't long before Nixon's comments at that speech were the subject of every headline in the country. Nixon, being a lawyer, knew that he shouldn't comment on any legal case that was in the midst of trial, as he could prejudice the outcome. Perhaps Nixon thought that because the jury was sequestered, they wouldn't have access to any news programs on television or newspapers, so they wouldn't know what he said, and it wouldn't matter. The Judge heard about what Nixon had said during the trial's lunch break, so when the Court reconvened, he dismissed the jury and discussed the situation with the attorneys. Naturally, Kanarek requested a mistrial, which the Judge denied. Then he asked for permission to question each of the jury members to see if they had heard anything the president had said. Judge Older rejected that request as well.

The following morning, it was Kanarek's turn to question Kasabian. He asked her about the amount of drugs she took and focused on questions relating to drug use.

In the meantime, another of the defense lawyers, Daye Shinn, entered the Court and sat down beside Manson. He slipped Manson a copy of the *Los Angeles Times*, whose headlines read "Manson Guilty, Nixon Declares." Instead of just reading the paper and keeping it to himself, Manson suddenly stood up, faced the jury, and held the front page directly in front of them. Just then, Atkins, Van Houten, and Krenwinkel stood up and stated loudly in perfect unison, "Your Honor, the President said we are guilty, so why go on with the trial?" The next morning, Manson entered the courtroom, and before he sat down at the defense table, he pulled out a handmade sign which read "Nixon's Guilty." The bailiffs grabbed it from him as soon as they saw it.

Kanarek spent the rest of the week questioning Kasabian. On the last day, he used the pictures taken by the police of the murder scene, putting them in Linda's face, while asking her questions. The jury became terrified by how he was yelling at Kasaian, as well as having to view the bloody pictures of the victims. He had turned everybody off in the courtroom, including Manson, who was so over Kanarek that he stood up to yell at him to stop.

The week concluded with the other defense attorneys questioning Kasabian. The testimony seemed dull, so Susan, Leslie, and Patricia grabbed some crayons and blank sheets of paper to doodle on and draw throughout. Perhaps it just seemed like mild questioning and testimony after the wild show that Kanarek had put on. Whatever it was, it was a welcome relief for everybody in the courtroom.

The morning of Tuesday, August 12th, came around as every other morning had before for everyone except for Manson. This morning, when the bailiffs came to escort him into the courtroom, he refused to go with them. He didn't fight them. He just lay there on his cot and wouldn't get up. At first, they asked him nicely, but he gave no response. Then the bailiffs moved in and took hold of him, trying to get him to respond in some way or at least stand up. But he remained unresponsive. Realizing that they had a problem, they called for backup. Soon, there were six bailiffs in Charlie's cell. They gave him a final warning before four of the guards, each taking one of Charlie's limbs, lifted him and carried him down into the courtroom. The Judge ordered them to bring Manson into his private chambers to see if he could resolve whatever issue there was with him.

The guards sat him in a chair which was across from the Judge's desk. When the Judge asked what the problem was, Charlie responded by saying that he was protesting his treatment by the American justice system. He was tired of them all looking at him in his cell and how they would even bring their sons into the prison to look at "the freak." Manson was distraught because they had taken away his right to make phone calls, and bailiffs were doing strip searches on him at least twice a day. The Judge listened and calmed him down, eventually persuading him to return to the courtroom.

The following day, Judge Older officially granted Kasabian immunity for completing her testimony. Before she left the courthouse, one of Manson's followers gave her a note that Charlie wrote. She then gave that letter to Bugliosi. When he approached Kanarek, he was told that Kasabian had stolen the letter from Manson. Kasabian remained in jail for a short time before being released. Upon release, she traveled to New Hampshire to live with her mother and her two children.

∾

Over the next few days, Manson created disturbances several times a day. He would be placed in the conference room until he calmed down again before being brought back into Court. Everyone knew that he was putting on a show as Manson liked to do because every time he was placed in that room, one of the bailiffs had to stay with him. Once they had gotten into the room, Manson would bum a smoke off the bailiff and plan and practice his future outbursts that he would do.

Next in the trial were a series of witnesses, including people who worked at Spahn Ranch, those who lived on Cielo Drive, detectives who worked on the case, and David Katsuyama, Deputy Medical Examiner. While the medical examiner was giving the details of wounds the victims had and explaining what they would have gone through to get those wounds and the pain associated with them, Susan Atkins began to moan loudly. She got louder and louder, and her attorney couldn't get her to be quiet. Everything stopped. Atkins claimed that she had a horrible stomachache, so the Judge sent her to be examined in the hospital. Doctors said that she had an impacted colon and gave her an enema, and after that, she was better. She returned to the Court.

When the Court started again, Atkins' attorney said that her client was in pain again and asked if she could be dismissed. The Judge retired and contacted the doctor who had administered the enema to Atkins, but the doctor told him that she was probably faking it. Judge Older returned to the Court and denied her request to leave, and the testimony resumed.

After the day concluded and Stovitz was leaving, one of the reporters in the court hallway asked him what he thought about Susan Atkins allegedly being sick again. Stovitz didn't stop as he was walking by the reporter and just shouted out, "It was a performance worthy of Sarah Bernhardt" (a famous French actress). Then he left the courthouse.

District Attorney Younger ordered both Stovitz and Bugliosi to come to his office immediately. Once there, he told Stovitz that he was off the Manson case for violating the gag order by talking to a reporter about Atkins. Stovitz and Bugliosi challenged Younger, telling him that it wasn't an interview, but rather a passing remark about her illness. That said, Stovitz did, in fact, ignore the gag order earlier when he interviewed about the case for *Rolling Stone Magazine*. When it came out, Younger immediately brought him in, reprimanded him, and warned him to say nothing to anyone, or he would be removed from the case entirely.

Younger had already made up his mind, and after removing Stovitz, he placed Stephen Kay, Deputy District Attorney, as second chair on the case. Bugliosi now had to take charge as well as train Kay on the case they were prosecuting. It wasn't going to be easy, as Kay and Bugliosi were two very different people. Bugliosi was aggressive, loud, and very direct, while Kay was more subdued and quiet.

~

Former Manson follower Barbara Hoyt was the next candidate for Squeaky to target in an attempt to keep her from testifying against Charlie. Squeaky phoned Hoyt a few times a day, begging her not to hurt the Family by testifying against them. Hoyt could go either way. She was still very close to many of the Family members and didn't want to hurt any of them, but she knew Charlie was bad.

During her September 5th phone call from Squeaky and Ruth Ann, Hoyt was finally convinced not to testify after being promised a free trip to Hawaii, all expenses paid. Hoyt jumped at the chance, and the following day, Ruth Ann and Hoyt were on a plane to Honolulu. They stayed in a beautiful hotel and had an excellent time for the first few days, going for walks on the beach and enjoying nice meals out.

On the third day, Ruth Ann suddenly told Hoyt that she had to leave and return to Los Angeles for an emergency. She said that Hoyt could stay there and have fun at the Family's expense. The two of them took a cab to the airport, and Squeaky went to buy her ticket while Hoyt grabbed them a table where they could sit and wait for the plane to board. When Ruth Ann returned, she had a hamburger that she said she had bought for Hoyt. The two sat and talked while Hoyt ate her burger. Soon, Ruth Ann's plane was called to board. She stood up and laughed while saying, "Just imagine if there were ten tabs of acid in there!" Then she boarded the plane. As Hoyt was heading towards the cabs parked in front of the airport, she lost control of her body and fell to the ground. People rushed over to see what had happened to her, and she pleaded for them to call Mr. Bugliosi.

Hoyt remained in the hospital for a few days while they treated her for a drug overdose. She had firmly made up her mind to take the stand to testify against Charlie. After all, he had tried to kill her. Once she was back in Los Angeles, Bugliosi had her placed where she could be protected, and then he had warrants issued for attempted murder against Ruth Ann, Squeaky, Gypsy, Clem, and Dennis Rice, who was the man who paid for the flights to Hawaii.

Hoyt's testimony after she finally recovered from the overdose was suitable for the prosecution because she told all of the stories about the killings that she heard from the other Family members. And there were a lot. Even when defense attorney Kanarek asked her why she followed Charlie and didn't leave, she told him that she was too scared not to obey him.

∾

Tex Watson had finally been extradited to Los Angeles on September 11th. Perhaps this was the reason why Ruth Ann had to return to California herself. Watson had a new look. He had his hair cut short and shaved, looking very respectable. When he finally appeared in Court before Judge Older, with Bugliosi watching, Watson was dressed conservatively, in a blue blazer jacket, gray dress pants, and nicely shined shoes.

While the Judge set the arraignment date for Watson for September 28th, Watson looked at the defendants and smiled at them. All the girls returned his smile. Kanarek stood up and objected, requesting a mistrial since the Court allowed Watson to be present in front of the jury. Manson didn't like that Watson was all clean cut now, and if they wanted to convince the jury that Watson was the mastermind for the murders, his new look wasn't good for them.

While in jail waiting for his trial to begin, Tex Watson started a hunger strike and always acted strangely when guards entered his cell. It was decided to send him to Atascadero State Hospital for evaluation. They needed to know if this was some ploy for his defense or not. When

Manson heard about what was happening with Tex, he asked the bailiff if he could speak with Bugliosi. During their short conversation, Manson told Bugliosi that if he could get about an hour with Tex, he would be able to get him straightened out and ready for trial. The request from Charlie elicited a loud and hearty laugh from Bugliosi, as there was no way he was going to let these two guys get together to talk about anything.

~

The next morning, Timothy Leary broke out of federal prison with the help of the Weathermen Underground. President Nixon once called him the most dangerous man in America, while the counterculture considered him to be the guru of psychedelic drugs. Leary had been serving two ten-year sentences to be served consecutively for two different marijuana possession convictions. He had begun serving his sentence earlier that same year, in January.

Leary had climbed out of the minimum security prison on a telephone line where the Weathermen were waiting for him with a truck. They smuggled him out of the United States and into Algeria, where they met up with Eldridge Cleaver and some of the other remaining members of the Black Panther Party.

The escape reenergized Manson and his Family as they started to believe that if Leary could escape prison, then so could Charlie.

After that, at least four random Family members showed up each day and sat outside the courthouse. They made sure to sit in the way of anyone who wanted to walk into or by the courthouse. They remained friendly, smiling, laughing, and chatting with anyone who would talk to them. Most passersby would try to avoid them, understanding who they were. The Family was easily identifiable, too, as each one had an X marked on their forehead and was shaven bald.

As the days went by, they started doing things to amuse themselves while waiting. They often played games such as pat-a-cake or sang songs. Some people felt sorry for them and brought them food and drinks, while others thought it was an absolute novelty and would come by to take pictures with them.

They weren't outside just for pleasantries with those who were passing by, though. Anytime members of the prosecution team had to walk by them, a scene would usually ensue. Once, when Bugliosi left the Court, Sandy followed him, playing with the handle of a knife she had stashed in the front of her pants. When Bugliosi saw that she had a knife, he turned around and told her, "Get away from me, you God damned bitch!" She immediately stopped and began to back away from Bugliosi so that she could keep her eyes on him.

The following day at trial, when the Court went into a recess, Charlie walked over to Bugliosi and told him, "Hey, don't be worried about Sandy and her knife. It was nothing, just Sandy being Sandy. I mean, if I had all the power and control over these people that you say I have, I could tell Sandy to go and get Bugliosi, and that would be it." He put on the large grin that he was known for and walked back to the defense table.

When the new prosecutor, Kay, was leaving one time, both Squeaky and Sandy walked up to him and told him that the same thing that happened at the Tate house could also occur at the Kay house. Then they both began laughing and walked away from him.

∿

On September 26th, a large fire consumed the Spahn Ranch, and even some of the horses died in it. While it was happening, the Family members who were living there at the time were all dancing around the fires and singing songs. Some of them were screaming out the warnings that this was the beginning of Helter Skelter, finally.

∿

After Barbara Hoyt finished her testimony, Spahn Ranch employee Juan Flynn took the stand to testify. Flynn explained how he saw Charlie, Tex, Susan Atkins, Linda, Patricia, Leslie, and Clem all drive off together the night that the LaBiancas were murdered on Waverly Drive. Before that, Flynn claimed that Susan was bragging about getting some fucking pigs, and Manson told him the night before that he was at the Cielo Drive house where Tate was murdered.

Whenever there was a witness like Flynn or Hoyt who had good evidence and was testifying against Manson, all of the Manson members who were on trial took turns standing and singing or making some statement. They aimed to halt the testimony's momentum or interrupt the jury sufficiently to cause them to lose track of what was being said.

The following week, on Monday, October 5th, Bugliosi had another detective, Paul Whitley, take the stand. After he finished questioning the detective, the defense declined to cross-examine him. When he left the stand and walked by the defense table, Charlie looked up at the Judge and asked if he was allowed to examine the witness. Judge Older flat-out refused him.

Charlie got angry and lashed out at the Judge, "You are going to use this courtroom to kill me, but I am going to fight for my life one way or another. You really should let me do that with words." The Judge stopped what he was doing and looked sternly at Manson and told him that if he kept speaking, he would be removed.

Charlie began to make a growling sound, then said, "I'll have you removed! I do have a system of my own for doing that, you know?" Judge Older, completely ignoring Manson, looked down at his journal, then looked up at Bugliosi. "Call your next witness, please." Bugliosi rose and started to call the next witness when suddenly Manson loudly interrupted him, "Do you think I'm kidding? He grabbed the pencil from his defense lawyer, quickly stood up, and leaped over the defense table towards the Judge sitting at the bench. Only a few feet away from reaching the Judge, two of the bailiffs grabbed him by his legs and pulled him to the ground.

As the guards were forcibly removing him, he kept yelling at the Judge, "In the name of Christian justice, someone should cut your head off." Just then, the three Manson Family female defendants stood and began to sing, so Older had them removed from the courtroom as well. Over the next four days, all the defendants were required to remain in a private room where they could hear everything that was happening in the trial, but they were unable to participate.

Bugliosi put his final witness, ex-Family member Dianne Lake, on the stand before resting on November 16th.

After twenty-two weeks, the prosecution presented three hundred and twenty pieces of evidence, including photos. The Court took a two-day recess before resuming on Thursday, November 19th, for the defense to present its case.

$\sim$

The defense attorneys began the morning by filing a motion to dismiss all charges against their clients. This type of motion is a standard request in such cases, and, like in most of them, the Judge rejected the motion.

The first lawyer to speak was Fitzgerald, who stood up and stated, "Your Honor, the defense rests." Right away, the commotion and talking started within the audience, and soon after, Patricia Krenwinkel, Susan Atkins, and Leslie Van Houten all stood up and began yelling at the Judge, stating that they wanted to testify and tell their stories too.

Judge Older started hammering away on his bench and demanded that the Court come to order, or he would clear the room. After things calmed down again, he ordered the three defense attorneys, Fitzgerald, Daye Shinn, and Ronald Hughes, to approach his bench. All three attorneys told the Judge that they didn't want any of the defendants to give testimony, as they would all admit that they were guilty and Manson had nothing to do with the murders. Bugliosi didn't want this to happen because it was precisely what Manson wanted. It was part of his plan to get free.

The Judge took some time to deliberate before making his decision. He knew it had to be done correctly within the law, or there would be an appeal of the ruling for sure. When Older returned to the bench, he ruled that all three defendants could testify in front of the Court, but only after the jury was removed. This way, regardless of what these defendants told the Court, only the admissible statements would be placed into the record for the jury to read.

Additionally, each attorney and the prosecutor had the right to decline to question any or all of the defendants. All three female defendants protested to the Judge, telling him that they had the right to testify in front of the jury, that they wanted to tell their story, and not have it edited. Judge Older rejected their requests, and so all three of them refused to testify at all.

As for Manson himself, he told the Judge that he didn't care if there was a jury or not. He would be more than happy to testify. He knew that there was an audience of people and the press in the courtroom who would watch and report on what he said, which was all he wanted. The other thing Manson requested was that his attorney, Kanarek, stay seated and say nothing the whole time Charlie was testifying, which the Judge agreed to.

35

CHARLIE'S TESTIMONY

If Charlie's testimony weren't going to be the true highlight of the case, then nothing else would. Charlie was a natural-born performer, so the anticipation of him taking the stand was high. Just before his first day of testimony, he had asked the judge if he could have his attorney refrain from asking him any questions so that he could speak directly to the court during his testimony, and Judge Older approved.

Manson talked for over an hour, which started with him attempting to make the jury feel sorry for him after he described his awful childhood. His poor upbringing is what led him to seek out and find other outcasts from society who were also living the same terrible childhood as he had. He claimed that it wasn't to lead them, but for companionship. Manson emphasized that all the children who lived with him were taught not to be like him but to be themselves. He added that if there was anybody to blame for their children being killers, it was their parents.

Manson knew how to cut deep with his words. He told the jury that he was only a reflection of who they were and that they had created him. He went on by telling them that if he could, he would kill every one of them. And that they deserved it.

Manson felt a key point for him to get across to the court was that he didn't murder anyone. It was the girls who did the killing, and he wasn't responsible for what they did. He believed that he was chosen by law enforcement because he was a nobody, and that they could get away with putting him to death because of that.

As for the Beatles and their music, Manson said that the song "Helter Skelter" was all about confusion, and those weren't his words or his music, so why was everyone blaming him for it?

Manson was now done speaking, and Bugliosi asked the judge for the right to cross-examine Manson. Older asked Manson if he wanted to answer the prosecution's questions. He refused.

After that, the court went into a ten-day recess to allow the attorneys to write their closing arguments.

On Monday, November 20th, the court reconvened. However, Leslie Van Houten's lawyer, Hughes, didn't show up. It caused further delays, and the judge had to appoint her a new lawyer, Maxwell Keith, making it December 21st before the court was ready to continue again. An exhaustive search began for the missing attorney, who had gone missing after leaving to go camping. It was another six weeks before they found Hughes' dead body in one of the streams near his campsite. Bugliosi automatically suspected that Manson had some of his Family members murder Hughes.

When the trial finally resumed, Leslie van Houten stood up and told the judge that she was not satisfied with the new attorney he had appointed to defend her. Before Older could respond, Charlie and the other two defendants also stood up and began complaining to the judge. Things were off to the same start as when the trial first began, with the Manson defendants all creating drama, only to end after the judge ordered them all removed.

Later that same day, the judge allowed them to return to the courtroom to listen to the prosecution deliver its closing statements. It wasn't long before they began to act up again. This time, Susan Atkins took the lead. All three girls began talking out of turn and very loudly.

The judge tried to stop them from speaking, but they wouldn't listen. So he had them removed again. This time, on their way out of the courtroom, Susan Atkins ran up to Bugliosi and took his closing argument speech, which was written down on a series of papers, and tore them in half in front of everyone. Bugliosi quickly responded by taking his papers back and calling her a "nasty little bitch" loudly enough so that even the jury heard him. After this scene, the judge decided that the whole lot of the Manson defendants would stay out of the courtroom until the jury needed to give them their verdict.

36

MANSON: IN HIS OWN WORDS

W hen Charlie was seated at the stand, the judge asked him if he had anything to say.

MANSON: Yes, I do. There has been a lot of things said about me and brought against me and brought against the co-defendants in this case, of which a lot could be cleared up and clarified to where everyone could understand exactly what the Family was supposed to have been, what the philosophies in regards to the families were, and whether or not there was any conspiracy to commit murder, to commit crimes, and to explain to you who think with your minds.

It is hard for you to conceive of a philosophy of someone who may not think. I have spent my life in jail and without parents. I have looked up to the strongest father figure, and I have always regarded people in the free world as good, while those inside the jail have been perceived as bad. I never went to school, so I never growed up in the respect to learn to read and write so good, so I have stayed in jail and I have stayed stupid. I have stayed a child while I have watched your world grow up, and then I look at the things that you do, and I don't understand.

I don't understand the courts, and I don't understand a lot of things that are brought against me. You write stuff about my mother in the newspaper that hasn't got anything to do with anything in particular. You invent stories, and everybody thinks what they do, and then they project it from the witness stand on the defendant as if that is what he did, for example, with Danny DeCarlo's testimony. He said that I hate black men, and he said that we thought alike, that he and I were a lot alike in our thinking.

Most of the people at the ranch that you call "The Family" were just people that you did not want., people that were alongside the road, that their parents had kicked them out, or they did not want to go to Juvenile Hall. So I did the best I could, and I took them up on my garbage dump. I told them this: that in love, there is no wrong. I don't care. I have one law, and I learned it when I was a kid in reform school. It's don't snitch. And I have never snitched, and I told them that anything they do for their brothers and sisters is good if they do it with a good thought. It is not my responsibility. It is your responsibility. It is the responsibility you have towards your own children, whom you are neglecting, and then you want to blame me again and again and again. Over and over, you put me in your penitentiary. I did not build the jail. I would not lock one of you up. I could not bring myself to lock another human being up.

You eat meat with your teeth, and you kill things that are better than you are, and in the same respect, you say how bad and even killers that your children are. You make your children what they are. I am just a reflection of every one of you. I have never learned anything wrong. In the penitentiary, I have never found a bad man. Every man in the penitentiary has always showed me his good side. And circumstances put him where he was. He would not be there. He is a good human, just like the policeman who arrested him is a good human. I have nothing against any of you. I can't judge any of you. But I think it's high time that you all started looking at yourselves and judging the lie you live in.

I sit and I watch you from nowhere, and I have nothing in my mind, no malice against you, and no ribbons for you. But you stand and you play the game of money. As long as you can sell a newspaper, some sensationalism, and you can laugh at someone and joke at someone and look down at someone, you know. You sell those newspapers for public opinion, just like you are all hung on public opinion, and none of you have any idea what you are doing.

You are just doing what you are doing for the money, for a little bit of attention from someone. I can't dislike you, but I will say this to you. You haven't got long before you are all going to kill yourselves because you are all crazy. And you can project it back at me, and you can say that it's me who cannot communicate. You can say that it's me that don't have any understanding, and you can say that when I am dead, your world will be better, and you can lock me up in your penitentiary, and you can forget about me.

But I'm only what lives inside of you, each and every one of you. These children: they take a lot of narcotics because you tell them not to. Any child you put in a room and tell them, "Don't go through that door," will never think of going through that door until you tell them to go through the door. You go to the high schools and you show them pills and you show them what not to take. How else would they know what it was unless you tell them? And then you tell them what you don't want them to do, in the hopes that they will go out and do it, and then you can play your game with them. You can also give them attention, because you don't give them any of your love. You only give them your frustration. You only give them your anger. You only give them the bad part of you, rather than the good part.

You should all turn around and face your children, then start following and listening to them. The music speaks to you every day, but you are too deaf, dumb, and blind to even listen to the music. You are too deaf, dumb, and blind to stop what you are doing. You point and you ridicule. But it's okay. It's all okay. It doesn't make any difference because we are all going to the same place anyway. It's all perfect. There is a God. He sits right over here beside me. That is your God. This is your God. But let me tell you something: there is another Father, and he has much more might than you imagine. If I could get angry at you, I would try to kill every one of you. If that's guilt, I accept it. These children did everything they have done out of love for their brother. Had you not arrested Robert Beausoleil for something he did not do...

I may have implied on several occasions to different people that I might be Jesus Christ, but I haven't decided yet what I am or who I am.

I was given a name and a number, and I was put in a cell. I have lived in a cell with a name and a number. I don't know who I am. I am whoever you make me, but what you want is a fiend. You want a sadistic fiend because that is what you are. You only reflect on me what you are inside of yourselves, because I don't care about any of you, and I don't care what you do.

I can stand here in front of this court and smile at you, and you can do anything you want to do with me. Still, you cannot touch me because I am only my love, and it is all for me. I give it to myself because I look out for myself first, and I like myself.

You can live with yourselves and your opinion of yourselves. I know what I have done. If I showed someone that I would do anything for my brother, including give my life for him on the battlefield, or do something else that I may want to do, then he picks up his banner and goes off to do what he does. That is not my responsibility. I don't tell people what to do. If we agree to build a house, I will help you build it and offer suggestions for the home, but I won't impose myself on you, as that is what made you weak, just as your parents have done.

You are not you. You are just reflections of yourself. You are reflections of everything that you think that you know, everything that you have been taught. Your parents have told you what you are. They made you before you were six years old, and when you stood in school and crossed your heart and pledged allegiance to the flag, they trapped you in truth because, at that age, you didn't know any lies until that lie was reflected to you.

No, I am not responsible for you. Your karma is not mine. My father is in jail. My father is your system, and each one of you is just a reflection of the other. You all live by yourselves. No matter how crowded you may think that you are in a room full of people, you are still by yourself, and you have to live with that self forever and ever and ever and ever.

To some people, this would be hell. To others, it would be heaven. I have mine, and each of you will have to work out yours. You cannot work it out by pointing fingers at people. I have eaten out of your garbage cans to avoid jail. I have worn your second-hand clothes. I have accepted things and given them away the next second. I have done my best to get along in your world, and now you want to kill me. And I look at you and I look at how incompetent you all are, and then I say to myself, "You want to kill me? Ha, I'm already dead. Have been all my life!" I've lived in your tomb that you built. I spent seven years on a thirty-seven-dollar check. I did twelve years because I didn't have any parents, and how many other sons do you think you have in there? You have many sons in there. Many, many sons in there. Most of them are black, and they are angry. They are mad, and they are mad at me. I look and I say, "Why are you mad at me?" He says, "I am mad at you because of what your father did." And I look at him and I say, "Well," and I look at my fathers, and I say, "If there was ever a devil on the face of this earth, I am him."

And he's got my head anytime he wants it, as all of you do too, anytime you want it. Sometimes I think about giving it to you. Sometimes I'm thinking about just jumping on you and letting you shoot me. Sometimes I think it would be easier than sitting here and facing you, in the contempt you have for yourself, the hate you have for yourself. It's only the anger you reflect at me, the anger you have for yourself. I do not dislike you, I cannot dislike you. I am you. You are blood. You are my brother. That is why I can't fight you. If I could, I would jerk this microphone out and beat your brains out with it because that is what you deserve. That is what you deserve.

Every morning, you eat that meat with your teeth. You're all killers. You kill things better than you. And what can I say to you that you don't already know? And I have known that there is nothing I can tell you. There is nothing I can say to any of you. It is you who has to say it to you, and that is my whole philosophy. You say it to you, and I will say it to me.

I live in my world, and I am my king in my world, whether it be a garbage dump, in the desert, or wherever it may be. I am a human being. You may restrain my body, and you may tear my guts out, do anything you wish, but I am still me, and you can't take that. You can kill the ego. You can kill the pride. You can kill the want, the desire of a human being. You can lock him in a cell, and you can knock his teeth out and smash his brain, but you cannot kill the soul. You never could kill the soul. It's always there, the beginning and the end. You cannot stop it. It's bigger than me. I'm just looking into it, and it sometimes frightens me.

The truth is now. The truth is right here. The truth is this minute, and this minute we exist. Yesterday, you cannot prove that yesterday happened today. It would take you all day, and then it would be tomorrow. And you can't prove that it happened last week. You can't prove anything except to yourself. My reality is my reality, and I stand within myself, accepting it. Yours is yours, and I don't care what it is. Whatever you do is up to you, and it's the same thing with anyone in my family. And anybody in my family is a white human being, because my family is of the white family. There is the black family, the yellow family, the red family, a cow family, and a mule family. There are all kinds of different families. We must first find ourselves, then God, and kindness next. And that is all I was doing. I was working on cleaning up my house, something Nixon should have been doing. He should have been on the side of the road picking up his children. But he wasn't. He was in the White House, sending them off to war.

I don't know the different people who have been on the stand. One friend said I put a knife to his throat. I did. I put a knife to his throat. And he said I was responsible for all of these killings. I have done the best I know how, and I have given all I can provide. I haven't got any guilt about anything because I have never been able to do anything wrong. I never found anything wrong. I looked at it wrong, and it's all relative.

Wrong is if you don't have any money. Wrong is if your car payment is overdue. Wrong is if the TV breaks. Wrong is if President Kennedy gets killed. Wrong is wrong. Wrong is wrong. You keep on, you pile it in your mind. You become belabored with it, and in your confusion, I've made up my mind. I think for myself. I look at you and I say, "Okay, you make up your mind. You think for yourself, then you see your mothers and your fathers and your teachers and your preachers and your politicians and your presidents, and you lay in your brain with your opinions, considerations, conclusions." And I look at you and I say, "Okay, if you are real to you, it's okay with me." But you don't look real to me. You only appear to be a composite of what someone told you you are.

You live for each other's opinion, and you have pain on your face, and you are not sure what you like, and you wonder if you look okay. And I look at you and I say, "Well, you look alright to me, you know," and you look at me and you say, "Well, you don't look alright to me." Well, I don't care what I look like to you. I don't care what you think about me, and I don't care what you do with me. I have always been yours anyway. I have always been in your cell. When you were out riding your bicycles, I was sitting in your cell looking out the window and looking at pictures in magazines and wishing I could go to high school and go to the proms, wishing I could go to the things you could do, but oh so glad, oh so happy, brothers and sisters, that I am what I am. Because when it does come down around your ears and none of you know what you are doing, you better believe I will be on top of my thoughts. I will know what I am doing. I will know exactly what I am doing.

If you ever let me go before you kill me. And then I don't care anyway, because I will still be there and I will still know what I'm doing. In my mind, I live forever. In my mind, I live forever, and I have always believed I do. I am only what you made me. I am only a reflection of you. I have done everything I was always told to do. I have mopped the floor when I was supposed to. And I have swept when I was supposed to sweep. I was smart enough to stay out of jail and too dumb to learn anything. I was too little to get a job there, and too big to do something over here. I have just been sitting in jail thinking about nothing. Nothing to think about.

Everybody used to come in and tell me about their past, their lives, and what they had done. But I could never tell anyone about my past or what my life was like or what I did, because I had always been confined to that room with a bed, a locker, and a table. So, then it moves on to awareness: how many cracks can you count in the wall? It moves to where the mice live and sees what the mice are thinking, and observes how clever they are.

And then, when you get on the outside, you look into people's heads. You put Linda Kasabian on the witness stand, and she testifies against her father. She never liked her father, and she has always projected her wrongs onto the male figure. Consequently, it is the man's fault again, and the woman turns around and blames him. The man made her do it. The man got her to do it. The man works for her. The enslaved men for her. The man does everything for her, and she lies around the house. And she tells him what he should do, because, generally, she is an extension of his mother. His mother taught him what to do and trained him for twenty years, then passed him on to his wife. Then the woman takes him and tells him what to wear, when to get up, and when to go to work. Then, when she gets on the stand, she says that when she looked in the man's eyes who was dying, she knew it was my fault.

She knew that it was my fault because she couldn't face death. And if she cannot face death, that is not my fault. Why should she blame it on me? I can face death. I have all the time. In the penitentiary, you live with it. With constant fear of death. Because it is a violent world in there, and you have to be on your toes constantly. So, it is not without violence that I live. It is not without pain that I live. I often look at the projection that comes from this witness stand for the defendants. It isn't what we said. It's what someone thought we said.

A word is changed: "in there" to "up there," "off of that" to "on top." The semantics become entangled in a word game in the courtroom to prove something that has passed in the past. It is gone in the past, and when it is gone, it is gone, sisters. It is gone, brother. You can't bring the past back up and postulate or mock up a picture of something that happened a hundred years ago, or 1970 years ago, as far as that goes. You can only live in the now, for what is real is now.

The words go in circles. You can say everything is the same, but it is always different. It is the same, yet always different. You can "but" it to death. You can say, "You are right, but, but, but." You sat here for nineteen days questioning that girl. She got immunity on seven counts of murder, she got. I don't know how much money she will make from magazines and other sources. You set her up to be a hero, and that is your woman. That is the thing that you worship. You have lost sight of God. You sing your songs to women. You put a woman in front of a man. A woman is not God. A woman is but a reflection of her man, supposedly. However, oftentimes, a man is a reflection of his woman. And if a man can't rise above a woman's thought, then that is his problem. It is not my problem. But you gave me this problem when you set this woman against me. You put this woman up here to testify against me. And she tells you a sad story about how she has taken every narcotic that is possible to take. She has only stolen, lied, cheated, and done everything that you have listed in that book. But it is okay. She is telling the truth now. She wouldn't have any ulterior motive, like immunity for seven counts of murder.

And then, comical as it may seem, you look at me, and you say, "You threatened to kill a person if they snitch." Well, that is the law where I am from. Where I am from, if you snitch, you leave yourself open to being killed. I could never snitch because I wouldn't want someone to kill me. So, I have always abided by that law. It is the only law that I know of, and it is the law that I have always abided by. But she will come up here, and you enshrine her. You put her above you, and you strive to be as good as something below you. It is circles that don't make any sense in my reality. But, of course, that is my reality, and it has nothing to do with you. Because you have your reality, and you have to live with what you believe in.

However, this woman has arrived and testified. She said she wasn't sure, but maybe. Then the magical mystery tour wouldn't be able to be explained to you. A magical mystery tour is when you pick up somebody else and play a part in their life. You may pick up a cowboy today, and you go around all day and play like a cowboy. You put on a hat, and you ride a horse.

This is all we have done. We have played like mom and dad. We have loved each other. We have done everything we could to stay outside the frame of the law, the shakedowns. Nothing has been stolen. I have got better sense than to break the law. I give to the law what it has coming. It is his law. If I break his law, he puts me back in the grave again. I haven't broken his law yet, but it seems as if somebody lies around and somebody needs to fill a spot. They snatch it up and say, "This will do. We will put this over here, and we can hang this on him. Or we can do this to that." Then the words take on another meaning and a deeper level of understanding. Why would a woman stand up and project herself onto a man and say, "Actually, he never told me anything, but I knew it all came from him." Her assumption. Am I to be found guilty on her assumption? You assume what you would do in my position, but that doesn't mean that is what I did in my position. It doesn't mean that my philosophy is valid. It's only valid to me. Your philosophies are whatever you think they are, and I don't particularly care what you think they are. But I know this: that in your hearts and your souls, you are as much responsible for the Vietnam War as I am for killing these people.

I knew a guy who used to work in the stockyards, and he used to kill cows all day long with a big sledgehammer, and then go home at night and eat dinner with his children and eat the meat that he slaughtered. Then he would go to church and read the bible, and he would say, "That is not killing." And I look at him and I say, "That doesn't make any sense. What are you talking about?" Then I look at the beast, and I say, "Who is the beast?" I am the beast. I am the beast. I am the most enormous beast walking the face of the earth. I kill everything that moves. As a man, as a human, I take responsibility for that. As a human, it won't be long, and God will ask you to take responsibility for it. It is your creation. You live in your creation. I never created your world. You made it.

You create it when you pay taxes. You create it when you go to work, and then you make it when you foster something like this trial. Only for vicarious thrills do you sell a newspaper, and do you kow-tow to public opinion. To sell your newspapers. You don't care about the truth. You take another Alka-Seltzer and another aspirin and hope that you don't have to think of the truth, and you wish that you don't have to look at yourself with a hangover as you go to a Helter Skelter party and make fun of something that you don't understand.

JUDGE OLDER: Mr. Manson, please confine your discussion to the issues of this case.

MANSON: The issues in this case? What are the problems in this case?

The issue is that Mr. Younger is the Attorney General, and I imagine he is a good man who does a good job. I don't know him. I can't judge him. But I know he has got me here. He set me in this seat. Mr. Bugliosi is doing his job for a paycheck. That is an issue. He is doing whatever he is doing. Whether he thinks it is right or not, I couldn't say. That is up to him. The only way that I have been able to live on that side of the road was outside the law. I have always lived outside the law. When you live outside the law, it's pretty hard. You can't call the man for protection. You have to protect yourself, for the most part. You can't live within the law and protect yourself. You can't knock the guy down when he comes over and starts to rape one of the girls, or starts to bring some speed or dope up there. You can't enforce your will over someone inside the law. I gave everything I could think of to that older man and the ranch to gain permission to stay there, and I have given the people who remained on that ranch my all. When no one wanted to go out in front and fight, I would go out and fight. When no one else wanted to clean the toilets, I would go and do it myself. People would see me and see what I do, and they would see the example that I set.

They see, when I am cleaning out a cesspool, that I am happy and smiling and making a game of it. Once upon a time, I was on a chain gang somewhere, and they would come and pass out the water. I make a game out of it, or I make a pleasure out of a job. We turn it into a magical mystery tour. We speed down the highway in a 1958 automobile that won't go but fifty, and an XKE Jaguar goes by, and I say to Clem, "Catch him, Clem, and we'll rob him or steal all of his money," you know. And he says, "What shall we do?" I say, "Hit him on the head with a hammer." We're on a magical mystery tour.

Then Linda Kasabian gets on the stand and says, "They were going to kill a man, they were going to kill a man in an automobile." To you, it seems serious. But Larry Kramer and I would get on a horse and ride over to Wichita, Kansas, and act like cowboys. We make it a game on the ranch. Like, Helter Skelter is a nightclub. Helter Skelter means confusion. Literally. It doesn't mean any war with anyone. It doesn't mean that those people are going to kill other people. It only means what it means. Helter Skelter is confusion.

I am not the person who projected it into your social consciousness, that sanity that you projected into your social consciousness, today.

You put so much into the newspaper, and then you expect people to believe what's going on. I say back to the facts again. How many witnesses do you have up here, projecting only what they believe in? What I believe in is what I believe in at this moment. I don't believe in anything beyond the present. I will speak to you from now on because there is nothing here to worry about. Nothing here to think about. Nothing here to be confused over. My house is not divided. My home is one with me, myself. Then I examine the facts that you have presented to this court, and I consider the twelve facts that are being used to judge me. If I were to judge them, what scale would that balance? Would the scale balance if I were to turn and judge you? How would you feel if I were to judge you? Could I judge you?

I can only judge you if you try to judge me. That is the fact. Mr. Bugliosi is a hard–driving prosecutor with a polished education. Semantics, words. He is a genius. He has everything that every lawyer would want, except one thing: a case. He doesn't have a case. Were I allowed to defend myself, I could have proven this to you. I could have called witnesses and shown you how these things lay, and I could have presented my picture. You are dealing with facts and positive evidence. If you are dealing with issues related to the matter at hand, then examine the facts. What else do you look at? Oh, the leather thong. How many people have ever worn moccasins with a leather thong in them? So, you have placed me in the desert wearing leather clothes, and you took a leather thong from my shoe. How many people could we take leather thongs from? That is an issue. Then you move on and say, "I had one around my neck." I always tie one around my head when my hair is long. It keeps it out of my eyes. And you pull it down on your neck. And I imagine many long-haired people do.

Numerous aspects of this case could be explored, revealing a great deal of truth and leading to a deeper understanding of the matter. It is a pretty hideous thing to look at: seven bodies, one hundred and two stab wounds. The prosecutor, or the doctor, gets up and shows how all the different stab wounds are one way, and then how all the other stab wounds are another way. But they are the same stab wounds in another direction. They put the hideous bodies on display, and they say, "If he gets out, see what will happen to you." Implying it. I am not saying he did this. This is implied. In my opinion, many diagrams are senseless in this case.

Then there is Paul Watkins' testimony. Paul Watkins was a young man who ran away from his parents and refused to return home. You could ask him to go home, and he would say no. He would say, "I don't have a place to live. Can I live here?" And I'd say, "Sure." So, he looks for a father image. I offer no father image. I say, "To be a man, boy, you have got to stand up and be your father." And he still hungers for a father image. So he goes off to the desert and finds a father image. When he gets on the stand, I forget what he said, whether it had any relative value. Oh, I was supposed to have said to get a knife and kill the Sheriff of Shoshone. Get a knife and kill the Sheriff of Shoshone? I don't know the Sheriff of Shoshone.

I don't think I have been there but once. I am not saying that I didn't say it, but if I did say it, at the time, I may have thought it was a good idea. Whether I said it in jest or joking, I can't recall. And reach back into my memory. I could say either way. I could say, "Oh, I was just joking," or I could say I was curious. But to be honest with you, I don't ever recall saying, "Get a knife and a change of clothes and go do what Tex said." Or I don't recall saying, "Get a knife and go kill the sheriff." I don't recall saying to anyone, "Go get a knife and kill anyone or anything." It makes me mad when someone kills snakes, dogs, cats, or horses. I don't even like to eat meat because that is how much I am against killing. So you have got the guy who is against killing on the witness stand, and you are all asking him to kill you. You are asking him to judge you. Because with my words, each of your opinions or diagrams, your thoughts, is dying.

What you thought was true is dying. What you thought was real is dying. Because you all know, and I know you do, and you know that I know you know. So, let's make that circle. You say, "Where do we start from there?" Back to the facts again. You say that the facts are elusive in my mind. They don't mean anything. The District Attorney can call them facts. They are facts. You are facts. But the facts of the case aren't even relevant, in my mind. They are relative to the Thirteenth Century. They are relative to the eighth century. They are relative to your age or the watch you wear on your arm. I have never lived in time. A bell rings, and I get up. A bell rings and I go out. A bell rings, and I live my life with bells. I get up when a bell rings, and I do what it says. I have never lived in time. When your mind is not in time, the whole thought is different. You view time as artificial.

And you say time is only relative to what you think it is. If you want to believe me guilty, then you can consider me guilty. And it's okay with me. I don't dislike any of you for it. If you want to believe me, I'm not guilty. It's okay with me. I know what I know, and nothing and no one can take that from me. You can jump up and scream, "Guilty!" and you can say what a no-good guy I am, and what a devil, fiend, eeky-sneaky slimy devil I am. It is your reflection, and you're right. Because that is what I am. I am whatever you make me.

You see, it's what happens inside the now that the words lose meaning. A motion is more real than a word. The Indians spoke with it. They could explain to you with motions what they felt. This is what I intended to do if I could represent myself. Explain to you what is inside of me, how I think about things. Because words are your words. You invented the words, created a dictionary, and gave it to me, saying, "These are what the words mean." Well, this is what they mean to you, but to someone else, they have a different dictionary. And things mean different things to other people, and to match the symbols up as you talk back and forth.

Then you put a witness up here to say what you said. I could never say what someone else said. I could only say what I said. You tell me something, and I'll try to repeat it tomorrow. If I didn't write it down, I couldn't tell you what you said. Let alone a year ago, let alone eight months ago, let alone a week ago. I am forgetful. I forget from one day to the next. I forget what day it is, what month it is, or what year it is.

I don't particularly care because all that is real to me is the present moment. But then, the case is real to me, and I say, "What do I have to do to make you people let me go back to the desert with my children?" You have your world. You will do with it whatever you do. I have no involvement with it. I don't have the schooling in it. I don't believe in your church. I don't believe in anything you do. I am not saying you are wrong, and I hope you will acknowledge that I am not mistaken for holding my beliefs.

Murder? Murder is another question. It is a move. It is a motion. You take another's life. Boom! and they're gone. You say, "Where did they go?" They are dead. You say, "Well, that person could have made the motion." He could have taken my life just as well as I took his. If a soldier goes off to the battlefield, he goes off with his life in front. He is giving his life.

Does that not permit him to take one? No. Because then we bring our soldiers back and try them in court for doing the same thing we sent them to do. We train them to kill, and they go over and kill. And we prosecute them and put them in jail because they kill. If you can understand it, then I bow to your understanding. But to my knowledge, I wouldn't get involved with it.

My peace is in the desert or the jail cell, and had I not seen the sunshine in the desert, I would be satisfied with the jail cell much more than your society, much more than your reality, and much more over your confusion, and much more over your world, and your word games that you play. And each witness got up here and testified only for what was best for themselves. They did not testify for what was best for me. They testified for what was best for them, their benefit. So you say, "Okay, and then what else did she say?" She says, "You only see in me what you want to see in me." You only see in her what you put in her, because when you take LSD enough times, you reach a stage of nothing. You get a stage of no thought.

An example of this: if you were to be standing in a room with someone and you were loaded on LSD, and the guy says, "Do you like my sports coat?" And you would probably not pay any attention to him. About two or three minutes later, the guy who is loaded on LSD will turn around and say, "My, you have a beautiful sports coat," because he is only reacting. He is only reacting to the individual terminology, the person he has in the room. As you would put two people in a cell, so would they reflect and flow on each other, like water seeking a level. I have been in a cell with an eighty-year-old man, and I listened to everything he said. "What did you do then?" And he explains to me his whole life, and I sit there and listen. Experiencing vicariously his entire being, his whole life. I look at him, and he is one of my fathers. But he is also another one of your society's rejects. Where does the garbage go, considering we have tin cans and garbage alongside the road, and oil slicks in your water? So, you have people, and I am one of them, and I am a garbage person. I am one of your motorcycle people. I am one of what you want to call hippies. I never thought about being a hippie. I don't know what a hippie is. A hippie is generally a pretty nice guy.

He will give you a shirt and a flower, and he will smile at you, and he will walk down the road. But don't try to tell him anything. He ain't listening to nobody. He got his thoughts. You try to tell him something, and he will say, "Well, if that's your bag." He is finding himself. Those children were finding themselves. Whatever they did, if they did whatever they did, is up to them. They will have to explain that to you. I'm just explaining to you what I am explaining to you. Everything is simple to me. It is what it is because that is what it is. It doesn't go any further. What? That is all there is. Why? Why? Why does it come from your mother? Your mother teaches you why, why, why. You go around asking your mother why, and she keeps telling you, "Because, because," and she fills your tiny brain with "because" and "because." "Why?" "Because." "Why?" And you don't know any different.

If you had two mothers, one to tell you one thing and one to say to you another, then your mind might be left where mine was. If you had a dozen parents that you went around with and couldn't believe anything you were told, and then you couldn't disbelieve anything you were told. And it's the same thing with this court. I don't believe what these witnesses say up here, but I don't disbelieve them either. I won't challenge them. If the guy says, "You're no good," I say, "Okay." If that's what you want me to believe, it's okay with me. I don't care what you believe. I know what I am. Do you care what I think of you? Do you care what I think of you? Do you care what my opinion is? No, I hardly think so. I don't believe that any of you care about anything other than yourselves, because when you find yourself, you see that everyone is out for themselves anyway. It looks that way to me here. The money that has been made, the things that I cannot talk about, and I know I can't talk about, I won't talk about, and I will keep quiet about these things.

How much money has been spent on this case? How sensational do you think that you have made this case? I never made it spectacular. I was hiding in the desert. You come and get me, remember? Or could you prove that? What could you prove? The only thing you can prove is what you can prove to yourselves, and you can sit here and build a lot in that jury's mind, and they are still going to interject their personalities on you.

They are going to interject their inadequate feelings. They are going to interject what they think. I look at the jury, and they won't look at me. So I wonder why they won't look at me. They are afraid of me. And do you know why they are so scared of me? Because of the newspapers. You projected fear. You projected fear. You made me a monster, and I have to live with that for the rest of my life because I cannot fight this case. If I could fight this case and present it, I would take that monster back and reclaim that fear. Then you could find something else to put your fear on, because it's all your fear. You look for something to project it on, and you pick a little old scroungy nobody who eats out of a garbage can, that nobody wants, that was kicked out of the penitentiary, that has been dragged through every hellhole you can think of, and you drag him up and put him into a courtroom. You expect to break me? Impossible! You broke me years ago. You killed me years ago. I sat in a cell, and the guy opened the door. He said, "You want out?" I looked at him and I said, "Do you want out? You are all in jail, and your entire procedure is underway. The procedure that is on you is worse than the procedure that is on me. I like it in there." I like it in there – it's peaceful. I don't like coming to the courtroom.

I want to get this over with as soon as possible. And I'm sure everyone else would like to get it over with as well. Without being able to prepare a case, without being able to confront the witnesses and to bring out the emotions, and to bring out the reasons why witnesses say what they say, and why this hideous thing has developed into the trauma that it's moved into, would take a bigger courtroom. And it would take a bigger public, a bigger press. Because you all, as big as you are, know what you are. As I see what you are, and I like you anyway.

I don't want to keep rehashing the same things over and over.

There are so many things that you can get into, Your Honor, that I have no thoughts on. It is hard to think when you don't care too much one way or the other.

I was released from the penitentiary, and I learned one lesson there: you don't tell anyone anything. You listen. When you are little, you keep your mouth shut, and when someone says, "Sit down," you sit down unless you know you can whip them. If you know you can whip them, you stand up, whip, and then tell them to sit down. Well, I pretty much sat down. I have learned to sit down because I have been reprimanded plenty of times for not doing so, and I have learned not to share something with people if they disagree with it. If a guy comes up to me and says, "The Yankees are the best baseball team," I am not going to argue with that man. If he wants the Yankees to be the best baseball team, it's okay with me. So I look at him and I say, "Yeah, the Yankees are a good ball club." And somebody else says, "The Dodgers are good." I will agree with that. I will agree with anything they tell me. That is all I have done since I was released from the penitentiary. I agreed with every one of you. I did my best to get along with you, and I have not directed any of you to do anything other than what you wanted to do.

I have always said this: You do what your love tells you, and I do what my love tells me. Now, if my love tells me to stand up there and fight, I will stand up there and fight if I have to. However, if there is any way my personality can circumvent it, I try my best to avoid anything that will disturb my peace. Because all I want is to be at peace, whatever it takes. Now, in death, you may find peace, and soon I may start looking to death to find my peace. I have reflected on your society, and each one of these young girls was without a home. Each one of these young boys was without a home. I showed them the best I could what I would do as a father and as a human being, so they would be responsible to themselves and not be weak, and not lean on me.

And I have told them many times, I don't want any weak people around me. If you are not strong enough to stand on your own, don't come and ask me what to do. You know what to do. This is one of the philosophies that everyone is mad at me for, because of the children. I always let the children go. "You can't let the children go down there by themselves." I say, "Let the children go down. If he falls, that is how he learns. You become strong by falling." They say, "You are not supposed to let the children do that. You are supposed to guide them." I say, "Guide them into what? Guide them into what you have got them guided into? Guide them into dope? Guide them into armies?" I say, "No, let the children loose and follow them." That is what I did in the desert. That is what I was doing, following your children, the ones you didn't want, each one of them. I never asked them to come with me – they asked me.

There's been a lot of talk about a bottomless pit. I found a hole in the desert that goes down to a river that runs North underground. And I call it a bottomless pit, because where could a river be going North underground? You could even put a boat on it. So I covered it up and hid it, and I called it "The Devil's Hole." We all laugh and joke about it. You could call it a Family joke about the bottomless pit. How many people could you hide down in this hole? Again, you have a magical mystery tour, where most of the time, there are forty or fifty people at the ranch playing Magical Mystery Tour. Randy Starr thought he was a Hollywood stuntman. He had a car all painted up, and it looked like he had never done any stunts. Another guy was a movie star, but he had never been in any movies, and everybody was playing a part, you know, like most people get stuck in one part, but like we were playing different parts every day. One day, you put on a cowboy hat and say, "Shoot somebody," or the next you might have a knife fighter, or go off in the woods for a month or two to be an Indian, or just like a bunch of little kids playing. Then you establish a reality within that reality of play acting. And then you get to conspiracy.

The power of suggestion is stronger than any conspiracy that you could ever enter into. The powers of the brain are so vast that it's beyond understanding. It's beyond thinking. It's beyond comprehension. So, to suggest a conspiracy might be to sit in your car and think evil thoughts about someone, then watch them have an accident in front of you. Or would it be a conspiracy for your wife to mention to you twenty times a day, "You know, you're going blind, George. You know how your eyes are. You're just going blind. We pray to God, and you're going blind, and you're going blind." And she keeps telling the older man he's going blind until he goes blind. Is that a conspiracy? Is it a conspiracy that the music is telling youth to rise against the establishment because the establishment is rapidly destroying things? Is that a conspiracy? Where does conspiracy come in? Does it come in that? I have shown people how I think by what I do. It is not as much what I say as what I do that counts, and they look at what I do and they try to do it also, and sometimes they are made weak by their parents and cannot stand up. But is that my fault?

Is it my fault that your children do what they do? Now the girls were talking about testifying. If the girls come up here to testify and they say anything good about me, you would have to reverse it and say that it was bad. You would have to say, "Well, he put the girls up to saying that. He put the girls up to not telling the truth." Then you say the truth is as I am saying it. But when it's gone, it's gone. Tomorrow, it changes. It's another day, and it's now a different truth, as it constantly moves thousands of miles an hour through space.

Hippie cult leader. Hippie cult leader. That is your words. I am a dumb country boy who never grew up. I went to jail when I was eight years old, and I got out when I was thirty-two. I have never adjusted to your free world. I am still that stupid, corn-picking country boy that I always have been. If you tend to compliment a contradiction about yourself, you can live in that confusion.

To me, it's all simple. Right here, right now, and each of us knew what we did, and I know what I did, and I know what I'm going to do, and what you do is up to you. I don't recognize the courtroom, I recognize the press, and I remember the people.

JUDGE OLDER: Have you completed your statement, Mr. Manson?

MANSON: You could go on forever. You can talk endlessly about words. It doesn't mean anything. I'm not sure it means anything. I can speak with the witnesses and ask them what they think about the situation. I can bring the truth out of other people because I know what the truth is, but I cannot sit here and tell you anything because all I want to do is try to explain to you what you are doing to your children. You see, you can send me to the penitentiary. It's not a big thing. I've been there all my life anyway. What about your children? These are just a few, but there are many, many more, and they're coming right at you.

JUDGE OLDER: Anything further?

MANSON: No. We're all our prisons. We're each our wardens, and we do our own time. I can't judge anyone else. What other people do is not my affair unless they approach me with it.

37

VERDICT

It only took the jury a matter of ten days to decide on the verdicts for the defendants. On Monday, January 25th, the Court returned to hear that all four defendants, Charles Manson, Patricia Krenwinkel, Susan Atkins, and Leslie Van Houten, were guilty on all charges. Judge Older then ruled that the penalty phase would start three days from then.

After two more months of testimonies and presentation of additional evidence, the jury retired to debate the appropriate sentences for the Manson Family members who were convicted. The following Monday, March 26th, they informed the Judge that they had all agreed on the sentences.

The Court reconvened, and everybody was waiting to hear what the defendant's fate was going to be. The Court Clerk stood up and started to read from the jury statement when suddenly Manson jumped out of his seat, sending his chair to the ground. He began yelling out while facing the jury, "You people have no authority over me! Half of you in here ain't as good as I am!" Almost immediately, three bailiffs jumped on Charlie and took him to the ground before handcuffing him and removing him from the courtroom.

The Judge called the Court to order, and the Clerk stood up again to read to the jury that all four Manson defendants were sentenced to death. Atkins, Krenwinkel, and Van Houten all faced the jury and began yelling at them to keep an eye out for their children, to lock their doors, as death was coming for them all.

Less than a month later, Judge Older officially gave each of the four defendants a sentence to die in the gas chamber.

≈

During Manson's stay in San Quentin prison, the California Supreme Court voted to abolish the death penalty on February 18, 1972. This allowed all previous death penalty sentences to be automatically reduced to a sentence of life imprisonment, and all previous death penalty inmates would now be eligible to apply for parole in seven years after their conviction.

≈

Manson had the problem of being moved from prison to prison because none of the wardens wanted him in their prisons. It was far too much trouble having him there, as Manson attracted way too much attention from the press and other prisoners. The few times when the warden attempted to put Manson in the general population, he got into fights. He was even beaten up badly once while in Folsom Prison.

Manson began a new faith in prison in 1974, called "The Order of the Rainbow." Members were not allowed to eat meat, smoke cigarettes, have sex, wear any make-up on their faces, or watch any movies or television programs that showed violence. He also instructed his followers not to display their bodies by wearing skimpy or tight clothing.

Out of this movement, Squeaky started a group that she named "People's Court of Retribution," which was a vigilante group for the environment whose mandate was to take revenge on those who pollute. In their press releases, they threatened companies that continued to destroy nature, telling them that they would die if they continued polluting.

A year later, Squeaky dressed up in a nun's outfit and, while concealing a gun, went to see President Gerald Ford, who was on a visit to meet with California Governor Jerry Brown. She mingled among the small crowd who were there to watch the political meeting between the two men. When Ford noticed her, he walked over to shake her hand and say hello. Squeaky removed her hand from her robe, looking like she was going to shake his hand, but instead she had a Colt .45 semiautomatic handgun in her hand. Quickly, the Secret Service tackled her to the ground, taking her gun from her. With Manson's newfound fame, the attempted assassination of Ford only reinforced the idea that he was still in control of his followers and that they would do anything for him.

∾

Meanwhile, Vincent Bugliosi's book *Helter Skelter*, which he co-authored with Curt Gentry, was released and became a bestseller, selling more than seven million copies. Two years later, in 1976, the book was adapted into a miniseries, which set television ratings records as the most-watched program of its time. Manson was in the spotlight once again.

∾

Manson remained in the Corcoran State Prison in California from 1998 until he died in 2017.

∾

The Cielo Drive home where Tate and her friends were murdered was torn down in 1994 after its last renter, Trent Reznor, from the band Nine Inch Nails, moved out. He said that he never knew about the murders until after he was already living in the house.

The Waverly Drive house where the LaBiancas were murdered still stands today.

PART IV

THE MANSON FAMILY

38

BOBBY BEAUSOLEIL

Robert "Bobby" Beausoleil was born to a middle-class family on November 6, 1947, and grew up in Santa Barbara, California. He frequently got into legal trouble for minor crimes, and by the time he was fifteen, he was sent to a reform school for ten months. After he was released in early 1964, he didn't return home. Instead, he became a transient, moving between San Francisco and Los Angeles. He joined rock bands and acted in local theaters until 1966, when he met Gary Hinman and joined his band, Milky Way.

Beausoleil met Charles Manson at the band's first practice, as he was also a member of the band. Manson was recently released from prison earlier that year and was living in Topanga Canyon.

The following year, in 1967, he met filmmaker Kenneth Anger and appeared in his film *Lucifer Rising*. After he completed his work on the film, Beausoleil moved into Gary Hinman's house in Topanga Canyon. While living there, he began meeting other members of Manson's Family, usually the female ones.

Hinman was believed to have inherited approximately $20,000, and after Manson heard this, he began sending his girls over to try to convince Hinman to move to Spahn Ranch with them. Manson even made a few visits to Hinman's house to try to convince him how much better his life would be if he came to join the commune. But Hinman wouldn't budge. He loved his life the way it was.

Manson decided that he could no longer wait to get Hinman's money. There was the looming pressure of Helter Skelter, and they needed the money to make their move to the desert and prepare for the race war. He told Beausoleil to get the cash from Hinman and take Susan Atkins and Mary Brunner with him.

The three of them arrived at the house just as they had gone out there before. Hinman let them in and offered them all drinks. Soon, Beausoleil became aggressive and told Hinman that they wanted the money. It's not precisely clear whether they asked for drug money or more, such as the twenty thousand dollars in inheritance, as different stories were told. After several hours of trying and even using force, Beausoleil was unable to get the money from Hinman, so he called Manson.

Manson showed up with Bruce Davis, and when Hinman answered the door, Manson took his sword and sliced the left side of his face, almost completely cutting off his ear. They dragged him back into the house, and while Manson threatened him, Davis was roughing him up. Manson and Davis decided to leave, but on his way out, Manson told Beausoleil, "You know what to do."

After Manson was gone, Beausoleil decided to try to sew up Hinman's ear with some dental floss he had lying around. Over the next three days, Beausoleil tried to force Hinman to give him the money by using force, hitting him, and even torture.

Beausoleil finally called Manson again. This time, he was told not only to murder Hinman, but to make sure that they left the house looking like the murder was done by the Black Panthers. He told Beausoleil to leave a panther paw print on Hinman's wall by sticking the palm of his hand in some of Hinman's blood and pressing it against the wall. Then Manson told him to take his finger and draw three panther prints on the wall as well, also with Hinman's blood.

Beausoleil kept stabbing Hinman until he tired. It seemed like no matter how many times he was stabbed, he wouldn't die. So, in between each attack that Beausoleil did, Atkins and Brunner would take turns sitting on top of him and holding a pillow over his face to try to suffocate him.

When Hinman finally died, Beausoleil did as Charlie told him. Using Hinman's blood, he created a panther-like paw print on the living room wall. The girls, whose identities are questionable, wrote "Political Piggie" on the wall as well. In Manson's thinking, "piggie" was what Blacks called the police at the time as a slur. But what he didn't realize was that most of the war protesters and revolutionaries also called the police "piggies" as well. In Manson's mind, having both the paw print and the word piggie would make police think that it was the Black Panthers who did the murder. He was wrong.

Before they murdered Hinman, Beausoleil forced Hinman to sign over both of his vehicles to him. The girls took one of the cars back to Spahn Ranch while Beausoleil took the other. On August 6th, while Beausoleil was out joyriding in Hinman's Fiat, he got tired. So he pulled the car over and went to sleep. A few hours later, a police cruiser saw the car parked and stopped to ensure the driver was okay. Once they ran the license plate, they discovered that it was stolen. They arrested Beausoleil and searched the vehicle. They found the knife, which had been used to murder Hinman, stuck in the tire well of the car.

On April 18, 1970, Beausoleil was convicted of murdering Gary Hinman in the first-degree and sentenced to the death penalty. Just as in the other murder cases tried before 1972 in California, all death sentences were commuted to life imprisonment.

Years later, while Beausoleil was giving an interview, he told the reporter a different scenario about the Gary Hinman murder. According to Beausoleil, he had conducted a drug deal with the biker gang, "The Straight Satans." He mentioned meeting several of their members who would often hang out at the ranch and party. Hinman was making mescaline out at his Topanga house, so it was perfect. Beausoleil would get the money from the biker gang, bring it to Hinman, pick up the drugs, return to the ranch, and give it to the gang. He could also take a bit of the drugs for himself and get a commission for the sale. Only the last time, when he brokered the deal and brought the drugs back to the bikers, they complained that the drugs were not good or there was something wrong with them after some of the guys who used them got sick.

He now claimed that this was the reason that he went, along with Atkins and Brunner, to Hinman's house. It was to get the drug money back for the Straight Satans for the harmful drugs that he had sold to them. He also said that Manson had never come to the house that night, and it was he who cut Hinman's ear, which happened by accident while they were struggling over a gun.

This story was never mentioned before by anyone, even during the trial. Even when Susan Atkins was asked about the drug-dealing tale, she said that she had never heard that before.

∾

In 1972, the famous author Truman Capote interviewed Bobby Beausoleil while he was in San Quentin Prison. The interview was published as a short story in 1980 and was called "Then it all Came Down" in his book *Music for Chameleons*. Beausoleil complained about the writing, saying that much of it was false and that Capote took gross literary license. Capote's biographer responded by saying that Capote rarely took actual notes when conducting these kinds of interviews and relied on his memory, which had been proven to be fallible in the past.

Then It All Came Down: Truman Capote Interviews Bobby Beausoleil. San Quentin, 1973. | Truman Capote

∾

Beausoleil was transferred from San Quentin to the Oregon State Penitentiary located in Salem, Oregon, in 1994. While he was serving time there, he met a woman who lived in Oregon, and the couple had four children together. Beausoleil was transferred again in the Summer of 2015 to the Deuel Vocational Institute, located in Tracy, California.

After several times being denied parole, Beausoleil finally got approved in January 2019, citing that he was only twenty years old when he committed the murder and should have been tried as a young offender. He had also had an excellent record while serving his time in prison. The prosecution office disagreed with the parole board's decision. By April 26, 2019, California Governor Gavin Newsom overturned the parole board's approval.

More recently, in January 2025, the parole board again approved Beausoleil for parole. However, as of this writing, Governor Newsom has not yet decided on the matter.

39

TEX WATSON

C harles Denton Watson was the youngest of three children born in Dallas, Texas, on December 2, 1945. He grew up close to Copeville and was not only an honor student in high school but also the editor of the school newspaper and captain of the football team. His family attended church regularly. In the Fall of 1964, he moved to Denton, Texas, to attend the University of North Texas.

Watson worked as a baggage handler at Braniff International, where he got free airline tickets to travel. On one of his trips, he flew to Los Angeles to visit one of his old fraternity brothers from university. While there, he was introduced to psychedelic drugs and hung out around the beach.

One day, when he was driving home from the beach, he picked up a hitchhiker who turned out to be Dennis Wilson, the Beach Boys' drummer. When they arrived at Wilson's house, Dennis invited him in for a drink. That's when he met Manson and a few of the Family members. At that time, they were already living with Wilson.

Watson eventually moved to Spahn Ranch with the Family when they left Wilson's home. During his time there, he started to believe in Manson's stories about the upcoming race war and that he was to take over, ruling the world after the Blacks defeated all the whites except them.

Sometime in December 1968, Watson left the Family at Spahn Ranch and moved in with a lover who had an apartment in Hollywood. They sold small amounts of drugs to survive. After only a few months, he decided to leave her and go back to Spahn Ranch.

After his return to the Family, Manson was telling his followers that they needed to get money so they could move out to the desert and hide away from the race war. Watson remembered a friend, Bernard Crowe, with whom he lived in Hollywood, and his lover. Eventually, Manson and Watson went to see Crowe, and after a brief fight, Manson shot Crowe in the stomach and left, thinking that he was dead. Watson would later use that same weapon in the Tate murders.

On August 9, 1969, Charles Tex Watson led three of the Manson Family girls, Susan Atkins, Linda Kasabian, and Patricia Krenwinkel, to the home of Roman Polanski and Sharon Tate located at 10050 Cielo Drive where they murdered four people who were in the house: Sharon Tate, Jay Sebring, Abigail Folger, and Fry Wykowski, and a fifth person outside of the house, Steven Parent.

On the following night of August 10th, Watson, along with Patricia Krenwinkel and Leslie Van Houten, went out again to the home of Leno and Rosemary LaBianca on Waverly Drive, Los Feliz, and murdered both occupants. On this trip, Manson accompanied them to ensure everything was done correctly, but left before anyone was murdered.

Two months later, on October 2, 1969, Watson left Spahn Ranch and returned to Texas, evading the law that was now searching for him. Months later, he was found and arrested for the murders and extradited to California.

On October 12, 1971, Watson was convicted of seven charges of first-degree murder: Sharon Tate, Abigail Folger, Jay Sebring, Wojciech Frykowski, Steven Parent, Leno LaBianca, Rosemary LaBianca, and one charge of conspiracy to commit murder. A week later, the jury sentenced him to death in the gas chamber. Watson avoided execution, though, after the California Supreme Court voided all death sentences that had been imposed before 1972.

Watson's autobiography, *Will You Die for Me?*, written by Raymond Hoekstra, was published in 1978.

~

Watson married Kristin Joan Svege, and the couple founded Abounding Love Ministries in 1980, as they were both Christians. Watson had converted back to Christianity in 1975 and was ordained as a minister in 1981. The couple were permitted to have conjugal visits and had three sons and one daughter.

However, in 1996, prisoners who were convicted of crimes and had been given a life sentence were no longer permitted to have conjugal visits with their spouses. The pair were divorced in 2003 after being married for twenty-four years. In that same year, Svege remarried. Watson and Svege have remained friends. Watson continued to take courses and study, and in 2009, he achieved a B.A. in Business Management.

~

Watson's attorney, Bill Boyd, died, and his law firm went into bankruptcy. While Watson was being tried for the murders, Boyd made several recordings with him, and now these recordings have become part of the bankruptcy proceedings. Watson didn't want these tapes released to the public, but when he went to court, the judge ruled that Watson had waived his attorney-client privilege by allowing his autobiographer to hear the recording while writing the book. Eventually, the LAPD gained possession of the tapes, which are reported to have Watson confessing to the murders, but offered no new information.

In 2014, Leslie Van Houten's lawyer subpoenaed the recording to be used for her parole hearings.

Watson first became eligible for parole on November 26, 1976, but his request was denied. During his first hearing, a petition was submitted that had over 80,000 signatures from people who opposed Watson's release from prison.

In the 1980s, Sharon Tate's mother, Doris, was behind the group

"Citizens for Truth," which gathered signatures for the petition. Years later, her other two daughters, Patricia and Debra, drove the petitions, which saw the signature base grow to around two million.

Watson has been denied parole eighteen more times since then. He remains locked up in San Diego County at the Richard J. Donovan Correctional Facility.

In 2023, Watson began producing a podcast of sermons delivered from 1977 to 1984 at the California Men's Colony.

40

BRUCE DAVIS

On December 2, 1970, Bruce Davis was the final member of the Manson Family to go on trial for the murder of Gary Hinman and Donald "Shorty" Shea. David had a strong interest in Scientology and hit it off right away with Manson. He joined the Manson Family in 1967.

∼

Bruce Davis was born in Monroe, Louisiana, on October 5, 1942, and grew up in Mobile, Alabama. He attempted college in Tennessee but dropped out after just one semester. In 1962, he headed to California and got a job in construction, becoming deeply immersed in the new hippie culture that was prevalent at the time.

One story about the Gary Hinman murder was that after Beausoleil was unable to get any money out of Hinman, he phoned Manson and told him that Hinman was holding out. Manson headed out to Himan's house, accompanied by Bruce Davis. Davis was a witness to Manson slicing off Hinman's ear and hearing Manson order the murder of Hinman directed at Beausoleil before Davis and Manson left.

Bruce Davis's account of what happened in the Donald Shea murder is as follows:

> "We were at the ranch early in the morning. Manson came down and said, "We're going to kill Shorty." I said, "What for?" "Well, he's a snitch." Charlie is there. Bill Bass is there. He says, "You guys take him. Ask him to take you down the hill to get some car parts and kill him on the way down the hill." I was in the car when Steve Grogan hit Shorty with the pipe wrench. Charles Watson stabbed him. I was in the back seat with...with Grogan.
>
> They took Shorty out. They had to go down the hill to a place. I stayed in the car for quite a while, but what...then I went down the mountain later, and that's when I cut Shorty on the shoulder with the knife after he was...well, I don't know if he was dead or not. He didn't bleed when I cut him on the shoulder.
>
> And I...I did touch Shorty Shea with a machete on the back of his neck. Didn't break the skin. I mean, I couldn't do it. And then I threw the knife, and he handed me a bayonet, and it...I just reached over, and I don't know which side it was on, but I cut him right about here on the shoulder, just with the tip of the blade. Sort of like saying, "Are you satisfied, Charlie?" And I turned around and walked away. And I...I was sick for about two or three days. I mean, I couldn't even think about what I...what I had done."

Davis is serving two life sentences for the murders of Gary Hinman and Donald Shea. He had been up for parole several times, and each time he was approved. However, it was always reversed by the Governor of California.

Davis has become a born-again Christian and earned a doctorate in Philosophy and Religion, ministering to the other inmates. He was also married and fathered a child while still being in prison at the San Luis Obispo, California Men's Colony.

In a 2017 documentary entitled *Manson Speaks: Inside the Mind of a Madman*, Detective Cliff Shepard posited that Bruce Davis might have been involved in the deaths known among Mansonites as "The Retaliation Murders." These deaths included Manson Family member

John Haught, a.k.a. Christopher Zero, Sandra Good's boyfriend Joel Pugh, Attorney Ronald Hughes, and Reet Jurvetson. Of course, being a fifty-year-old case, Shepard failed to turn up any objective evidence of Davis' involvement. Indeed, though, some strange and compelling facts suggest there's more to the story.

41

STEVE "CLEM" GROGAN

S teve Grogan was born in Los Angeles on July 13, 1951, and had a difficult childhood, dropping out of school as a young teenager. His parents were frustrated and let him go live and work at the Spahn Ranch, hoping that it would help him. This was long before the Manson Family went to live there.

Donald Shea, who ran the ranch, liked him and protected him, as most of the others at the ranch considered him unintelligent and nicknamed him "Scramblehead."

On the night of August 10, 1969, Grogan rode along when members of the Manson Family—Tex Watson, Patricia Krenwinkel, and Leslie Van Houten—were dropped off at Leno and Rosemary LaBianca's house. Manson, Grogan, Susan Atkins, and Linda Kasabian continued to Venice Beach.

After arriving at the beach, Manson sent Grogan, Atkins, and Kasabian to kill actor Saladin Nader. Kasabian didn't want to be involved in another murder and took them all to the wrong apartment. After realizing they were in the wrong place, they gave up and went back home.

Grogan would later be involved with the murder of Donald Shea with Manson and Bruce Davis. The three were charged and convicted, with Manson and Davis both getting life sentences while Grogan received the death penalty. Later, a judge would commute Grogan's sentence to life as he considered Grogan to be too stupid to have decided anything on his own.

Years later, Grogan helped authorities find Shea's remains by drawing them a map. He had learned the details from Manson while they were serving time together. His help in finding the body benefited Grogan in getting parole on November 11, 1985.

Grogan met a woman while serving time and was allowed conjugal visits, during which the couple had two children. He is now living in Northern California with his family.

42

LESLIE VAN HOUTEN (LULU)

Leslie Van Houten was born in Los Angeles, California, to her auctioneer father, Paul Van Houten, and schoolteacher mother, Jane Edwards, on August 23, 1949. She had one older brother, Paul, and her parents also adopted two younger orphans, one boy and one girl, both from Korea. The family lived together in Altadena, a middle-class suburb of Los Angeles. By the time Leslie turned fourteen, her parents had divorced. Leslie then lived with her mother.

At the age of fifteen, Leslie began to use drugs like marijuana and LSD and was often skipping school, going out to parties, and meeting up with boys. After she met Robert Mackie, the two began dating. She became pregnant at the age of fifteen. Leslie later claimed that her mother forced her to have an abortion and bury the remains in the backyard where they lived. From that time, Leslie was no longer close to her mother and slowly drifted into a hippie commune lifestyle.

At the age of seventeen, Leslie decided to run away with her boyfriend at the time, but she returned a few months later so she could complete high school in 1967. After that, she enrolled in a secretarial school and joined the Self-Realization Fellowship group, which studies spirituality through yoga. She became a nun for the group.

Only a year later, Leslie became bored with her new lifestyle as a nun and decided to leave the group and travel around the country. While in California, she met a musician named Bobby Beausoleil, and they began a romantic relationship. One of Bobby's friends, Catherine Share, told her about a great Family run by Charlie Manson, so Leslie went to meet him and became a follower quickly afterwards.

After Leslie began to live with the Manson Family, she claimed that she became "saturated in acid" and was unable to understand the difference between real life and a psychedelic one. Leslie was never as close to Manson as many of the other girls, and Manson always referred to her as one of Bobby's girls.

Van Houten joined Manson, Tex Watson, and Patricia Krenwinkel on the night of August 10, 1969. Leslie said she wasn't aware of what was going to happen that evening, but felt that she had to go along with it and, hopefully, Manson would be more accepting of her.

Once they arrived at the LaBianca house on Waverly Drive, Charlie and Tex left the girls in the car while they went into the house. After a while, Charlie returned and told the girls to go into the house through the front door and follow Tex's instructions.

After they both entered the house, Tex instructed them to go upstairs to the bedroom and attend to the women there. Once they got to the room, they saw Rosemary LaBianca lying on the bed with her hands tied behind her back and a pillowcase placed over her head with the power cord of the table lamp tied around her neck.

Leslie and Krenwinkel remained still, unsure of what they were supposed to do. The tied and gagged woman was still alive as she was moving around on the bed and moaning. Suddenly, they all heard loud yelling from two men coming down the stairs. "No! Stop stabbing me! They're killing me!"

Instantly, Rosemary got herself up off the bed and began trying to find her way to the bedroom door. She also began to answer her husband, yelling that she was on her way. Both Leslie and Krenwinkel grabbed Rosemary, but even together, they weren't strong enough to pull her down or stop her from going for the door. Krenwinkel then began to scream for help from Tex.

Minutes later, Tex burst into the room to see both girls trying to hold on to Rosemary as she made her way around the room, even though she was still tied and had the pillowcase over her face. Tex walked right over to the three women and pushed hard on them, causing both Leslie and Krenwinkel to fall to the ground.

Rosemary somehow managed to remain standing and started moving towards the door again. Tex grabbed the cord, which was hanging from her neck, and pulled it hard until she fell to the ground. He then jumped on her, pulled out his knife, and began stabbing her.

Krenwinkel got up and walked over to Tex and Rosemary, got down on her knees, and began to stab Rosemary as well. Leslie just stood there in shock, watching and saying nothing. Before long, Rosemary stopped moving or making any noises. Tex and Krenwinkel both stood up and began to wipe the blood that had splashed onto their faces.

Tex remembered that Manson had ordered him to make sure that everyone took part in the murders, so he handed his bloody knife to Leslie and told her to stab the bitch. Leslie knelt on one knee and looked at Rosemary, who was now lying on her stomach, but didn't move. Tex then let out a loud yell, "Fucking do it, now!"

Out of fear, Leslie began stabbing without looking at the woman. She ended up stabbing Rosemary sixteen times in her lower back and buttocks. Later, when testifying, she said she couldn't tell if Rosemary was still alive when she was stabbing her. There was no way for her to tell, she said. The medical exam showed that Rosemary had been stabbed several times after she was already dead.

After Manson and the Family had been arrested and she was charged with the LaBianca murders, the court assigned her an attorney, Donald Barnett. A few weeks later, Manson got into an argument with Barnett, and Leslie fired him.

The court assigned her a second attorney, Marvin Part, who wanted to declare that Leslie was insane and that was the reason she was involved in the murders. Leslie and Part began arguing over this as she didn't think that she was insane.

During the trial, when Part was questioning a doctor about how LSD affected someone, the doctor began answering that the person using the drug could easily be controlled. Leslie yelled out to the court, "That's a big lie! The only thing that influenced me was the Vietnam War on TV." Leslie then fired Part.

The court appointed her a third attorney, Ronald Hughes, who argued to the court that Leslie's capacity for any rational thought had been diminished because of the amount of LSD she had been using. He also claimed that she had to obey the orders to commit these murders from Manson, who had a significant influence over her at the time.

The jury took into account the fact that Leslie was constantly giggling and smiling in court throughout the trial. When she testified, she admitted to murdering the two victims but told the court that Charlie had nothing to do with them and that he didn't tell her to murder anybody.

Leslie was convicted of murder along with the other Family members who were charged in this trial, Manson, and Krenwinkel. During the sentencing part, Leslie was sent for a psychiatric evaluation. She told the psychiatrist that she was involved in another murder, which Charlie had nothing to do with. Even though Leslie was never engaged in this other murder, she wanted the psychiatrist to believe that she was capable of murdering somebody on her own.

During the sentencing phase of the trial, Ronald Hughes wanted to show that Leslie had remorse for the murders. In front of the jury, he asked her if she felt sorry for her actions in the murder, and Leslie answered by saying, "Sorry is only a five-letter word, and you can't undo something that is done."

Leslie then went on by telling the court, "I stabbed her of my own free will. Charlie had nothing to do with it." Hughes then asked her if she could tell if Rosemary was still alive when she stabbed her. "Of course she was, I could feel her moving around as I was stabbing her in the spine, and she would let out screams." The autopsy showed that Rosemary had been stabbed several times after she was already dead. Krenwinkel and/or Leslie probably inflicted these wounds, but it couldn't be determined.

Before the sentence was handed down, Hughes went missing and was later found dead. Leslie was sentenced to death, which made her not only the youngest ever to be sentenced to death, but also the first woman. The prison had to build a death row for females, as they had never needed one before.

The California Institute for Women built a special unit for the killer females. Leslie Van Houten, Patricia Krenwinkel, and Susan Atkins were all housed there, but kept apart from the general prison population. Later in 1975, all three women were moved to the general population part of the prison.

The 1972 Supreme Court decision resulted in all previously imposed death sentences being commuted to life in prison. Leslie's sentence was automatically changed to life in prison, and she became eligible for parole after seven years of serving.

By 1978, Leslie was eligible to apply for parole, and if granted, she would have been released. The Governors didn't gain the power to rescind paroles they disagreed with until 1988.

One year before Leslie was up for her first parole hearing in 1977, her conviction was overturned because the court that initially tried her should have called a mistrial when her attorney was found dead. As well, the jury foreman of her trial told reporters that they couldn't decide from the evidence they heard whether Leslie's judgment was impaired enough to convict her of first-degree murder or if it should be manslaughter.

In 1978, a second trial took place. The prosecution added charges of theft of clothing, food, and money, all of which had been taken from the house. The additional charges made it a felony murder, which undermined the idea of Leslie being of diminished capacity. Leslie and her cohorts were committing felonies, and the thefts and murders happened in the commission of those felonies.

Leslie was out on bond during the second trial, which lasted about six months. The jury returned a guilty verdict, and later she was sentenced to life in prison with the possibility of parole. A year later, Leslie claimed that she was high almost the whole trial because she was getting LSD in prison.

Leslie van Houten was finally released on parole on July 11, 2023, after serving fifty-two years. She was sent to the transitional living facility, where she will be supervised for up to three years. Her first scheduled leave was in 2024. Leslie had been rejected for parole a total of 23 times.

43

LINDA KASABIAN

Linda Kasabian grew up in Milford, New Hampshire, but her father moved out while she was still very young to remarry another woman. Her mother also remarried Jake Byrd, who, according to Linda, was abusive to her and her mother. By the time Linda was sixteen, she had decided to marry Robert Peasley, but the marriage lasted only a few months before they got divorced. Linda then headed to Miami, where her father had been living with his new wife. Things didn't work out very well for them, as his new wife didn't want Linda around her house.

Linda then met Robert Kasabian, and they were married on September 20, 1967. They had met while both were living in a hippie commune in the Boston area. Early in 1968, the couple had a daughter named Tanya. Linda and Robert began arguing, and Linda took her daughter and moved back home with her mother. Later that same year, Robert called Linda at her mother's house and asked her to return to California to try to reconcile. She agreed and moved in with him in Topanga Canyon.

Robert and Linda began to fight regularly, just as they had when they were living together before. Feeling rejected, Linda decided to take her daughter, Tanya, and stay with a girlfriend of hers, Gypsy, who had been living in a hippie commune on a ranch. This move would ultimately lead to her joining the Manson Family, living on Spahn Ranch, led by Charlie Manson.

Now part of the Family, on the night of August 8, 1969, Linda headed into town with Tex Watson, Susan Atkins, and Patricia Krenwinkel to what she believed would be another "creepy-crawley." A creepy-crawley was where they would break into someone's home, rearrange items, consume some of their food, and cause damage. They weren't out to hurt anybody, but they thought it funny to freak people out who would later return home, and things were all moved around.

Watson told her where to drive. She was the driver because she was the only one who had a driver's license. Once they arrived at 10050 Cielo Drive, Linda was told to wait outside. The other three got out of the car and began making plans.

Just then, a car started to drive away from the house and towards them. Tex suddenly got enraged and ran out in front of the vehicle to stop it. The car stopped, and Tex went over to the car window, pulled a gun out of his pants, and shot the driver four times.

The following night, the LaBianca murders happened. Shortly after that, Linda became terrified. She took one of the cars and drove away. She left the commune and went into hiding. She was unable to bring her daughter, Tanya, with her at the time.

Weeks later, when Manson and some of the Family were arrested and charged with murder, Linda claimed possession of her daughter. She agreed to testify against Manson and some of the others for immunity. During the trial, when Linda was testifying, Manson or the Family members would repeatedly disrupt her testimony. One time, Manson ran his finger across his throat as if to say, "This is what is going to happen to you if you keep talking." Susan Atkins would whisper the words, "You're Killing Us."

Linda gave birth to a baby boy on March 10, 1970. The father was missing at that time, and Tanya was in an undisclosed location.

44

PATRICIA KRENWINKEL

P atricia Krenwinkel was born on December 3, 1947, in Los Angeles, where she lived with her father, who was an insurance salesman, her stay-at-home mother, and stepsister Charlene.

Krenwinkel always struggled with her weight, and because she had an endocrine issue, she had an excessive amount of hair on her face. She would often be teased and laughed at by her classmates during school, and never really formed a group of friends.

Charlene got Patricia some diet pills, which back then consisted mainly of high amounts of caffeine, and when she lost some weight, she still didn't like her looks at all. Patricia then started to look for boys that she could have sex with to help fill her insecurities.

At the age of seventeen, in 1964, her parents divorced. Patricia stayed in Los Angeles with her father until she graduated from high school. She then moved to Alabama to attend a Catholic college there, but dropped out at the end of the first semester and returned to California.

Patricia returned to Los Angeles and moved in with her stepsister, Charlene, who had an apartment on Manhattan Beach. She got a job as a clerk. At the time, Charlene was using heroin regularly and starting to become addicted.

In the Fall of 1967, Patricia came home after work to find that Charlene was having a party in their apartment. Charles Manson was there. He had approached her and began to talk to her in his "Charlie way," making her feel that she was everything to him. They would spend the night together. During their romance, he would constantly tell her how beautiful she was, which would often bring tears to her eyes. As a result, she would become one of his most devoted followers.

Patricia Krenwinkel became Charlie's third follower to join him after Mary Brunner and Lynette Fromme. The four-member Family decided to go to Seattle. Manson didn't like the vibes of the city, so he took the girls and moved to San Francisco.

Soon, the Family grew, and Charlie found an old school bus that they painted and decorated to look very psychedelic. They toured around the country for a year and a half before settling back in Los Angeles. Patricia Krenwinkel would later say that these were the best times for them, as all they did was have fun by running through the trees and putting flowers in their hair. It was as if they had no cares in the world.

After they returned to Los Angeles, Charlie had the girls go out to look for celebrities or rock stars for him, as he was trying to make a connection to have his music heard and secure a record contract. One of the things he had them do was to go out on Sunset Drive and hitchhike around so that they could meet people.

During the Summer of 1968, Krenwinkel was out hitchhiking with Ella Bailey, another member of the Family. A handsome man drove up and asked them if they would like to go back to his house and have some raw milk and cookies. They both said yes and then jumped in his car.

The man ended up being the drummer for the rock band, the Beach Boys, Dennis Wilson. All of them returned to his place and had milk and cookies. Dennis was serious about that, and he did give them raw milk, as that was the only kind of milk he would drink. Later in the afternoon, Wilson had to go to his recording studio to work on some music with his band, so the girls left.

When Krenwinkel and Bailey returned to see Charlie, he told them who they had been picked up by. Charlie got excited and loaded several of the girls into the car, telling them to lead the way to Wilson's house.

The girls had never heard of the Beach Boys before, but Manson was familiar with them.

Later that night, around midnight, Wilson returned to his home to find the Manson Family had moved into his house. When he walked into the house, many of the girls were naked or only wearing their underwear, eating his food, drinking his liquor, and playing Beatles albums on his record player.

The Family ended up staying at Wilson's house for several months before Dennis told them that they had to leave because he was giving up the house and going on tour for a while. Manson and his followers would move to Spahn Ranch, located in the hills of the San Fernando Valley.

On the night of August 8th, Krenwinkel accompanied Tex Watson, Susan Atkins, and Linda Kasabian to the house on Cielo Drive, which was owned by Sharon Tate and her husband, Roman Polanski. She participated in the killings that went on there more than the other two women did.

After they entered the Tate house, Frykowski was woken up shortly after midnight by Charles Tex Watson. When he asked him what time it was, Tex proceeded to kick him in the head. Frykowski got up off the floor and asked him who he was. Tex said, "I'm the devil, and I'm here to do the devil's business."

While this was going on, the Manson girls searched the house to find everyone and bring them all back to the living room.

Krenwinkel entered Abigail Folger's bedroom, where she had been lying on her bed reading. Krenwinkel told her to get out of bed and follow her out into the living room. Folger believed Krenwinkel was a high partygoer looking for someone else at the house, so she refused her.

Krenwinkel got mad and walked over to Folger on the bed, grabbed her by the hair, and pulled her off. Folger started to get up and began to fight back when Krenwinkel pulled her knife out and swiped it at Folger's face. Folger dropped to the floor, and Krenwinkel grabbed Folger's left leg near her foot and dragged her out into the living room without any struggle.

Once they got there, and Krenwinkel let go of her leg, Folger got up

268 | PEACE, LOVE & MURDER

and began to fight with her. The two wrestled and fell to the ground. Krenwinkel was starting to lose control, so she began to stab Folger. Once she believed that Folger was dead, she got back up, only to have Folger run out of the room and out into the back lawn. Krenwinkel chased her and tackled her. Once they both fell again, she started to stab her some more. Krenwinkel began to weaken and could no longer control Folger, so she yelled for Tex, who ran outside behind them. He ended up killing Folger.

The following night, Krenwinkel joined Manson, Tex Watson, and Leslie Van Houten at the home of Leno and Rosemary LaBianca on Waverly Drive. During the events of this night, Krenwinkel felt empowered because of the prior evening's killings. This time, she did not need to be ordered to do the killing. In fact, she stabbed Rosemary LaBianca with vigor. She also got excited to be able to write on the walls with the blood from their victims. She seemed to enjoy getting the blood as well. Krenwinkel even left a carving fork in Leno LaBianca's stomach after carving the word "War" across his chest.

When the police raided Spahn Ranch on August 16th, they were looking for stolen vehicles. Three days later, the charges were dropped because the search warrant had the wrong date written in it.

Manson relocated to Barker Ranch, which was situated farther out in the desert of Death Valley. He thought that it would be better to move out there to get away from the police, and it would help to isolate his Family from outside influences.

While out in Death Valley, the Family spent most of their time stealing vehicles and converting them for desert use or stealing dune buggies. Everyone was preparing for the upcoming race war between the Blacks and Whites. As Manson had told them about a hidden place in the desert that they needed to find to be safe from the Blacks, many members would spend their day out searching for it.

October 10th came, and in the early morning, police raided the Manson Family yet again, also looking for stolen vehicles. Krenwinkel's father came and bailed her out of jail. He sent her to stay with her aunt, who lived in Mobile, Alabama.

Over the next month, Susan Atkins, who remained in jail, began to tell police about the Tate and LaBianca murders. Warrants for the arrest for murder were issued for many of Manson's followers, including Krenwinkel. Police found her at her aunt's on December 1, 1969, and the following day, she was indicted for seven counts of murder in the first degree.

For the next two months, Krenwinkel fought extradition to Los Angeles, claiming that Manson would kill her, and that was the reason she moved to Alabama in the first place.

In February the following year, Krenwinkel was finally sent to Los Angeles to stand trial along with Manson, Van Houten, and Susan Atkins. Tex Watson wasn't located and extradited until much later, so he stood trial on his own.

During the trial, Krenwinkel appeared to show little interest in anyone being questioned on the stand or in what the attorneys were telling the jury. Instead, she was focused on drawing pictures or doodling the whole time, seldom looking up. All three female Manson defendants, Krenwinkel, Atkins, and Van Houten, followed Manson's instructions well. They walked to the court together, holding hands and singing songs. Once, they even shaved their heads bald. Another time, they painted an "X" on their foreheads. All of these acts were intended to demonstrate the Family's unity.

After their nine-month trial was over, Krenwinkel was convicted on all seven charges of murder: the August 9th Cielo Drive killings of Abigail Folger, Steven Parent, Sharon Tate, Jay Sebring, and Wojciech Frykowski, and for the August 10th killings of Leno and Rosemary LaBianca.

Krenwinkel was sentenced to death on March 29, 1971. But like the other Manson Family members who were convicted of murder, her sentence was later commuted to life in prison due to the Supreme Court decision in 1972.

Krenwinkel's first parole hearing was in July 1978. It was denied. There were another fourteen parole hearings for Krenwinkel, and she was rejected in all of them. At the last parole hearing, her attorney claimed that she was dealing with battered woman syndrome, which Manson had inflicted. She claimed that he often beat her during the time of the murders. A year later, the parole board declined her application.

On her fifteenth attempt, on May 26, 2022, Krenwinkel was granted parole. However, on October 14, 2022, California Governor Gavin Newsom reversed that decision. Patricia Krenwinkel remains in prison today.

On May 21, 2025, Krenwinkel was again approved for parole. However, at the time of this writing, she hasn't yet been released. The Governor has yet to decide whether to reverse that decision.

When Krenwinkel was initially sent to prison, she remained close to Susan Atkins and Leslie Van Houten. The three of them followed Manson completely without question. After serving a couple of years, Krenwinkel started to become weary of Manson and began to distance herself from the other girls.

Over time, Krenwinkel joined Alcoholics Anonymous and Narcotics Anonymous and began studying correspondence courses through the University of La Verne, earning her bachelor's degree in human services. Her degree led her to teach other illiterate prisoners how to read. She has also become very social, participating in sports and attending dances in prison.

45

SUSAN ATKINS

S usan Denise Atkins was born in San Gabriel, California, on May 8, 1948, and lived with her parents, Edward and Jeanne Atkins, and two siblings in San Jose, California. She was known as a quiet, self-conscious girl at school who belonged to both the school's glee club and the family's church choir. Her mother died in 1961, when Susan was only thirteen years old, and her father moved them to Los Banos, California.

A few months after that, Edward got a job working on the new San Luis Dam construction project and needed to move there, so he left Susan behind to take care of her younger brother, Steven. Relatives were also helping to take care of Susan and her brother, but Susan had to get a job as well to help support them financially.

In 1966, when the Christmas school break began, she ran away to San Francisco with two friends she had attended school with. Early in 1967, Susan took a job as a stripper in Los Angeles and became immensely popular. Even the leader of the Church of Satan, Anton LaVey, hired her for a performance.

Later in 1967, Susan attended a house party, where a man named Charlie Manson was playing guitar for the crowd. They met at this party and struck up a friendship. A couple of weeks later, the house where

Susan was renting was raided by police, and she had to find a new place to live. Charlie invited her to come with him and his Family, who had a bus and were going to take a trip across America.

Susan accompanied the Family on their trip, and Manson dubbed her "Sadie Mae Glutz." She even had a false identification made for her under that same name. During the Family bus trip, Susan started to believe that Manson was the second coming of Jesus. Soon afterwards, Manson and his Family moved to live on the Spahn Ranch, located in Southern California's San Fernando Valley.

On October 7, 1968, Susan gave birth to a son, whose father was Bruce White, a member of the Family. The son was named Zezozose Zadfrack Glutz by Manson.

When the Summer of 1969 came, Manson was desperate to get enough money and dune buggies to move his followers out to Barker Ranch in the Death Valley Desert. Police were also becoming suspicious of the Manson Family because they were hearing rumors about them being behind some of the car thefts.

Manson was also encouraging his members to sell drugs to make some money as well. One of their suppliers was a man named Gary Hinman, who made mescaline in the basement of his home. During some of the visits by different Family members to Hinman's home, they heard that he had inherited a substantial amount of money. At first, Manson tried to convince him to come out and join his commune, but Hinman wasn't interested. He liked living alone.

One of Manson Family regulars, Bobby Beausoleil, wasn't officially part of the commune. Still, he partied at the ranch a lot and would often arrange drug sales to different bikers who partied at Spahn Ranch with the Family. He got the drugs from Hinman.

On one of the sales he made to the Straight Satan biker gang at Spahn Ranch, he took their money and went to Hinman's house and exchanged it for the drugs. Then he returned and gave it to the bikers. Beausoleil often did this for a cut of the money and some drugs. But with this sale he made in July, the bikers came back to him and told him the drugs were bad, so he would have to get their money back for them.

When he told Charlie what was going on, Manson told him to bring Susan Atkins and Mary Brunner with him when he went out to

Hinman's house. After they arrived at the house, Beausoleil told him that they wanted the drug money back, but Hinman said that he didn't have it anymore. So Beausoleil beat him up.

They called Manson and told him what was going on. Manson, along with Bruce Davis, showed up at Hinman's a few hours later. When Hinman opened the door, Manson took his sword and sliced Hinman's ear off. He then threatened Hinman. Before he left, he told Beausoleil, "You know what to do."

After more beating and torture, all Beausoleil managed to do was to get Hinman to sign the titles to his two cars over to him. Neither vehicle was worth very much, perhaps totaling around $2,000 combined.

Beausoleil had left the room, leaving Susan Atkins alone with Hinman, who got up and began to fight with her, so she started to stab him. Atkins wasn't able to control Hinman, so she screamed out for Beausoleil. When he came back into the room, he tackled Hinman and began to stab him as well. Beausoleil would eventually stab him to death.

Then they wrote "Political Piggie" on the wall with Hinman's blood. They also left what appeared to be a panther paw print on the wall. The print mark was to try to make it look like the murder was committed by the Black Panther group.

Later that summer, on August 7th, Beausoleil was found asleep in the back of one of Hinman's cars. He was still wearing the same clothes that he had worn when he stabbed Hinman to death, and he was still all covered in blood. Police searched the car and found the knife that was used to murder Hinman in the tire well. He was taken in and arrested for the murder.

The day after Beausoleil's arrest, August 8th, Manson decided that to get Beausoleil free, they would do a copycat style murder. They would do the murders in much the same way and leave a bloody panther paw behind. This time, Manson wanted to murder people who were either rich or celebrities so that the murders would make a big splash with the press.

Manson had Tex Watson take the lead and bring Susan Atkins, Linda Kasabian, and Patricia Krenwinkel with him. Manson told the girls firmly that they were to do anything Tex told them to do, without question.

After the murders, they returned to Spahn Ranch and told Charlie what happened. Manson was upset and didn't trust that they left things the way they should have. He got into the car and drove them all back to Cielo Drive, making sure everything was in order.

The next day, after the news broke, and Manson wasn't hearing what he thought he would from the press, that there were murders of some rich celebrity-type people by the Black Panthers, he knew that he had to strike again.

That evening, he would go himself, and this time he brought Tex Watson, Susan Atkins, Patricia Krenwinkel, Linda Kasabian, Leslie Van Houten, and Steve Grogan with him. He took them to the La Biancas' home, located on Waverly Drive. He entered the house with Tex and approached Leno LaBianca. Tex tied him up.

Once he explained to Tex what he wanted done and how the place needed to be left, he went back to the car and sent Krenwinkel and Van Houten into the house before leaving with the others.

On August 16th, less than a week after the LaBianca murders, police raided the Spahn Ranch looking for stolen cars. They found some of the stolen vehicles they were looking for, but because of an error in the date on the search warrant, all charges were dropped three days later.

Manson moved most of his followers to Barker Ranch in Death Valley to escape outside influences and distance himself from the police. They resumed stealing more vehicles, just as they had before. Eventually, police caught up with them again, and in October 1969, police raided Manson and his followers again at his new location, Barker Ranch.

~

While Atkins was in jail for car theft, she met up with two of her friends from before, Virginia Graham and Ronnie Howard. Over the following weeks, she would tell them about the murders that she and the Family were part of and many of the other illegal activities they did. One key highlight that Atkins bragged about was how she responded to Sharon Tate when she pleaded for her unborn baby's life. "Look bitch, I don't care about you. I don't care about your baby. You're going to die, and I don't feel a thing about it."

As with many murder cases that happen, we are left with the killers to tell us who did what. Atkins initially said that she stabbed Tate, but later said that she was lying and that it was Tex Watson who stabbed her. Later, Tex would take responsibility for Tate's murder. Is he just protecting Atkins? Was he trying to look big by saying that he murdered Tate? We know that Atkins couldn't help but brag about anything she did to anyone who might listen.

Both Graham and Howard were so sickened from the stories that Atkins had told them, they both went to the prison authorities and told them. The auto theft charges were soon elevated to murder. Eventually, both Graham and Howard would get the $25,000 reward that Tate's husband, Roman Polanski, offered for information leading to the conviction of her murderers.

Initially, the detectives offered Atkins a plea deal for her giving evidence and testimony to convict Charles Manson. They would, in turn, give her complete immunity. When Vincent Bugliosi took over the case, he immediately said, "No! We don't need to give that gal anything at all! We will do it without her. She needs to pay for her involvement!"

Later, Bugliosi would alter his plan slightly. Instead of complete immunity, he would take the death penalty off the table and only go for a life imprisonment penalty against Atkins in return for her testimony. After Atkins was convicted of first-degree murder, and the jury went into deliberation for the penalty phase of the crime, they returned with a death sentence for Atkins. They refused to go along with Bugliosi based on Atkins' testimony because she seemed to take pleasure in her descriptions of murdering the victims. The jury could do this legally because Atkins had filed a statement claiming that what she had said to Bugliosi was not true. As a result, it also meant that Atkins did not cooperate with the prosecution, and her immunity 'no death penalty' deal was therefore void.

Later, Atkins would say that she backed away from the agreement only because Manson had told her, through messages, that it would be "better for her son" if she didn't testify against any of the Family members.

As Atkins told the jury about holding Tate down when Tex was stabbing her, Atkins seemed to want the jury to say to her what a great job she did, even though Tate put up such an aggressive struggle. She was able to keep her under control so that Tex could "get the job done."

Atkins also described when Tate pleaded for her unborn baby's life, and she replied, "Woman, I have no mercy for you!" Even though it had been softened for the jury, they still found it too horrific.

Atkins claimed that the words she spoke to Tate were not directed at her but rather meant for herself and to help reassure her that she was doing the right thing. Atkins later tried to change her story by claiming she lied to both Howard and Graham when she said that she had tasted Tate's blood.

Atkins was also tried and convicted for the Gary Hinman murder, where she pleaded guilty and testified that she was there, but she had no idea that they were going to kill Hinman. She believed that they were there only to get money. Later in Atkins' book, she said something different. She said she knew what they were going to do, and she took some part in the murder as well.

As with the other Manson girls, she was sent to the newly built death row for women on April 23, 1970. Atkins' sentence was also commuted to life imprisonment after the California Supreme Court decision of 1972, which, in effect, invalidated all previous death sentences given in California before 1972.

In 1974, while Atkins was in her cell, she claimed that her cell door opened, and out of nowhere, a bright light came over her. She believed that it was the light of Jesus, and he told her that God had forgiven her for all of her sins. Atkins would write about these experiences in a book published in 1977, titled *Child of Satan, Child of God*.

After this, she became a model prisoner and participated in several prison programs, even receiving two commendations for her assistance to guards. Atkins was also married twice during her incarceration. One of her marriages, which only lasted a few months, was to Donald Lee Laisure on September 2, 1981. They originally met through letters sent by mail. Laisure was a famed conman, and Atkins was his thirty-sixth wife. He divorced Atkins so that he could marry his thirty-seventh wife.

In the Summer of 1987, Atkins got married again to a Harvard Law

School graduate, James W. Whitehouse, who would also be her legal counsel during her parole hearing until she died. At the time of their marriage, Atkins was thirty-eight and Whitehouse was fifteen years younger at twenty-four.

Laisure filed a lawsuit against the Federal Court, believing that Atkins was a political prisoner, and this was why she had always been denied parole. These proceedings resulted in a three-year ban from Atkins, preventing her from reapplying for parole.

On June 1, 2005, Atkins was given a special parole hearing based on compassion, as she was now ill with brain cancer and was given only six months left to live. She was denied again.

In April 2008, Atkins was permanently hospitalized, and her left leg had to be amputated. The operation ultimately cost taxpayers over $1.15 million for medical expenses and over $300,000 for the cost of full-time guards to protect her in the hospital.

Atkins died while in prison at the Central California Women's Facility in Chowchilla, California, on September 24, 2009. She had lost her parental rights to her son after she was convicted of murder. At that time, none of her relatives would take the boy, so the court changed his name and placed him for adoption. Susan never saw him again.

46

RUTH ANN MOOREHOUSE

Protestant Minister Dean Allen Moorehouse, who was living in Toronto, Canada, with Audrey Sirpless, had Ruth Ann on January 6, 1953. When they were living in Minnesota previously, they had three other children: two girls and a boy. Soon after Rutn Ann was born, the family moved to Campbell, California, where she attended Westmont High School.

In the Spring of 1967, when Dean Moorehouse was driving home from work, he picked up a hitchhiker, who ended up being Charles Manson. The two men got along well, and Moorehouse invited Manson over to his house, now in San Jose, for dinner.

That night, the two of them sang religious tunes, with Charlie playing the piano, and they discussed scripture. Manson spent the night, and the next morning, Moorehouse told Manson that he was always welcome in his house.

Manson began visiting the Moorehouse home a couple of times a week. During one of his visits, the only person home was Ruth Ann, who was fourteen at the time. He invited her to accompany him on a trip to the coast. Manson had gotten a Volkswagen Microbus on an earlier visit from one of the neighbors in exchange for a piano, which had belonged to Dean Moorehouse.

When Dean and Audrey returned home later that day and found out what had happened, they called the police to report their daughter as a runaway. A few days after that, on June 28, 1967, police found them at the beach. Manson was arrested for trying to interfere with the police, and Ruth Ann was brought back home.

Right after this, trouble began between Dean and Audrey. They started fighting over Dean's friendship with Manson. She thought he was weird and a bad influence on their daughter, Ruth Ann. She began to worry about her other children. Eventually, Audrey decided she would leave and move in with her sister.

The following Spring, on May 20, 1968, Ruth Ann married Edward Heuvel Horst, a twenty-three-year-old bus driver in Santa Cruz. Ruth Ann wanted to escape her father, and at fifteen, this was the only way she could think of to do it. Manson had given her this idea so that she could come and live with him. The day after she was married, she left for Los Angeles and the Manson Family.

When Dean heard that Ruth Ann had left her husband after just one day and moved to Los Angeles, he decided to go down there and see what was going on with her. He soon learned that Manson and the girls were all living with Beach Boy drummer Dennis Wilson at his house on Sunset Drive, so he went there looking for his daughter.

Dean parked his car on the road in front of Wilson's house and walked to the front door, and rang the doorbell. Manson joyously answered the door and was thrilled to see Dean. He bent down on his knees and began to kiss Dean's toes. Once Dean entered the house, Manson gave him a hit of LSD. He stayed there all summer, trading a room in Wilson's guesthouse for landscaping the property. When Manson left the Wilson estate and took his Family to Spahn Ranch, Dean followed them there as he was slowly becoming a devout Manson follower. Yet Dean ended up leaving the Family within a year.

When Manson met Terry Melcher, he had some of his girls with him, including Ruth Ann. Melcher liked her, and the two began to have a sexual relationship. Soon after that, Melcher offered her a job at his home, which at that time was the Cielo Drive house, which would later be the scene of the Tate murders. When Ruth Ann showed up to start her first day of work there, Melcher's live-in girlfriend at the time, Candice Bergen, told her to leave and never come back again.

Ruth Ann became a valuable Family member to Manson, not only for her ability to earn a substantial income through panhandling or stealing food, but also because she was skilled with children. She would ultimately become the Family's full-time caretaker for the kids.

When the police first raided Manson and his Family, it was at Spahn Ranch on August 16, 1969. They were looking for stolen vehicles, and Ruth Ann was one of the followers they arrested. The police wrote the search warrant with he wrong date on it, so all charges were dropped, and everyone was released three days later.

Ruth Ann was one of the followers that Manson sent to live at Barker Ranch out in the desert, because all the children went there too. While she was living there, Susan Atkins told her the story about the murders that she was involved in at Cielo Drive. It was said that Ruth Ann was excited about what they had done and wanted to get involved. She just couldn't wait to make her first kill.

When the police did their second raid, this time at the Barker Ranch, Ruth Ann, along with twelve others, including Manson, were arrested. She was released after a couple of weeks and decided to move in with her mother, who was now remarried and living in Minnesota. Out of sight, out of mind, at least that's how it was for Ruth Ann, who stopped hearing from any of the Manson Family for about six months.

Then, out of the blue one day, Squeaky began to contact her. Of course, this wasn't just Squeaky all of a sudden remembering how much she loved Ruth Ann and felt it was time to call her. No, instead, it was the beginning of the Tate and LaBianca murder trials against Charlie and some of the other girls. Squeaky needed to rally the troops, garner as much support as possible for Charlie, and at the same time ensure that the prosecution hadn't turned any of the former Family members.

Eventually, Squeaky talked Ruth Ann into returning to Los Angeles, where she would become part of the regular support squad of Manson girls with an X on their foreheads, standing outside the courthouse and chanting about love. Ruth Ann was slowly being pulled back into a loyal following of Manson again.

Once Squeaky had learned that Bugliosi was getting ex-Family member Barbara Hoyt to testify against Charlie in the Fall of 1970, she planned to stop that from happening. At first, Squeaky thought that she could meet with Hoyt and talk her out of it. But after several phone calls and still being unable to convince Hoyt not to testify, she offered her a free trip to Hawaii.

When Hoyt heard this, she was excited. She had never been there before, so she agreed. Squeaky arranged for Hoyt and Ruth Ann to obtain free plane tickets, as well as credit cards under the aliases of Amy Riley and Jill Morgan. Soon, the two of them were off to Hawaii for a fun time.

The first couple of days went well for them. They stayed at a beautiful hotel, where they had the opportunity to order all the food and drinks they wanted, walk on the beach, and go shopping. It was wonderful.

On day three, September 9th, Ruth Ann came up to Hoyt and told her that she had to leave and return to Los Angeles that day. Hoyt could stay in Hawaii as long as she wanted, and it would still be all free for her.

They took a cab to the airport, and while they were waiting, they each ordered something to eat. When the food came up, Hoyt paid for it while Ruth Ann took it outside. When Hoyt got outside, Ruth Ann gave her the hamburger that she had ordered, and she ate it. The boarding announcement came over the loudspeaker, so Ruth Ann stood up. Before she left to catch the plane, she said, "Could you imagine what it would be like if there were ten tabs of acid in that burger?" She laughed and quickly ran away.

Hoyt got a cab back to the hotel where she had been staying, but when she got out of the cab, she started to feel strange. Hoyt had felt this feeling before when she had been high on acid. Then she realized that Ruth Ann had drugged her. She ran into the lobby bathroom and began to put her fingers down her throat to make herself throw up.

Hoyt seemed to calm down a bit and decided she would go outside for some fresh air. As she slowly walked, the dizziness returned, this time with even greater intensity. So, she walked into the first building she saw, which happened to be the Salvation Army.

A man there asked her if there was anything that he could do for her, as she didn't look very well. Hoyt told the man to call Mr. Bugliosi and then passed out. An ambulance was called, and she was taken to the hospital.

She was now ready to testify against Charlie, who tried to have her killed.

On December 18, 1970, when police made arrests for the attempted murder of Barbara Hoyt, Ruth Ann Moorehouse was one of them. She also had to take the stand on the Tate and LaBianca murder cases in February 1971, and at this time, she was around eight months pregnant.

A month later, Ruth Ann pleaded no contest to conspiracy to dissuade a witness, Barbara Hoyt, and the attempted murder charges were dropped. She was sentenced to serve ninety days in jail, but she failed to appear at the hearing. Instead, she had run away and gone to live with her sister in Carson City, Nevada, where she gave birth to her daughter on April 10, 1971.

Ruth Ann moved to Reno after meeting and marrying Harold Fowler, a construction worker, and they had a daughter together in 1973. Two years later, the FBI found her. She was arrested for fleeing her jail sentence and was now charged again with the attempted murder of Barbara Hoyt. Her lawyer argued that she only ran before because she was nine months pregnant and didn't want to have to give birth to her baby in prison. In November, the judge set her free because of the hard life she had lived.

After her release, Ruth Ann moved back to Minnesota and married for a third time, Dale Warren Geist. The couple had a daughter who only lived until 1981. She was only seven years old at the time. The couple ended their marriage in divorce. She also had plastic surgery to have the scar of the swastika on her forehead removed.

47

SANDRA GOOD

S andra Good was born on February 20, 1944, in San Diego, California. After she finished high school, Sandra spent seven years in various colleges, including California State University in Sacramento, San Francisco State College, and the University of Oregon. Still, she would never complete a degree in any of her studies.

While attending San Francisco State College, she met Joel Pugh, a lab technician. The two began dating and became extremely close in a short time.

In the Spring of 1968, Good met Manson at a party, and his spiritual beliefs captivated her. Before long, she began following Manson everywhere that he went. But Joel didn't like that, nor did he like Manson, whom he thought was a fraud.

In the Summer, when Manson and his Family moved to Spahn Ranch, Good joined them, leaving Joel behind. Manson didn't like Joel either, and he began to tell Good that Joel was an evil man and she should stay away from him. Manson had his eye on the $2,000 trust fund that Good was living off for his use.

Joel became unhappy with losing Good. He quit his job at the university, gave up his apartment, and moved back to Minnesota to live with his parents. One day, out of the blue, Good appeared at Joel's parents' home to see him. Good was pregnant, and she wanted to use Joel's last name for the baby. He didn't like that and told her no.

Good had the baby on September 16th, naming him Ivan Pugh. She used Joel's last name for the baby's birth certificate soon after Joel left the country to travel around the world. Later, it was determined that Ivan's father was Bobby Beausoleil, who was convicted of murdering Gary Hinman.

The week before the Cielo Drive murders happened, Charlie had sent Good and Mary Brunner out to get some clothes and supplies. They were arrested for using stolen credit cards to make purchases and were subsequently taken into custody and then transported to jail.

Good was released on August 12th and went back to the ranch. Both the Tate and LaBianca murders had already happened, but she wasn't aware of who committed them or that any of the Family was involved. Four days later, the police conducted a raid on Spahn Ranch, searching for stolen cars, and Good was one of the followers arrested that day. She was released in three days, as all charges against her had been dismissed. The police had dated the search warrant incorrectly, making it invalid. Therefore, anything they found in the search couldn't be used in court.

On December 1, 1969, Joel Pugh's dead body was found in London, England, in the Hotel Talgart. Both of his wrists and throat had been sliced with a knife. Police took note of writing on his bedroom mirror, but there was nothing mentioned about committing suicide. Detectives would rule his death a drug-induced suicide.

Bugliosi heard about the death of Joel Pugh and became suspicious about his death because one of Manson's crew, Bruce Davis, who was also a Scientologist, was there working for the church at the same time Pugh was found dead. Bugliosi kept a close eye on Davis, but no charges were ever filed against him.

After the trials of the Manson Family members were completed, several of his followers who were on the outside remained faithfully devoted to Manson. They continued to do everything they could to try to get him free by causing trouble wherever they could. Squeaky Fromme was standing in the public area of the California State Capitol grounds while President Gerald Ford, who was on his way to see the

Governor on September 5, 1975. As Ford walked by, Squeaky raised her arm, and in her hand was an M1911 gun. She pointed it directly at his head and pulled the trigger, but she didn't chamber the round, so it never fired.

Just after Squeaky was arrested, Good was interviewed on the A.M. radio station *WWL* in New Orleans, where she told the interviewer that the Ford assassination attempt was just the first of many more to come. Good now claimed that she was part of a group called the International People's Court of Retrobution. She would go on to name different business executives whom she accused of polluting the country. Good would threaten the lives of these executives and their families on air that day.

By December 1975, Good, along with another Family member, Susan Murphy, was arrested and charged with conspiracy to send threatening letters through the mail in Sacramento, California. The pair had collectively threatened the lives of more than one hundred and seventy people. After only three months of trial, they were both found guilty, and Good received a fifteen-year prison sentence on April 13, 1976.

She served a ten-year term of her sentence in West Virginia at the Federal Correctional Institution for Women. One of the conditions of her parole was that she couldn't live in California, so she moved to Vermont and changed her name to Sandra Collins. She remained under this alias until 1999, when someone discovered her true identity.

After Good completed her parole, she moved back to California in Hanford, because it was close to where Manson was in prison, even though she wouldn't ever be allowed to visit him as she was a convicted felon. Good then started *Access Manson*, a website promoting Charlie, which made her feel good because she was doing something to help him out. Even during her last public interview in 2019, Good was still worshipping Charlie and everything he had done.

48

LYNETTE "SQUEAKY " FROMME

Lynette Fromme was born in Santa Monica on October 22, 1948. Her father was an aeronautical engineer, William Millar Fromme. Her mother, Helen, took the time to train Lynette in dance, and she became part of the Westchester Lariats, which toured both the United States and Europe. They ended up becoming famous enough to play the White House and appear on the popular *Lawrence Welk Television Show*.

When Lynette turned fifteen in 1963, her family moved to Redondo Beach. After entering high school there, she started to experiment with drugs and drinking alcohol, and soon she began skipping school, and her grades went down fast. She graduated in 1966 and moved away from home, staying with some of her friends.

Lynette's father had her move home and attend college, a decision that lasted only about two months. He kicked her out of the house because she was constantly screaming and swearing at her parents and refused to do anything they asked her to do. Lynette dropped out of college and moved to Venice Beach, where she would spend her nights.

Often during the day, she sat on road curbs or at bus stops to pass the time. One day, Charles Manson got off the bus and he noticed her sitting alone and walked up to her and asked, "Your parents threw you out, didn't they?" He then turned around and began walking away from her. Lynette grabbed her bags and followed him. This chance encounter was in 1967, just after he was released from Terminal Island Prison. Lynette would become his second long-term follower.

Manson was living with Mary Brunner in her apartment at the time, and when Manson brought Lynette back to their apartment, Mary was at work. The two ended up having sex, and when Mary returned home, she was angry at Charlie. Eventually, he persuaded Mary to let Lynette live with them. When the Manson Family moved to Spahn Ranch, the owner, George Spahn, gave Lynette the nickname "Squeaky," which stuck from then on.

After the arrests of Manson and his followers in 1969, those involved with the Tate–LaBianca murders, Squeaky remained one of Charlie's leading outside actors. She constantly received messages from him while he was in jail and passed them on to the intended recipient. She was also the one who would locate Family members who had left and moved away, ensuring they weren't involved in the trial and would not cause any further problems for Charlie. Squeaky was also one of Manson's followers who would camp outside of the courthouse with her head shaved and an X marked onto her forehead. She preached to anyone who walked by and stopped to listen.

Squeaky was never involved in any of the murders, and so she was never arrested ot charged for them. Later, she was accused of attempting to prevent witnesses from testifying in court, and when she was subpoenaed to testify, she refused to do so. As a result, the judge charged her with contempt of court. On both occasions, she would only receive sentences of less than a year in prison.

After the trials of Manson were over in 1973, Squeaky began to write a book on the Manson Family, which also included some of her photos and drawings about the murders that happened, which were quite incriminating, so she decided that she wasn't going to have it published. This book was later published in 2018 under the title *Reflexion*.

In the early morning of September 5, 1975, Squeaky went to the Capitol Building in Sacramento because she heard that President Gerald Ford was going to be there to visit Governor Jerry Brown. As Ford walked by, Squeaky, who was standing among the crowd of people on the grounds, pulled out her Colt M1911 .45 caliber semi-automatic pistol and aimed it at his head. Standing only a couple of feet away, she pulled the trigger. But nothing happened. Though she had four bullets loaded in the magazine, there were no rounds in the chamber, so the gun didn't fire. The Secret Service immediately grabbed her and threw her to the ground.

Squeaky was arrested, tried, and convicted of attempting to assassinate the president, and she was sentenced to a life term in prison. While in prison, she was constantly in fights with other inmates.

On December 28, 1987, Squeaky escaped from prison to meet Manson but was captured two days later.

Squeaky became eligible for parole in 2005, at which time she waived her right to a hearing. She was eventually approved for parole in 2008, but remained in prison because she had to serve out her sentence for her attempt to escape back in 1987.

Squeaky was finally released from prison on August 14, 2009, and she moved to Mercy, New York, with her boyfriend, Robert Valdner.

REFERENCES

1. The Times | UK News, World News and Opinion
2. "Manson Family Members and Associates". *Helter Skelter*. 0-553-14683-1
3. "Ex-Manson follower Susan Atkins dies". *www.cnn.com*
4. Fox, Margalit (September 26, 2009). "Susan Atkins, Manson Follower, Dies at 61". *The New York Times*.
5. *Child of Satan, Child of God: Her Own Story, Susan Atkins*. Menelorelin Dorenay's Publishing. ISBN 978-0-9831364-8-4.
6. Transcript of Atkins's 2005 parole hearing.
7. Johnston, Lori (July 27, 2019). *Gary Hinman: The Forgotten Manson Family Victim*. Medium. New York City: A Medium Corporation.
8. "Charles Manson, leader of murderous cult, dead at 83". *CBS News*. New York City: CBS Corporation. November 20, 2017
9. "Transcript of Atkins's Grand Jury Testimony" Archived October 22, 2012, at the Wayback Machine, *Manson Family Today*.
10. Grand Jury Proceedings: Susan Denise Atkins Archived October 22, 2012, at the Wayback Machine, December 15, 1969, *mansonfamilytoday.info*.
11. CDCR, "History of capital punishment in California."
12. "Susan Atkins: I'm a Political Prisoner". *TalkLeft*. May 31, 2003
13. "Judge Dismisses 'Political Prisoner' Suit By Manson Associate". *Legal Reader*. November 30, 2003.
14. "Terminally ill Manson follower Susan Atkins dies in prison". *TheGuardian.com*.
15. "Manson's family member Patricia Krenwinkel recommended for parole". *The Guardian*. Reuters.
16. Meares, Hadley (October 22, 2014). "The Story of the Abandoned Movie Ranch Where the Manson Family Launched Helter Skelter".
17. Vronsky, Peter (2007). *Female Serial Killers: How and Why Women Become Monsters*. New York City: Penguin Publishing. p. 420. ISBN 978-0-425-21390-2.
18. "Parole Hearing: Patricia Krenwinkel" (Transcript). *cielodrive.com*. Corona, California. December 29, 2016.
19. "Manson follower Patricia Krenwinkel denied parole". CNN. January 21, 2011. Archived from the original on January 22, 2011
20. "Patricia Krenwinkel Granted Parole". *cielodrive.com*. May 26, 2022.
21. "CDCR Inmate Information – Krenwinkel, Patricia"
22. Juzwiak, Rich (August 7, 2014). "Manson Girl, Patricia Krenwinkel, Gives Prison Interview". *Gawker*.

23. "Mother Accepts Blame Over Linda". United Press International. August 24, 1970.

24. Watson, Charles (1978). "You Were Only Waiting for This Moment". *Will You Die for Me?* ISBN 0-8007-0912-8.

25. Watkins, Paul; Soledad, Guillermo (1979). *My Life with Charles Manson*. Bantam Books. ISBN 0-553-12788-8.

26. King, Greg (2016). *Sharon Tate and the Manson Murders*. Open Road Media. ISBN 9781504041720.

27. "Tacoma-Pierce County death notices for January 2023". *The News Tribune*. February 19, 2023

28. Sailor, Craig. "Manson Family cult member who provided crucial murder trial testimony dies in Tacoma". *TheNewsTribune.com*.

29. Transcript of Subsequent Parole Consideration Hearing. State of California. Hearing September 6, 2017. Transcribed September 16, 2017

30. Weber, Christopher (July 11, 2023). "Leslie Van Houten, follower of cult leader Charles Manson, released from California prison". *AP News*.

31. Guinn, Jef:. *Manson: The Life and Times of Charles Manson*

32. Interview with Leslie Van Houten". *CNN. Larry King Weekend*. February 1, 2009.

33. Linder, Douglas O. (2014). "The Influence of the Beatles on Charles Manson". Famous Trials. University of Missouri–Kansas City School of Law.

34. Melnick, Jeffrey: "Keeping Faith With the Manson Women," *The New Yorker*, August 1, 2018

35. Karlene Faith, *The Long Prison Journey of Leslie Van Houten: Life Beyond the Cult* (Northeastern University Press, 2001

36. California governor again rejects parole for Manson follower Van Houten". *UPI*. June 4, 2019.

37. "Manson follower Leslie Van Houten could be freed after court overrules Newsom". *Los Angeles Times*. May 30, 2023

38. Waters, John (August 3, 2009). "Leslie Van Houten: A Friendship". *Huffington Post*.

39. "Steve Grogan - Clem", *TateMurders.com.com*

40. "Steve Dennis Grogan profile", *cielodrive.com*

41. "Manson Family – Special Report Part 4 Steve Grogan Paroled". *Youtube.com*. July 23, 2006.

42. Elias, Thomas D. (April 3, 2019). *After death penalty reprieves, multiple Manson's confront Newsom*. Antelope Valley Press

43. "Charles Manson follower Leslie van Houten released from prison a half-century after grisly killings". *Associated Press*. July 11, 2023.

44. "Charles Manson's 'right-hand man' recommended for parole". *Los Angeles Times*. October 5, 2012

45. George, Edward; Matera, Dary (July 16, 1999). *Taming the Beast: Charles Manson's Life Behind Bars*. Macmillan. ISBN 9780312209704.

46. Keith Rovere (April 2023). "S1E22 - Bruce Davis: Scientology, Murder, and Manson". Spotify (Podcast). *The Lighter Side of Serial Killers with Keith Rovere*

47. Sanders, Ed (April 11, 2023). *The Family*. Hachette Books. ISBN 9780306834226.

48. "CDCR Today: Parole Granted for Former Manson Family Member Bruce Davis". Archived from the original

49. "Parole Hearing: Bruce Davis 2014" *cielodrive.com*

50. "Parole Hearing: Bruce Davis 2019" *cielodrive.com*

51. Governor Denies Parole for Former Manson Family Follower". June 18, 2021.

52. (CDCR), California Department of Corrections and Rehabilitation. "State of California Inmate Locator". *inmatelocator.cdcr.ca.gov*

53. Linder, Doug (2014). "The Charles Manson (Tate–LaBianca Murder) Trial". University of Missouri–Kansas City School of Law

54. "Where Are the Manson Family Members Now? Inside Their Lives Over 50 Years After Their Killing Spree". *People.com*.

55. Watson, Charles. "FAQs". Abounding Love Ministries.

56. Neiswender, Mary (June 13, 1971). "Tex Watson, Honor Student, Athlete: Accused Mass Killer's Profile"

57. DeLong, William (February 19, 2024). "Methodist To Murderer: How A Young Texas Boy Became Charles Manson's Right-Hand Man". *All That's Interesting*

58. "Who Is Manson Family Member Charles 'Tex' Watson?". *Oxygen*. July 24, 2019.

59. Watson, Charles (2019). *Cease to Exist* (1 ed.). Santa Monica: 12AX7 Press. pp. 69–98. ISBN 9781083079879.

60. Waxman, Olivia B. (July 26, 2019). "Why Did the Manson Family Kill Sharon Tate? Here's the Story Charles Manson Told the Last Man Who Interviewed Him". *Time magazine*. Archived

61. Watson Convicted Of Tate Murders; Faces Sanity Trial" *The New York Times*. October 13, 1971.

62. "Charles 'Tex' Watson 1978 Parole Hearing Transcript". *www.cielodrive.com*

63. Watson, Charles. "Will You Die For Me?". Abounding Love Ministries. p. 96. Archived from the original on April 5, 2007.

64. Watson Sentenced to Death For a Part in Tate Murders". *The New York Times*. October 22, 1971. ISSN 0362-4331

65. Childress, Deirdre M. (April 30, 1984). "Slain actress Sharon Tate's mother – with tears rolling..." *upi.com*

66. "Abounding Love Podcast with Former 'Tex Watson". Official page for the *Abounding Love Podcast* (Podbean). Podbean

67. Martinez, Michael; Cary, Michael (June 13, 2012). "Judge declines to reverse order giving Manson follower tapes to police". *CNN*

68. O'Neill, Tom (2019). *Chaos: Charles Manson, the CIA, and the Secret History of the Sixties*. Little, Brown. ISBN 978-0-316-47757-4.

69. Hamilton, Matt (October 16, 2021). "Manson follower Tex Watson denied parole for Tate/La Bianca killings". The Mercury News. Archived from the original on October 19, 2021

70. Anderson, Lessley. "Lucifer, Arisen". *SF Weekly*.

71. "Informal Q & A, 2017". Bobby BeauSoleil Reference Archive. February 2017

72. Breznikar, Klemen: (July 27, 2014). "Bobby BeauSoleil interview (The Orkustra)". *It's Psychedelic Baby! Magazine*.

73. "Bobby Beausoleil". *Biography.com*. A&E Television Networks.

74. Sederstrom, Jill: (September 18, 2018). "The Story Behind The Murder That Set Off The Manson Family". *Oxygen*.

75. Yuko, Elizabeth: (January 4, 2019). "Manson Family Associate Bobby Beausoleil Recommended for Parole". *Rolling Stone*.

76. "Manson's Pal Found Guilty Of Murder," *The San Bernardino Sun-Telegram*, San Bernardino, California, Sunday, April 19, 1970,

77. Sobel, Barbara: (April 30, 2019). "Bobby Beausoleil, Manson Family Member, Parole Reversed by Governor". *Guardian Liberty Voice*.

78. Levenda, Peter: (June 1, 2011). *Sinister Forces—The Manson Secret: A Grimoire of American Political Witchcraft*. Trine Day. ISBN 978-0984185832.

79. "The Farcical Capote Interview". Bobby BeauSoleil Reference Archive. December 2016.

80. Keefe, Patrick Radden: (March 22, 2013). "Truman Capote's Co-Conspirators". *Newyorker.com*

81. "Gary Hinman | Charles Manson Family and Sharon Tate-Labianca Murders". *cielodrive.com*

82. Gary Hinman's Family Reacts to Charles Manson's Death. *people.com*

83. What were the events that led up to the Tate murders?. *britannica.com*

84. Bobby Beausoleil and the Last Manson Mystery. *rollingstone.com*

85. Peterson, Bettelou: (August 14, 1969). "Jay Sebring, Man with a Successful Idea". *Detroit Free Press*.

86. White, Carrie: (2011). *Upper Cut: Highlights of My Hollywood Life*. Atria Books ISBN 9781439199091.

87. Tannen, Mary: (August 18, 2002). "Message In A Shampoo Bottle". *The New York Times*.

88. Would you pay $50 for a haircut?". *Star-News*. August 3, 1963

89. "Manson Victim's Friend Posits Alternative Motive: "I Never Bought into the Race War Theory"". *The Hollywood Reporter*.

90. Jay Sebring Documentary Lands at Shout! Studios (Exclusive). *The Hollywood Reporter*. February 26, 2020.

91. "Jay Sebring Is the Godfather of Men's Hairstyling. So Why Haven't You Heard of Him?". *Esquire*. October 1, 2020.

92. "Remembering Jay Sebring, Hollywood's First Celebrity Hairstylist". *Vogue.* September 22, 2020

93. Tate–LaBianca murders - Wikipedia

94. "Frykowski, Wojciech | friend of Polanski". *britannica.com*

95. "Wojciech Frykowski - Helter Skelter". *charlesmanson.com*

96. Abigail Folger | Ultimate Pop Culture Wiki | Fandom

97. Romano, Aja: (August 7, 2019). "The Manson Family murders, and their complicated legacy, explained".

98. "Sharon Tate Autopsy"

99. Bishari, Nuala Sawyer: (July 9, 2018) [July 9, 2018]. "Yesterday's Crimes: The Helter Skelter Heiress". *SFWeekly*

100. California Abolishes Death Penalty". *The Journal* (Ogdensburg, N.Y.). AP. February 18, 1972.

101. Woo, Elaine: (September 26, 2009). "Susan Atkins dies at 61; imprisoned Charles Manson follower". *Los Angeles Times.*

102. "Donald 'Shorty' Shea". *www.cielodrive.com*

103. Montaldo, Charles: (3 July 2019). "Manson Family Murder Victim Donald 'Shorty' Shea's Revenge". *ThoughtCo.*

104. Steven Parent | Tate murders victim | Britannica. *britannica.com*

105. Petruzzello, Melissa. "Sharon Tate". *Encyclopedia Britannica.*

106. Sandford, C. (2009). *Polanski: A Biography.* St. Martin's Press. ISBN 978-0-230-61176-

107. Paul Tate, 82; Investigated Murder of Daughter Sharon Tate". *Los Angeles Times.* May 24, 2005

108. Kraemer, Kristin (July 26, 2019). "A cult murdered this Richland beauty queen. Sharon Tate is featured in a new Hollywood film". *Tri-City Herald*

109. Sanders, Ed (2002). *The Family.* Thunder's Mouth Press. ISBN 1-56025-396-7.

110. Hughes, David (August 14, 2019). "Sharon Tate murder: the true story of the actress portrayed in Once Upon a Time in Hollywood, killed by the Manson Family". *The i Paper.*

111. Dunne, Dominick (1999). *The Way We Lived Then: Recollections of a Well-Known Name Dropper.* Crown Publishers. ISBN 0-609-60388-4.

112. "The Story of the Tate Family". Tate Family Legacy website

113. How a Music Producer Was Tied to Charles Manson — and Possibly Evaded His Murder". *Oxygen.* November 15, 2024

114. Vulliamy, Ed; Vulliamy, By Ed (March 7, 1999). "Manson set to defend himself, 30 years on". *The Guardian.* ISSN 0261-3077.

115. "Long Before Little Charlie Became the Face of Evil". *The New York Times. August 7, 2013*

116. *Lansing, H. Allegra (July 11, 2019).* "Son of Man: The Early Life of Charles Manson". *Medium. Boston, Massachusetts: A Medium Corporation*

117. Maslin, Janet (August 6, 2013). "Long Before Little Charlie Became the Face of Evil". *The New York Times.* New York City

118. Charles Manson – Diane Sawyer Documentary.

119. Smith, David E; Luce, John (1971). *Love Needs Care: A History of San Francisco's Haight-Ashbury Free Medical Clinic and Its Pioneer Role Treating Drug-abuse Problems*. Boston, Little, Brown.

120. Melnick, Jeffrey Paul: (2018). *Creepy Crawling: Charles Manson and the Many Lives of America's Most Infamous Family*. Arcade. ISBN 978 1628728934.

121. Emmons, Nuel (1988). *Manson in His Own Words*. Grove Press. ISBN 0-8021-3024-0.

122. Bitette, Nicole (August 31, 2016). "Beach Boy Mike Love alleges bandmate watched Charles Manson carry out murder". *New York Daily News*.

123. Gill, Lauren (November 16, 2017). "Remember, Charles Manson Was a White Supremacist". *Newsweek*

124. Thompson, Desire (November 20, 2017). "Charles Manson & His Obsession with Black People". *Vibe*. New York City

125. Whitehead, John W. (August 3, 2010). "Helter Skelter: Racism and Murder". *HuffPost*.

126. Beckerman, Jim (August 9, 2019). "Charles Manson: 50 years later, murders have a racist link to recent mass-killings". *The Record*.

127. Waxman, Olivia B. (July 26, 2019). "Why Did the Manson Family Kill Sharon Tate? Here's the Story Charles Manson Told the Last Man Who Interviewed Him". *Time magazine*.

128. Did The Manson Family Have Other Victims?". *CBS News*. March 16, 2008.

129. Romano, Aja (August 7, 2019). "The Manson Family murders, and their complicated legacy, explained". *Vox*.

130. Pelisek, Christine (February 22, 2019). "Did Charles Manson Have 4 More Victims? 'There's an Answer There Somewhere,' Says LAPD Detective". *People*.

131. "Would-Be Assassin 'Squeaky' Fromme Released from Prison". *ABC. August 14, 2009.*

132. "Manson moved to a tougher prison after a drug charge". *Sun Journal*. Lewiston, Maine. AP. August 22, 1997

133. Hedegaard, Erik (November 21, 2013). "Charles Manson Today: The Final Confessions of a Psychopath". *Rolling Stone*.

134. "Charles Manson Dead at 83". *Rolling Stone*.

135. Dillon, Nancy (November 24, 2017). "Battle erupts over control of Charles Manson's remains, estate". *New York Daily News*.

136. Feldman, Kate (November 28, 2017). "Charles Manson's secret prison pen pal Michael Channels wants murderer's body". *New York Daily News*.

137. "Charles Manson: The Incredible Story of the Most Dangerous Man Alive". *Rolling Stone*. August 8, 2017

138. Lusher, Adam (November 20, 2017). "Charles Manson: Neo-Nazis hail

serial killer a visionary and try to resurrect fascist movement created on his orders". *The Independent*. London, United Kingdom.

139. Dennis Wilson interview Archived December 15, 2007, at the Wayback Machine *Circus Magazine*, October 26, 1976.

140. "Charles Manson Issues Album Under Creative Commons". *PC Magazine*. July 10, 2009.

141. "Watch This Chilling Manson Documentary from 1973". *vice.com*. November 20, 2017

142. Stebbins, Jon (2000). *Dennis Wilson: The Real Beach Boy*. ECW Press. ISBN 978-1-55022-404-7.

143. Bugliosi, Vincent; Gentry, Curt (1974). *Helter Skelter: The True Story of the Manson Murders* (1992 ed.). Norton. ISBN 0-09-997500-9.

144. Udo, Tommy (2002). *Charles Manson: Music, Mayhem, Murder*. Sanctuary Records. ISBN 1-86074-388-9.

145. LeBlanc, Jerry; Davis, Ivor (1971). *5 to Die*. Holloway House Publishing. ISBN 0-87067-306-8.

146. Gilmore, John (2000). *Manson: The Unholy Trail of Charlie and the Family*. Amok Books. ISBN 1-878923-13-7.

147. 'Then It All Came Down': Truman Capote Interviews Bobby Beausoleil. San Quentin, 1973. | Truman Capote

148. "Obituaries: Terry Melcher". *The Daily Telegraph*. November 23, 2004.

149. Oliver, Myrna (November 22, 2004). "Terry Melcher helped create the surf music sound". *Los Angeles Times*.

150. Rogan, Johnny (1998). *The Byrds: Timeless Flight Revisited* (2nd ed.). Rogan House. ISBN 978-0-9529-5401-9.

151. Cozzen, R. Duane (August 11, 2015). "BRUCE & TERRY, Bruce Johnston & Terry Melcher, Singles (45's)". *Surf & Hot Rod Music of the '60s* ISBN 978-1-3294-0033-7.

152. Paul Werner, *Polański. Biografia*, Poznań: Rebis, 2013

153. Berendt, Joanna (6 December 2016). "Roman Polanski Extradition Request Rejected by Poland's Supreme Court". *The New York Times*.

154. *Polanski, Roman; Bernstein, Catherine (5 May 2006). "Mémoires de la Shoah: témoignage de Roman Polanski, enfant de déporté, enfant caché, né le 18 août 1933"*

155. "Sharon Tate's family bares 'Restless Souls'" Archived 25 June 2012 at the Wayback Machine, *USA Today*.

156. Bradshaw, Peter (15 July 2005). "Profile: Roman Polanski, The Guardian, Guardian Unlimited". *The Guardian*. London

157. "Roman Polanski, UXL Newsmakers, Find Articles at BNET.com". *Findarticles.com*

158. "Biography". Movies.*yahoo.com* 2009

159. Cronin, Paul (2005). *Roman Polanski: Interviews*. University Press of Mississippi. ISBN 1578067995.

160. Polański, Roman (1984). Roman. Morrow (ibidem). p. 73. ISBN 0688026214.

161. Glazer, Mitchell. *Rolling Stone Magazine*, 2 April 1981

162. "Polanski Seeks Sex Case Dismissal – 3 December 2008". *Thesmokinggun.com*.

163. Ain-Krupa, Julia, Roman Polanski: A Life in Exile, ABC Clio, Santa Barbara, California, 2010

164. Sandford, Christopher, *Polanski: A Biography*, 2008, Palgrave Macmillan

165. Romney, Jonathan (5 October 2008). "Roman Polanski: The truth about his notorious sex crime". *The Independent*. London

166. "Timeline of Director Roman Polanski's Life". *The Washington Post*. Associated Press. 28 September 2009.

167. "Roman Polanski First Interview After Arrest – Diane Sawyer – video Dailymotion"

168. "Alleged victim defends Polanski and criticises 'opportunistic' protesters". *Irish News*. 8 April 2020

169. "Polanski charged with rape". *Eugene Register-Guard*. (Oregon). UPI. 13 March 1977.

170. "Polanski Pleads Not Guilty in Drug-Rape Case". *Los Angeles Times*. 16 April 1977

171. Romney, Jonathan (5 October 2008). "Roman Polanski: The truth about his notorious sex crime". *The Independent*. UK

172. "Polanski ducks out on court". *Spokesman-Review*. (Spokane, Washington). Associated Press. 2 February 1978

173. "Polanski in Paris; extradition unlikely". *Eugene Register-Guard*. Associated Press. 2 February 1978

174. "Polanski Victim Blames Media" Archived 4 March 2016 at the Wayback Machine *ABC News* video, 10 March 2011

175. Smith, Dave (January 26, 1971). "Mother Tells Life of Manson as Boy". *Los Angeles Times*.

176. Lansing, H. Allegra (July 11, 2019). "Son of Man: The Early Life of Charles Manson". *Medium*. Boston, Massachusetts: A Medium Corporation

177. Maslin, Janet (August 6, 2013). "Long Before Little Charlie Became the Face of Evil". *The New York Times*. New York City.

178. Smith, David E; Luce, John (1971). *Love Needs Care: A History of San Francisco's Haight-Ashbury Free Medical Clinic and Its Pioneer Role Treating Drug-abuse Problems*. Boston, Little, Brown

179. Roberts, Steven V. (December 7, 1969). "Charlie Manson, Nomadic Guru, Flirted With Crime in a Turbulent Childhood". *The New York Times*. p. 84.

180. Nolan, Tom (November 11, 1971). "Beach Boys: A California Saga, Part II". *Rolling Stone*.

181. Atkins, Susan, with Bob Slosser. *Child of Satan, Child of God*. Bantam, 1978.

182. Bishop, George. *Witness to Evil: The Uncensored Inside Story of Charles Manson and His Murderous Family*. Dell, 1972.

183. Bravin, Jess. *Squeaky: The Life and Times of Lynette Alice Fromme*. Buzz Books/St. Martin's, 1997.

184. *How to Win Friends and Influence People*. Simon & Schuster, 1936.

185. *The White Album: Essays*. Farrar, Straus & Giroux, 1979.

186. Emmons, Nuel (as told to by Charles Manson). *Manson in His Own Words: The Shocking Confessions of "The Most Dangerous Man Alive."* Grove, 1986.

187. Hotchner, A. E. *Doris Day: Her Own Story*. Bantam, 1976.

188. Livsey, Clara. *The Manson Women: A "Family" Portrait*. Richard Marek, 1980.

189. Perry, Charles. *The Haight-Ashbury: A History*. Wenner Books, 2005. (Originally published in 1984.)

190. Rudd, Mark. *Underground: My Life with SDS and the Weathermen*. William Morrow, 2009.

191. Selvin, Joel. *Summer of Love: The Inside Story of LSD, Rock & Roll, Free Love and High Times in the Wild West*.

192. Watson, Tex, as told to Chaplain Ray. *Will You Die for Me? The Man Who Killed for Charles Manson Tells His Own Story*. Fleming H. Revell, 1978.

193. Talbot, David. *Season of the Witch: Enchantment, Terror, and Deliverance in the City of Love*. Free Press, 2012.

194. Wilson, Brian. *Wouldn't It Be Nice: My Own Story*. HarperCollins, 1991.

195. Federal Bureau of Investigation Charles Manson File (obtained through Freedom of Information Act)

196. *www.aboundinglove.org*. Official site of Charles "Tex" Watson's ministry.

197. *www.susanatkins.org*. Maintained by Susan Atkins's husband, James Whitehouse.

198. "The Manson Murders at 40: 'Helter Skelter' Author Vincent Bugliosi Looks Back." *Newsweek*, August 1, 2009

ABOUT THE AUTHOR

Alan R Warren is a Bestselling Author, Producer, and host of the popular NBC Radioshow *House of Mystery* and *Inside Writing*, both heard on the 106.5 F.M. Los Angeles/102.3 F.M. Riverside/ 1050 A.M. Palm Springs/ 540 A.M. KYAH Salt Lake City/ 1150 A.M. KKNW Seattle/Tacoma and Phoenix.

His bestselling true crime books in Canada include *Beyond Suspicion: The True Story of Colonel Russell Williams*, which will be featured on CNN's *Lies, Crimes, & Videos* (Season 4), and *Murder Times Six: The True Story of the Wells Gray Park Murders*. In America, his bestsellers include *The Killing Game: Serial Killer Rodney Alcala*, which was featured on several television shows such as *Very Scary People with Donny Walberg*, Oxygen's *Mark of a Killer*, Reelz' *Killer Trophies*, and soon to be included in a four-part Sundance Channel documentary called *Death's Date*. His bestseller, *Doomsday Cults: The Devil's Hostages*, was featured on Vice's *Dark Side of the '90s*.

His latest series, *Killer Queens*, is a six-part book series covering murders that affect the Gay Community. So far, it includes Book 1 - Leopold & Loeb, Book 2 - Butcher of Hanover: Fritz Haarmann, Book 3 - Grindr Serial Killer: Stephen Port, and Book 4 - Bruce McArthur: Toronto Gay Killer.

ALSO BY ALAN R. WARREN

VOLUME 8 of The House of Mystery Interview Series: CHARLES MANSON

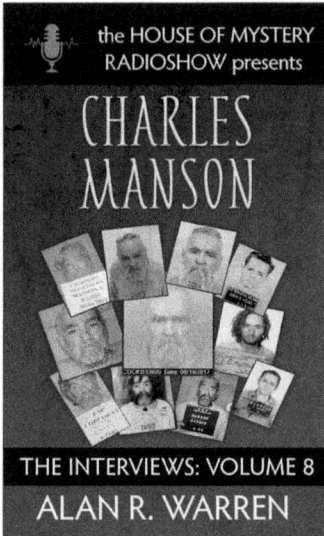

The *House of Mystery Radio Show* has been on the air for ten years, starting as a way to interview guests knowledgeable in many of the world's mysteries involving crime, science, religion, history, paranormal, conspiracies, etc. The *House of Mystery Interview Series* is a curated collection of interviews from the show. Each volume focuses on one of the mysteries, providing the background and reproducing the main points discussed in the interviews. There will be no committed answer at the end, as the Interviews series does not attempt to solve the case. Instead, it provides the most compelling aspects of each theory held by different experts. This series is an excellent reference for researchers and a good overview for those unfamiliar with the case. Online links to the actual interviews are included.

In *Charles Manson: The Interviews*, presented by the *House of Mystery Radio Show*, true crime author and show host Alan R. Warren delves deep into the twisted legacy of Charles Manson and his murderous cult—not from the headlines or familiar facts, but through the minds of those who've studied him most closely.

In this exciting collection, Warren talks with some of the most respected authors and investigative journalists who have written extensively about Manson and his devoted followers. These candid, often chilling interviews peel back the layers of myth and media frenzy to expose the psychological, cultural, and criminal underpinnings of one of the most infamous cases in American history.

The interviews with first-hand researchers of the Manson case offer the stories behind their books, unique insights into Manson's manipulative charisma, the vulnerability of his followers, and the lingering impact of the Tate-LaBianca murders on America.

Charles Manson: The Interviews presents an essential exploration of the minds that have tried to make sense of madness. It's not just a book about Charles Manson—it's a discussion about how we understand evil.

PEN AND BLOOD: Conversations with Killers

Step into the darkest corners of the human mind with bestselling true crime author Alan R. Warren as he uncovers chilling words from some of the most notorious killers of our time. *Pen and Blood* offers a rare and unflinching look at the thoughts, motivations, and disturbing realities behind crimes that shocked the world.

Through exclusive letters and interviews, Warren brings readers face-to-face with convicted UK murderers Stephen Port and Ian Brady, both responsible for the brutal sexual assault and murder of young victims. The book also features in-depth interviews with Canadian child killer David Shearing, offering a deeply unsettling glimpse into the psyche of a man who annihilated three generations of an entire family.

These are not just crime stories or opinions, but direct communications from those who committed the unthinkable. Warren provides critical context to these firsthand accounts, exploring the psychology, manipulation, and hidden patterns behind their monstrous acts.

Pen and Blood is not for the faint of heart. It is a sobering, investigative journey into the minds of predators—and a stark reminder of evil that can hide in plain sight.

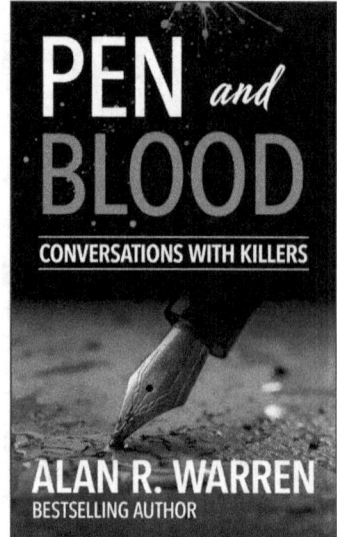

MURDER TIMES SIX: The True Story of The Wells Park Murders

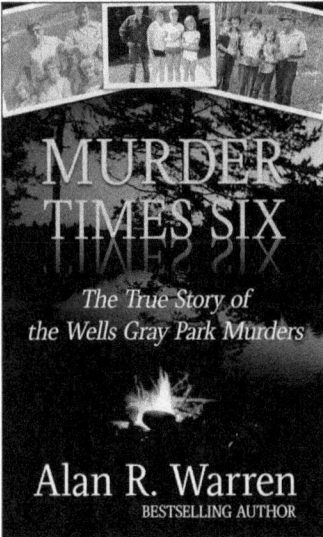

"The author even had me (who conducted the interview) on the edge of my seat as I was turning the pages as "the Detective" was trying to unearth the unspeakable truth."

— *SGT. MIKE EASTHAM R.C.M.P.*

It was a crime unlike anything seen in British Columbia. The horror of the "Wells Gray Murders" almost forty years ago transcends decades.

On August 2, 1982, three generations of a family set out on a camping trip – Bob and Jackie Johnson, their two daughters, Janet, 13, and Karen, 11, and Jackie's parents, George and Edith Bentley. A month later, the Johnson family car was found off a mountainside logging road near Wells Gray Park, completely burned out. In the back seat were the incinerated remains of four adults, and in the trunk were the two girls.

But this was not just your average mass murder. It was much worse. Over time, some brutal details were revealed; however, most are still only known to the murderer, David Ennis (formerly Shearing). His crimes had far-reaching impacts on the family, community, and country. It still does today. Every time Shearing attempts freedom from the parole board, the grief is triggered as everyone is forced to relive the horrors once again.

Murder Times Six shines a spotlight on the crime that captured the attention of a nation, recounts the narrative of a complex police investigation, and discusses whether a convicted mass murderer should ever be allowed to leave the confines of an institution. Most importantly, it tells the story of one family forever changed.

THE KILLING GAME: The True Story of Rodney Alcala

Beginning in 1968 and continuing into the 1970s, a predator stalked California and New York, torturing, raping, and murdering young girls and women. But who was the monster behind these tragedies?

Eventually, a suspect emerged, but he didn't look like a monster. Indeed, Rodney Alcala was a handsome, charming photographer who'd once studied film at New York University under director Roman Polanski. With his wit, easy self-confidence, and humor, he'd even been selected as the "winner" on the popular television show "The Dating Game." But his real game was much more sinister.

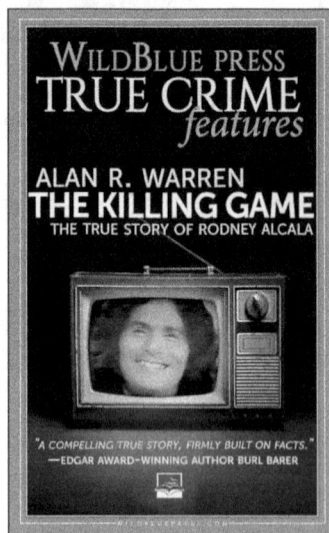

WILDBLUE PRESS
TRUE CRIME
features
ALAN R. WARREN
THE KILLING GAME
THE TRUE STORY OF RODNEY ALCALA

"A COMPELLING TRUE STORY, FIRMLY BUILT ON FACTS."
—EDGAR AWARD-WINNING AUTHOR BURL BARER

In 2010, Alcala was convicted of murdering five women in California during the 1970s; then, in 2013, as he waited on Death Row, he confessed to the murder of two more in New York. Yet, that might not be the end of the nightmare he caused. At his arrest, police found his "portfolio" with thousands of nude and erotic photographs of women and boys, who may also be among his victims.

In *The Killing Game*, bestselling true crime author and radio show host Alan R. Warren reveals the shocking details of Alcala's brutal crimes, as well as the trials and appeals that stretched on for decades and may still not be over.

The "compelling true story" of "The Dating Game Killer" by the radio host and bestselling author of Drinks, Dinner & Death.

— BURL BARER, EDGAR AWARD-WINNING
AUTHOR

BEYOND SUSPICION: Russell Williams–A Canadian Serial Killer

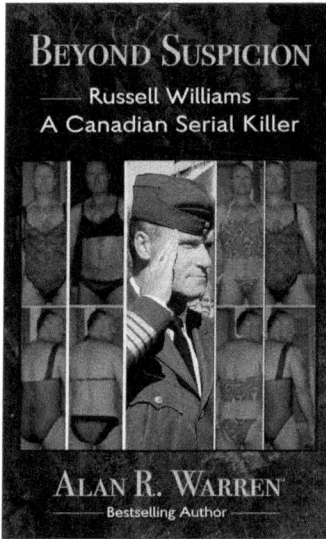

Young girl's panties started to go missing; sexual assaults began to occur, and then female bodies were found! Soon, this quiet town of Tweed, Ontario, panicked. What's even more shocking was when an upstanding resident stood accused of the assaults. This was not just any man but a pillar of the community, a decorated military pilot who had flown Canadian Forces VIP aircraft for dignitaries such as the Queen of England, Prince Philip, the Governor-General, and the Prime Minister of Canada.

This is the story of serial killer Russell Williams, the elite pilot of Canada's Air Force One, and the innocent victims he murdered. Unlike other serial killers, Williams seemed very unaffected by his crimes and leading two different lives.

Alan R. Warren describes the secret life, including the abductions, rape, and murders that were unleashed on an unsuspecting community. Included are letters written to the victims by Williams and descriptions of the assaults and rapes as seen on videos and photos taken by Williams during the attacks.

This updated version also contains the full brilliant police interrogation of Williams and his confession. Also, the twisted way Williams planned to pin his crimes on his unsuspecting neighbor.

KILLER QUEEN SERIES BOX SET (Books 1 - 4)

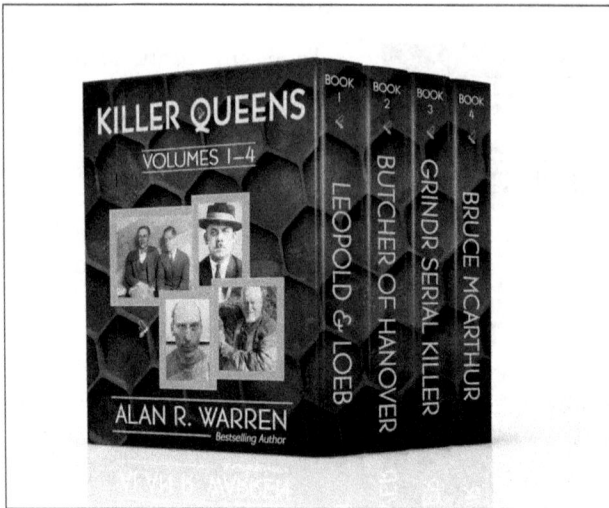

The Killer Queens is a new series of historical fiction books based on true stories. Sources, such as police reports and newspaper articles, are examined to gather as many facts as possible surrounding each case. As with any work of fiction, some creative additions are made when telling these stories, usually within the conversations between the personalities involved. The various sources are the basis of these conversations and, hopefully, make them come alive for the readers to help understand what was meant by those words.

Book 1 of the series focuses on what has been called "The Crime of the Century" in the 1920s United States. At the center of this murder case were Nathan Leopold Jr. and Richard Loeb – two wealthy University of Chicago students who, in May of 1924, kidnapped and murdered 14-year-old Bobby Franks.

Book 2 of the series focuses on the serial killer of at least 27 young men and boys in Germany in the post-World War 1 era. At the center of this murder case were Fritz Haarmann and Hans Grans, who were lovers while committing these murders. It wasn't until the skulls and bones started washing ashore from the Leine River in Hanover that Germany realized they had a cold-blooded serial killer in their country.

Book 3 focuses on more modern times. It is based on the case of Stephen Port, a serial murderer in London, U.K., who was convicted of drugging, raping, and murdering four young men. He was also convicted of drugging and raping several other men. His victims were found through a new type of gay sex parties called 'Party N Play' or 'Chemsex' parties that have become all the rage.

Book 4 This book is based on Toronto's Gay Village and the few times serial killers reigned terror upon it. As much as this series wants to point out the negative aspects of murders in the gay community in countries that don't respect gay people, it's also important to reveal its effects in countries that seemingly support gay people.

KILLER CRIME SERIES BOX SET (Books 1 - 8)

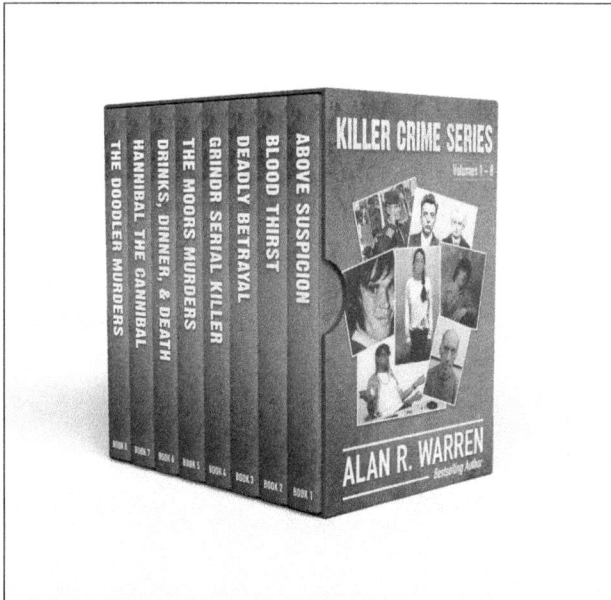

Step into the chilling depths of human depravity with this meticulously crafted box set from bestselling author Alan R. Warren, renowned for his captivating explorations of real-life crimes. This collection of eight unflinching narratives draws readers into the shadowed minds and actions of some of the world's most notorious criminals. From the twisted motivations behind Colonel Russell Williams' crimes in Above Suspicion to the shocking story of Jennifer Pan in Deadly Betrayal, who plotted a tragic betrayal against her own family, Warren delivers each tale with an unmatched intensity that will keep readers riveted.

In Blood Thirst, Warren examines the "Vampire Killer" who terrorized Canada, while Doodler Murders sheds light on the mysterious unsolved murders that haunted 1970s San Francisco. The Grindr Killer follows the grim story of

Stephen Port, whose use of dating apps led to tragedy, and in The Moors Murders, Warren revisits the notorious crimes of Ian Brady and Myra Hindley. Rounding out the collection is Hannibal the Cannibal, exploring the dark legacy of one of history's most infamous criminals.

This box set is a journey into the darker side of human psychology, weaving together cases from across different eras and places. Warren's unparalleled storytelling sheds light on these shocking events while honoring the victims and dissecting the minds of those who dared to defy the boundaries of morality and humanity.

www.ingramcontent.com/pod-product-compliance
Lightning Source LLC
LaVergne TN
LVHW051223080426
835513LV00016B/1384